The Art of Java

Herbert Schildt, James Holmes

McGraw-Hill/Osborne

New York   Chicago   San Francisco
Lisbon   London   Madrid   Mexico City   Milan
New Delhi   San Juan   Seoul   Singapore   Sydney   Toronto

The McGraw·Hill Companies

McGraw-Hill/Osborne
2100 Powell Street, 10ᵗʰ Floor
Emeryville, California 94608
U.S.A.

To arrange bulk purchase discounts for sales promotions, premiums, or fund-raisers, please contact
McGraw-Hill/Osborne at the above address. For information on translations or book distributors
outside the U.S.A., please see the International Contact Information page immediately following the
index of this book.

The Art of Java

1234567890 FGR FGR 019876543
ISBN 0-07-222971-3

Publisher	Brandon A. Nordin
Vice President & Associate Publisher	Scott Rogers
Editorial Director	Wendy Rinaldi
Project Editor	Jennifer Malnick
Acquisitions Coordinator	Athena Honore
Technical Editor	James Holmes
Copy Editor	Emily Rader
Proofreader	Emily Hsuan
Indexer	Sheryl Schildt
Composition	Tara A. Davis, Lucie Ericksen
Illustrators	Kathleen Fay Edwards, Melinda Moore Lytle, Lyssa Wald
Series Designer	Roberta Steele
Cover Designer	Jeff Weeks

This book was composed with Corel VENTURA™ Publisher.

Contents

About the Authors

Herbert Schildt is a leading authority on the Java, C, C++, and C# languages, and is a master Windows programmer. His programming books have sold more than three million copies worldwide and have been translated into all major foreign languages. He is the author of numerous bestsellers, including *Java 2: The Complete Reference, Java 2: A Beginner's Guide, Java 2 Programmer's Reference, C++: The Complete Reference, C: The Complete Reference*, and *C#: The Complete Reference*. Schildt holds a master's degree in computer science from the University of Illinois. He can be reached at his consulting office at (217) 586-4683.

James Holmes is a recognized leader in Java programming. He was named 2002 Oracle Magazine Java Developer of the Year and is a Committer on the Jakarta Struts open source project. He is currently an independent Java consultant, Sun Certified Java Programmer, and Sun Certified Web Component Developer. James can be reached via e-mail at james@ jamesholmes.com. You can also visit his Web site at http://www.JamesHolmes.com.

Preface

by Herbert Schildt

Beginning in 1991 at Sun Microsystems, James Gosling, along with Patrick Naughton, Chris Warth, Ed Frank, and Mike Sheridan, began work on a new language that would eventually rock the foundations of programming. Originally called Oak, this new language was renamed Java in 1995—and computing hasn't been the same since.

Java changed the course of programming in two important ways. First, Java incorporated features that facilitated the creation of Internet-enabled applications. Thus, Java was the world's first truly Internet-ready language. Second, Java advanced the state of the art in computer language design. For example, it redefined the object paradigm, streamlined exceptions, fully integrated multithreading into the language, and created a portable object code called bytecode that enabled programs to run on a variety of different platforms.

Java's importance to computing, therefore, lies firmly on two pillars: its built-in support for the Internet, and its advances in computer language design. Either one of these would have made Java a good language, but it is the combination that made Java a great language and ensured its place in computing history.

This book shows some of the reasons why Java is such an extraordinary language.

What's Inside

This book is different from most other books on Java. Whereas other books teach the basics of the language, this book shows how to apply it to some of computing's most interesting, useful, and, at times, mysterious programming tasks. In the process, it displays the power, versatility, and elegance of the Java language. Thus, it is through the *art* of Java that the *artistry* of Java's design is displayed.

As you might expect, several of the applications, such as the download manager in Chapter 4 or the e-mail subsystem in Chapter 5, relate directly to the Internet. However, many of the chapters develop code that illustrates the expressiveness of Java independently of the Internet. For example, the language interpreter in Chapter 3, or the AI-based search routines in Chapter 10, are what we call "pure code" examples. Neither of these applications relies on the Internet or uses a GUI interface. They are the type of code that in the past one might have expected to find written in C++. The ease by which these types of programs can be written in Java demonstrates the versatility and agility of the language.

ix

Each chapter develops code that you can use as-is, without changes. For example, the expression parser in Chapter 2 makes an excellent addition to many applications. However, the real benefits result when you use the applications as starting points for your own development. For example, the Web crawler developed in Chapter 7 can be adapted for use as a Web-site archiver or broken-link detector. In general, think of the various programs and subsystems as launching pads for your own projects.

Knowledge of Java Is Assumed

This book assumes that you have a solid grounding in the fundamentals of the Java language. You should be able to create, compile, and run Java programs. You should be able to use the most common parts of the Java API, handle exceptions, and create a multithreaded program. Thus, this book assumes that you have the skills that one would acquire in a first course on Java.

If you need to refresh or enhance your basic knowledge, I recommend the following books:

▶   *Java 2: A Beginner's Guide*
▶   *Java 2: The Complete Reference*

Both are published by McGraw-Hill/Osborne.

A Team Effort

I have been writing about programming for many years now and I seldom work with a coauthor. However, this book is a bit of an exception. Because of a rather unexpected but happy turn of events, I was able to team up with one of the brightest new talents in computing: James Holmes. James is an outstanding programmer with several impressive accomplishments, including being Oracle's Java Developer of the Year, and being a Committer for the Jarkarta Struts project. Because of James' unique knowledge of Web-based programming, I thought that it would be great if he could contribute several chapters to this book—fortunately, I was able to convince him to do so. As a result, James wrote chapters 4, 5, 6, and 7, which contain the most Internet-intensive applications. His contributions added greatly to the success of this project.

James is now working on an in-depth book about Struts called *Struts: The Complete Reference*, which will be available by the end of 2003.

Don't Forget: Code on the Web

Remember, the source code for all of the examples and projects in this book is available free of charge on the Web at **www.osborne.com**.

More From Herb Schildt

The *Art of Java* is just one in a series of Herb Schildt programming books. Here are some others that you will find of interest.

To learn more about Java programming, we recommend the following:

► *Java 2: The Complete Reference*

► *Java 2: A Beginner's Guide*

► *Java 2: Programmer's Reference*

To learn about C++, you will find these books especially helpful:

► *C++: The Complete Reference*

► *C++: A Beginner's Guide*

► *Teach Yourself C++*

► *C++ From the Ground Up*

► *STL Programming From the Ground Up*

To learn about C#, we suggest the following books:

► *C#: A Beginner's Guide*

► *C#: The Complete Reference*

If you want to learn more about the C language, the foundation of all modern programming, then the following titles will be of interest:

► *C: The Complete Reference*

► *Teach Yourself C*

More From James Holmes

To learn about Struts, the open-source framework for Web development, we recommend the following book by James Holmes:

► *Struts: The Complete Reference*

The Genius of Java

By Herb Schildt and James Holmes

Histtory in the large view is mirrored on a smaller scale by the history of programming. Just as the first societies sprang from simple beginnings, so too did programming. Just as great civilizations rose, flourished, and declined, so too have programming languages. Yet, throughout the rise and fall of nations, mankind progressed. In similar fashion, as each new language replaced its predecessor, the ongoing refinement of programming proceeded. Throughout history, there have been pivotal events, such as the fall of the Roman Empire, the invasion of Britain in 1066, or the first nuclear explosion, which transformed the world. The same is true for programming languages, albeit on a smaller scale. For example, the invention of FORTRAN changed forever the way that computers would be programmed. Another such pivotal event was the creation of Java.

Java is the milestone that marks the beginning of programming's Internet age. Designed expressly for creating applications that would run anywhere there was an Internet connection, Java's "write once, run anywhere" philosophy defined the new programming paradigm. What Gosling, et al., initially saw as the solution to a relatively small class of problems became a force that defined the programming landscape for the next generation of programmers. Java so fundamentally altered how we thought about programming that the history of computer languages can be divided into two eras: Before Java and After Java.

Programmers in the Before Java world created programs that ran on a stand-alone machine. Programmers in the After Java world create programs for a highly distributed, networked environment. No longer does a programmer think in terms of a single computer. Instead, the network *is the computer* and today we programmers think in terms of servers, clients, and hosts.

Although the development of Java was driven by the needs of the Internet, Java is not simply an "Internet language." Rather, it is a full-featured, general-purpose programming language designed for the modern, networked world. This means that Java is suitable for nearly all types of programming. Although sometimes overshadowed by its networking capabilities, Java also incorporated many innovative features that advanced the art of programming. These innovations still ripple through computing today. For example, several aspects of C# are modeled on elements first mainstreamed by Java.

Throughout this book we will demonstrate the wide-ranging capabilities of Java by applying it to a varied cross section of applications. Some of the applications demonstrate the power of the language, independent of its networking attributes. We call these "pure code" examples because they show the expressiveness of the Java syntax and design philosophy. Others illustrate the ease with which sophisticated networked programs can be developed using the Java language and its API classes. Collectively, the applications show the power and scope of Java.

Before we begin our exploration of Java, we will take some time in this first chapter to point out several of the features that make it a remarkable programming language. These are features that reflect what we call the "genius of Java."

Simple Types and Objects: The Right Balance

One of the greatest challenges facing a designer of an object-oriented computer language is how to handle the object vs. simple type dilemma. Here is the problem. From a conceptually pure point of view, every data type should be an object, and every type should descend from a universal parent object. This makes all data types work the same, with each sharing a common set of inherited traits. The trouble is that making the simple types, such as **int** or **double**, into objects can cause a decrease in performance because of the added overhead incurred by the object mechanism. Because the simple types are often used to control loops and conditional statements, this extra overhead would have wide-ranging, negative consequences. The trick is to find the right balance between the "everything is an object" desire and the "performance counts" reality.

Java solves the object, simple type problem in an elegant manner. First, it defines eight simple types: **byte**, **short**, **int**, **long**, **char**, **float**, **double**, and **boolean**. These types translate directly into binary values. Thus, a variable of type **int** can be operated on directly by the CPU without any added overhead. The simple types in Java are as fast and efficient as they are in any other language. Therefore, a **for** loop controlled by an **int** runs at full speed, unencumbered by any object-related issues.

Aside from the simple types, all other types in Java are objects that inherit the universal superclass **Object**. Thus, all other types share inherited functionality. For example, all objects have a **toString( )** method because **toString( )** is a method defined by **Object**.

Because simple types are not objects, Java is free to treat objects and nonobjects a bit differently. This is where the real genius of Java's design becomes apparent. In Java, all objects are accessed through a reference, rather than directly, as is the case for the simple types. Thus, your program never operates on an object directly. By using this approach, several benefits follow, not the least of which is garbage collection. Because all objects are accessed via a reference, garbage collection can be efficiently implemented: when there is no reference to an object, it can be recycled. Another benefit is that an object reference of type **Object** can refer to any object in the system.

Of course, accessing every object through a reference adds overhead. The reason is that a reference is, essentially, an address (i.e., a pointer). Thus, every object access occurs indirectly, through that address. Although modern CPUs handle indirect accesses efficiently, indirect accesses are not as fast as operating directly on the data itself, as is the case with the simple types.

Although the simple types are quite efficient, there are still times when an object equivalent of a simple type is needed. For example, you might want to create a list of integers at runtime and have those integers recycled (garbage collected) when no longer needed. To handle this type of situation, Java defines the simple type wrappers, such as **Integer** and **Double**. These wrappers enable the simple types to participate in the object hierarchy when necessary.

Java's resolution to the object vs. simple type problem captures the right balance. It allows efficient programs to be written, but at the same time it allows the object model to be implemented without concern about negatively impacting the performance of the simple types.

Memory Management Through Garbage Collection

Garbage collection as a memory management technique has been around a long time, but in Java it took on a new life. In languages such as C++, memory must be managed manually, with the programmer explicitly releasing unused objects. This is a source of problems because it is common to forget to release a resource after it is no longer needed, or to release a resource that is still being used. Java prevents these problems by managing memory for you. This can be done in an efficient manner because *all objects* in Java are accessed through a reference. Thus, when the garbage collector finds an object to which there is no reference, it knows that the object is unused and can be recycled. Had Java allowed objects to be operated on directly (in a fashion similar to the simple types), then such an efficient means of garbage collection would not have been possible.

Java's use of garbage collection reflects the philosophy of Java in general. The Java designers took great pains to create a language that would prevent some of the problems typical of other programming languages. By using garbage collection, it is not possible for the programmer to forget to release a resource or to mistakenly release a resource that is still in use. Thus, garbage collection heads off an entire class of problems.

A Wonderfully Simple Multithreading Model

Java's designers saw early on that the future of programming involved language-level support for multithreaded multitasking. Recall that there are two basic types of multitasking: process-based and thread-based. In process-based multitasking, the smallest schedulable unit is a process. A process is, essentially, a program that is executing. Thus, process-based multitasking is the feature that allows a computer to run two or more programs at the same time. In thread-based multitasking, a thread is the smallest schedulable unit. A thread defines a path of execution within a program. Thus, one process can contain two or more threads of execution, and a multithreaded program can have two or more parts of itself executing simultaneously.

Although process-based multitasking is mostly a function of the operating system, thread-based multitasking benefits greatly from language-level support. For example, C++, which has no built-in support for multithreaded programming, must rely completely on operating system functions to handle multithreading. This means that to create, begin, synchronize, and end threads requires numerous calls to the operating system. As a result, multithreaded code in C++ is not portable. It also makes multithreading unwieldy in a C++ program.

Because Java builds in support for multithreading, much of what must be done manually in other languages is handled automatically in Java. One of the most elegant parts of Java's multithreading model is its approach to synchronization. Synchronization is based on two innovative features. First, in Java, all objects have built-in monitors that act as mutually exclusive locks. Only one thread can own a monitor at a given time. The locking feature is turned on by modifying a method with the **synchronized** keyword. When a synchronized method is called, the object is locked and other threads wanting access to the object must wait.

The second part of Java's support of synchronization is found in **Object**, the universal superclass of all other classes. **Object** declares the following synchronization methods: **wait( )**, **notify( )**, and **notifyAll( )**. These methods support interthread communication. Thus, all objects have built-in support for interthread communication. When used in combination with a synchronized method, these methods allow a high-level of control over the way threads interact.

By making multithreading an easy-to-use, built-in part of the language, Java changed the way that we thought about the fundamental architecture of a program. Before Java, most programmers conceptualized programs as monolithic structures that had a single path of execution. After Java, we think of programs as collections of parallel tasks that interact with one another. This change to parallelism has had a wide-ranging effect on computing, but perhaps its greatest impact has been to facilitate the use of software components.

Fully Integrated Exceptions

The conceptual framework for exceptions predates Java. So, too, does the incorporation of exceptions into other programming languages. For instance, exceptions were added to C++ several years before Java was created. What makes Java's approach to exceptions important is that they were part of the original design. They were not added after the fact. Exceptions are fully integrated into Java and form one of its foundational features.

A key aspect of Java's exception mechanism is that its use is not optional. In Java, handling errors through the use of exceptions is the rule. This differs from C++, for example, in which exceptions are supported but are not fully integrated into the entire programming environment. Consider the common situations of opening or reading from a file. In Java, when an error occurs during one of these operations, an exception is thrown. In C++, the methods that open or read from a file report an error by returning a special error code. Because C++ did not originally support exceptions, its library still relies on error return codes rather than exceptions, and your program must constantly check for possible errors manually. In Java, you simply wrap the file-handling code within a **try/catch** block. Any errors will automatically be caught.

Streamlined Support for Polymorphism

Polymorphism is the attribute of object-oriented programming that allows one interface to be used by multiple methods. Java supports polymorphism with a variety of features, but two stand out. The first is the fact that every method (other than one marked **final**) can be overridden by a subclass. The second is the **interface** keyword. Let's examine each a bit closer.

Because methods in a superclass can be overridden by those in a derived class, it's trivially easy to create class hierarchies in which subclasses are specializations of the superclass. Recall that a superclass reference can be used to refer to any subclass of that superclass. Furthermore, a call to a method on a subclass object, through a superclass reference, automatically executes the overridden version of that method. Thus, a superclass can define the form of an object and provide a default implementation. This default implementation can then be customized by a subclass to better meet the needs of a specific situation. Thus, the same interface, in this case the one defined by the superclass, can be the basis for multiple implementations.

Of course, Java takes the concept of "one interface, multiple methods" a step further. It defines the **interface** keyword, which allows you to fully separate a class' methods from their implementations. Although an **interface** is abstract, you can still declare a reference of an **interface** type. This reference can then be used to refer to any object that implements the interface. This is a very powerful concept because it streamlines and facilitates the use of polymorphism. As long as a class implements an interface, an object of that class can be used by any code that requires the functionality provided by the interface. For example, assuming an interface called **MyIF**, consider the following method:

```
void myMeth(MyIF ob) {
  // ...
}
```

Any object that implements the **MyIF** interface can be passed to **myMeth( )**. It doesn't matter what other capabilities (if any) that object has. If it implements **MyIF**, then **myMeth( )** can operate on it.

Portability and Security Through Bytecode

Despite all of its powerful features, Java may not have been much more than a footnote in programming history if it were not for one important but nearly transparent part of the language: bytecode. As all Java programmers know, the output of the Java compiler is not machine code that can be directly executed by a CPU. Instead, it is a highly optimized set of portable instructions, called *bytecode,* which are executed by the Java Virtual Machine (JVM). The original JVM was simply an interpreter for bytecode. Today, the JVM also applies on-the-fly compilation of bytecode into executable code. Whatever process is used to execute bytecode, its advantages are enormously important to the success of Java.

The first advantage is portability. By compiling a Java program into bytecode, it can be executed on any computer, with any type of CPU (and operating system) as long as a JVM is available for that environment. In other words, once a JVM has been implemented for a specific environment, any Java program can run in that environment. It is not necessary to create a separate executable for each different environment. The same bytecode can be run in all environments. Therefore, through the use of bytecode, Java offered programmers the ability "to write once, run anywhere."

The second advantage achieved by bytecode is security. Because execution of the bytecode is under the control of the JVM, the JVM can prevent a Java program from performing malicious acts that affect the host machine. The ability to ensure the security of the host computer was crucial to the success of Java because it enabled the creation of the applet. Because an applet is a small, dynamically downloaded program that comes across the Internet, some mechanism to prevent applets from doing harm was necessary. The combination of bytecode and the JVM provided the mechanism by which applets could be downloaded safely. Frankly, without bytecode, the Web would be a much different place today.

The Richness of the Java API

Conceptually, computer languages consist of two parts. The first is the language proper, defined by the keywords and syntax. The second is the standard library, which contains a set of classes, interfaces, and methods that are available to the programmer. Although all of the major languages today provide large libraries, the one defined by Java stands out because of the richness and diversity it offers to the programmer. When Java was first created, its library contained a set of core packages, such as **java.lang**, **java.io**, and **java.net**. With each new release of Java, classes and packages have been added. Today, Java gives the programmer access to a truly amazing array of functionality.

Since the beginning, one of the key elements that differentiated the Java library from that provided by other languages was its support for networking. At the time of Java's creation, other languages, such as C++, did not (and still do not) provide standard library elements that handle networking. By providing classes that easily handled connecting to and using the Internet, Java helped spark the Internet revolution. With Java, the Internet was open to all programmers, not just those that specialized in networking. The functionality in **java.net** transformed computing.

Another key package of the core Java library is **java.awt**, which supports the Abstract Window Toolkit (AWT). The AWT enables the programmer to create portable, GUI-based code. That is, by using the AWT classes, it is possible to create a windowed application that uses the various standard GUI elements, such as scroll bars, check boxes, and radio buttons. Because of the AWT, it is possible to create a GUI application that can run in any environment that supports the Java Virtual Machine. This level of GUI portability was unknown prior to Java.

Java's inclusion of the AWT revolutionized the way programmers thought about the application environment. Before Java, GUI-based programs had to be specifically written for their execution environments. This meant that a Windows program, for example, would need to be substantially recoded to run in an Apple computer. After Java, a programmer could write one program that would execute in both environments. By defining a portable GUI, Java unified the programming environment.

In later years, a lightweight alternative to the AWT was added to Java: Swing. The Swing components are contained in **javax.swing** and its subpackages. Swing offers the programmer a rich set of GUI components that have enhanced portability. As many of the examples in this book show, both the AWT and Swing give the programmer the ability to produce highly effective, portable GUI-based applications.

Today, the Java library has grown substantially from its initial core. Each new release of Java has been accompanied with additional library support. New packages have been added, and new functionality has been added to existing packages. The Java library has been in a constant state of transformation because it has been responsive to the rapidly evolving computing environment. This ability to adapt and change in short order is part of the genius of Java.

The Applet

Although taken for granted today, the applet is one of Java's more revolutionary features because it allowed the creation of portable, dynamically downloaded programs that could safely execute within the confines of a browser. In the Before Java world, executable content was always suspect because of the harm a malicious program could do to the client's computer. Furthermore, code compiled for one type of CPU and operating system would not work on another type of system. Because there are a wide variety of CPUs and operating systems connected to the Internet, it was not practical to create a unique version of a program for all environments. The Java applet provided a solution to both problems. With the applet, the Web programmer was able to easily add dynamic content to the rather static world of HTML. Java applets made the Web move, and there was no going back.

In addition to changing the way that we thought about Web content, the applet had another important effect—or perhaps side effect. It helped propel the move to component software. Because applets are small programs, they usually represent small units of functionality, which is the same thing that a software component does. Once we began to think in terms of applets, it was a small step to Beans, and beyond. Today, the component-oriented architecture, in which an application consists of an interacting set of components, has largely replaced the monolithic model that typified the past.

The Continuing Revolution

There is one more aspect of Java that reflects its genius, although it isn't actually part of the language. Java brought with it a culture of innovation that welcomed new ideas, and a process by which these new ideas could be rapidly assimilated. Whereas many other computer languages change slowly, Java is constantly evolving and adapting. Furthermore, this process is open to the entire Java community through the Java Community Process (JCP). The JCP offers a mechanism by which users of Java help influence the future direction of the language, tools, and associated technologies. Thus, the people that actually use the language have input into its ongoing development.

From the start, Java revolutionized programming—and the revolution hasn't stopped. Java is still at the forefront of computer language development. It is a language that has earned a lasting place in the history of computing.

A Recursive-Descent
Expression Parser

by Herb Schildt

How do you write a program that will take as input a string containing a numeric expression, such as $(10 - 5) * 3$, and compute the proper answer? If there is still a "high priesthood" among programmers, it must be those few who know how to do this. Many otherwise accomplished programmers are mystified by the way a high-level language converts algebraic expressions into instructions that a computer can execute. This procedure is called *expression parsing*, and it is the backbone of all language compilers and interpreters, spreadsheets, and anything else that needs to convert numeric expressions into a form that the computer can use.

Although mysterious to the uninitiated, expression parsing is a well-defined task for which there is a rather elegant solution. This is because the problem is well defined and expression parsing works according to the strict rules of algebra. This chapter develops what is commonly referred to as a *recursive-descent parser* and all the necessary support routines that enable you to evaluate numeric expressions. Once you have mastered the operation of the parser, you can easily enhance and modify it to suit your needs.

Aside from being a useful piece of code in itself, the parser was chosen as the first example in this book because it illustrates the power and range of the Java language. A parser is a "pure code" subsystem. By this, I mean that it is not network-oriented, does not rely on a GUI interface, is neither an applet nor servlet, and so on. It is the type of code that one might expect to find written in C or C++, but not Java. Because Java was a revolutionary force that fundamentally changed the way we program for the Internet, we sometimes forget that it is not limited to that environment. Instead, Java is a full-featured language that can be applied to nearly any programming task. The parser developed in this chapter proves this point.

Expressions

Because the parser processes an expression, it is necessary to understand what constitutes an expression. Although there are many different types of expressions, this chapter deals with only one type: numeric expressions. For our purposes numeric expressions are composed of the following items:

- ► Numbers
- ► The operators +, –, /, *, ^, %, =
- ► Parentheses
- ► Variables

Here, the operator ^ indicates exponentiation (not the XOR as it does in Java) and = is the assignment operator. These items can be combined in expressions according to the rules of algebra. Here are some examples:

$$10 - 8$$
$$(100 - 5) * 14/6$$
$$a + b - c$$
$$10\char`^5$$
$$a = 10 - b$$

Assume this precedence for each operator:

Highest	$+ -$ (unary)
	$\wedge$
	$* / \%$
	$+ -$
Lowest	$=$

Operators of equal precedence evaluate from left to right.

The parser developed here will be subject to a few constraints. First, all variables are single letters (in other words, 26 variables, **A** through **Z**, are available). The variables are not case sensitive (**a** and **A** are treated as the same variable). Second, all numeric values are assumed to be **double**, although you could easily modify the parser to handle other types of values. Finally, to keep the logic clear and easy to understand, only rudimentary error checking is included.

Parsing Expressions: The Problem

If you have not thought much about the problem of expression parsing, you might assume that it is a simple task, but it isn't. To better understand the problem, try to evaluate this sample expression:

$10 - 2 * 3$

You know that this expression is equal to the value 4. Although you could easily create a program that would compute that *specific* expression, the problem is how to create a program that gives the correct answer for any *arbitrary* expression. At first you might think of an algorithm something like this:

```
a = get first operand
while(operands present) {
    op = get operator
    b = get second operand
    a = a op b
}
```

This approach gets the first operand, the operator, and the second operand to perform the first operation, and then gets the next operator and operand to perform the next operation, and so on. However, if you try this basic approach, the expression $10 - 2 * 3$ evaluates to 24 (that is, 8 * 3) instead of 4 because this procedure neglects the precedence of the operators. You cannot just take the operands and operators in order from left to right because the rules of algebra dictate that multiplication must be done before subtraction. Some beginners think that this problem can be easily overcome, and sometimes, in very restricted cases, it can. But the problem only gets worse when you add parentheses, exponentiation, variables, unary operators, and the like.

Although there are a number of ways to write the code that processes an expression, the one developed here is the approach most easily written by a person. It is called a *recursive-descent parser*, and in the course of this chapter you will see how it got its name. (Some of the other methods used to write parsers employ complex tables that are usually generated by another computer program. These are sometimes called *table-driven parsers*.)

Parsing an Expression

There are a number of ways to parse and evaluate an expression. For use with a recursive-descent parser, think of expressions as *recursive data structures*—that is, expressions that are defined in terms of themselves. If, for the moment, we assume that expressions can only use +, −, *, /, and parentheses, all expressions can be defined with the following rules:

> expression → term [+ term] [− term]
> term → factor [* factor] [/ factor]
> factor → variable, number, or (expression)

The square brackets designate an optional element, and the → means produces. In fact, the rules are usually called the *production rules* of the expression. Therefore, for the definition of *term* you could say: "Term produces factor times factor or factor divided by factor." Notice that the precedence of the operators is implicit in the way an expression is defined.

Here is an example. The expression

> 10 + 5 * B

has two terms: 10 and 5 * B. The second term contains two factors: 5 and B. These factors consist of one number and one variable.

On the other hand, the expression

> 14 * (7 − C)

has two factors: 14 and (7 − C). The factors consist of one number and one parenthesized expression. The parenthesized expression contains two terms: one number and one variable.

This process forms the basis for a recursive-descent parser, which is a set of mutually recursive methods that work in a chainlike fashion and implement the production rules. At each appropriate step, the parser performs the specified operations in the algebraically correct sequence. To see how the production rules are used to parse an expression, let's work through an example using the following expression:

> 9/3 − (100 + 56)

Here is the sequence that you will follow:

1. Get the first term, 9/3.
2. Get each factor and divide the integers. The resulting value is 3.

3. Get the second term, (100 + 56). At this point, start recursively analyzing this subexpression.

4. Get each term and add. The resulting value is 156.

5. Return from the recursive evaluation of the second term.

6. Subtract 156 from 3. The answer is –153.

If you are a little confused at this point, don't feel bad. This is a fairly complex concept that takes some getting used to. There are two basic things to remember about this recursive view of expressions. First, the precedence of the operators is implicit in the way the production rules are defined. Second, this method of parsing and evaluating expressions is very similar to the way humans evaluate mathematical expressions.

The remainder of this chapter develops two parsers. The first will parse and evaluate floating point expressions of type **double** that consist only of literal values. This parser illustrates the basics of the recursive-descent method of parsing. The second adds the ability to use variables.

Dissecting an Expression

In order to evaluate an expression, a parser needs to be fed the individual components of that expression. For example, the expression

$$A * B - (W + 10)$$

contains these individual parts: A, *, B, –, (, W, +, 10, and). In the language of parsing, each component of an expression is called a *token*, and each token represents an indivisible unit of the expression. Since *tokenizing* an expression is fundamental to parsing, let's look at it before examining the parser itself.

To render an expression into tokens, you need a method that sequentially returns each token in the expression individually, moving from start to finish. The method must also be able to determine the type of a token and detect the end of the expression. In the parser developed here, the method that performs this task is called **getToken( )**.

Both parsers in this chapter are encapsulated within the **Parser** class. Although this class is described in detail later, the first part of it needs to be shown now so that the workings of **getToken( )** can be explained. **Parser** begins by defining the **final** variables and fields shown here:

```
class Parser {
  // These are the token types.
  final int NONE = 0;
  final int DELIMITER = 1;
  final int VARIABLE = 2;
  final int NUMBER = 3;

  // These are the types of syntax errors.
```

```
final int SYNTAX = 0;
final int UNBALPARENS = 1;
final int NOEXP = 2;
final int DIVBYZERO = 3;

// This token indicates end-of-expression.
final String EOE = "\0";

private String exp;    // refers to expression string
private int expIdx;    // current index into the expression
private String token;  // holds current token
private int tokType;   // holds token's type
```

Parser first defines the values that indicate the type of a token. When parsing an expression, each token must have a type associated with it. For the parsers developed in this chapter, only three types are needed: variable, number, and delimiter. These are represented by the values **VARIABLE**, **NUMBER**, and **DELIMITER**. The **DELIMITER** category is used for both operators and parentheses. The **NONE** type is just a placeholder value for an undefined token.

Next, **Parser** defines the values that represent the various errors that can occur when parsing and evaluating an expression. **SYNTAX** represents a broad category of errors that result in a malformed expression. **UNBALPARENS** indicates unbalanced parentheses. **NOEXP** is the error reported when no expression is present when the parser is executed. **DIVBYZERO** indicates a divide-by-zero error.

The **final** variable **EOE** is the token that indicates that the end of the expression has been reached.

A reference to the string that holds the expression being parsed is stored in **exp**. Thus, **exp** will refer to a string such as "10+4". The index of the next token within that string is held in **expIdx**, which is initially zero. The token that is obtained is stored in **token**, and its type is stored in **tokType**. These fields are **private** because they are used only by the parser and should not be modified by outside code.

The **getToken( )** method is shown here. Each time it is called, it obtains the next token from the expression in the string referred to by **exp** beginning at **expIdx**. In other words, each time **getToken( )** is called, it obtains the next token at **exp[expIdx]**. It puts this token into the **token** field. It puts the type of the token into **tokType**. **getToken( )** uses the **isDelim( )** method, which is also shown here:

```
// Obtain the next token.
private void getToken()
{
  tokType = NONE;
  token = "";

  // Check for end of expression.
  if(expIdx == exp.length()) {
    token = EOE;
    return;
```

```
    }

    // Skip over white space.
    while(expIdx < exp.length() &&
      Character.isWhitespace(exp.charAt(expIdx))) ++expIdx;

    // Trailing whitespace ends expression.
    if(expIdx == exp.length()) {
      token = EOE;
      return;
    }

    if(isDelim(exp.charAt(expIdx))) { // is operator
      token += exp.charAt(expIdx);
      expIdx++;
      tokType = DELIMITER;
    }
    else if(Character.isLetter(exp.charAt(expIdx))) { // is variable
      while(!isDelim(exp.charAt(expIdx))) {
        token += exp.charAt(expIdx);
        expIdx++;
        if(expIdx >= exp.length()) break;
      }
      tokType = VARIABLE;
    }
    else if(Character.isDigit(exp.charAt(expIdx))) { // is number
      while(!isDelim(exp.charAt(expIdx))) {
        token += exp.charAt(expIdx);
        expIdx++;
        if(expIdx >= exp.length()) break;
      }
      tokType = NUMBER;
    }
    else { // unknown character terminates expression
      token = EOE;
      return;
    }
  }

// Return true if c is a delimiter.
private boolean isDelim(char c)
{
  if((" +-/*%^=()".indexOf(c) != -1))
    return true;
  return false;
}
```

Look closely at **getToken( )**. After the first few initializations, **getToken( )** checks if the end of the expression has been reached by seeing if **expIdx** is equal to **exp.length( )**. Since **expIdx** is an index into the expression being analyzed, if it equals the length of the expression string, the expression has been fully parsed.

If there are still more tokens to retrieve from the expression, **getToken( )** first skips over any leading spaces. If trailing spaces end the expression, then the end-of-expression token **EOE** is returned. Otherwise, once the spaces have been skipped, **exp[expIdx]** contains either a digit, a variable, or an operator. If the next character is an operator, it is returned as a string in **token**, and **DELIMITER** is stored in **tokType**. If the next character is a letter instead, it is assumed to be one of the variables. It is returned as a string in **token**, and **tokType** is assigned the value **VARIABLE**. If the next character is a digit, the entire number is read and stored in its string form in **token** and its type is **NUMBER**. Finally, if the next character is none of the preceding, **token** is assigned **EOE**.

To keep the code in **getToken( )** clear, a certain amount of error checking has been omitted and some assumptions have been made. For example, any unrecognized character can end an expression as long as it is preceded by a space. Also, in this version, variables can be of any length, but only the first letter is significant. You can add more error checking and other details as your specific application dictates.

To better understand the tokenization process, study what it returns for each token and type in the following expression:

$$A + 100 - (B * C) / 2$$

Token	Token Type
A	VARIABLE
+	DELIMITER
100	NUMBER
–	DELIMITER
(	DELIMITER
B	VARIABLE
*	DELIMITER
C	VARIABLE
)	DELIMITER
/	DELIMITER
2	NUMBER

Remember that **token** always holds a string, even if it contains just a single character.

One last point: Although Java contains some very useful, built-in tokenizing capabilities, such as those supported by the **StringTokenizer** class, for the parser, it is better to handle this job ourselves, using a dedicated tokenizer, such as **getToken( )**.

A Simple Expression Parser

Here is the first version of the parser. It can evaluate expressions that consist solely of literals, operators, and parentheses. Although **getToken( )** can process variables, the parser does nothing with them. Once you understand how this simplified parser works, we will add the ability to handle variables.

```
/*
   This module contains the recursive descent
   parser that does not use variables.
*/

// Exception class for parser errors.
class ParserException extends Exception {
  String errStr; // describes the error

  public ParserException(String str) {
    errStr = str;
  }

  public String toString() {
    return errStr;
  }
}

class Parser {
  // These are the token types.
  final int NONE = 0;
  final int DELIMITER = 1;
  final int VARIABLE = 2;
  final int NUMBER = 3;

  // These are the types of syntax errors.
  final int SYNTAX = 0;
  final int UNBALPARENS = 1;
  final int NOEXP = 2;
  final int DIVBYZERO = 3;

  // This token indicates end-of-expression.
  final String EOE = "\0";

  private String exp;    // refers to expression string
```

```java
  private int expIdx;    // current index into the expression
  private String token; // holds current token
  private int tokType;  // holds token's type

  // Parser entry point.
  public double evaluate(String expstr) throws ParserException
  {
    double result;
    exp = expstr;
    expIdx = 0;

    getToken();
    if(token.equals(EOE))
      handleErr(NOEXP); // no expression present

    // Parse and evaluate the expression.
    result = evalExp2();

    if(!token.equals(EOE)) // last token must be EOE
      handleErr(SYNTAX);

    return result;
  }

  // Add or subtract two terms.
  private double evalExp2() throws ParserException
  {
    char op;
    double result;
    double partialResult;

    result = evalExp3();

    while((op = token.charAt(0)) == '+' || op == '-') {
      getToken();
      partialResult = evalExp3();
      switch(op) {
        case '-':
          result = result - partialResult;
          break;
        case '+':
          result = result + partialResult;
          break;
      }
    }
```

```java
    return result;
  }

  // Multiply or divide two factors.
  private double evalExp3() throws ParserException
  {
    char op;
    double result;
    double partialResult;

    result = evalExp4();

    while((op = token.charAt(0)) == '*' ||
          op == '/' || op == '%') {
      getToken();
      partialResult = evalExp4();
      switch(op) {
        case '*':
          result = result * partialResult;
          break;
        case '/':
          if(partialResult == 0.0)
            handleErr(DIVBYZERO);
          result = result / partialResult;
          break;
        case '%':
          if(partialResult == 0.0)
            handleErr(DIVBYZERO);
          result = result % partialResult;
          break;
      }
    }
    return result;
  }

  // Process an exponent.
  private double evalExp4() throws ParserException
  {
    double result;
    double partialResult;
    double ex;
    int t;

    result = evalExp5();
```

```
  if(token.equals("^")) {
    getToken();
    partialResult = evalExp4();
    ex = result;
    if(partialResult == 0.0) {
      result = 1.0;
    } else
      for(t=(int)partialResult-1; t > 0; t--)
        result = result * ex;
  }
  return result;
}


// Evaluate a unary + or -.
private double evalExp5() throws ParserException
{
  double result;
  String  op;

  op = "";
  if((tokType == DELIMITER) &&
      token.equals("+") || token.equals("-")) {
    op = token;
    getToken();

  }
  result = evalExp6();

  if(op.equals("-")) result = -result;

  return result;
}

// Process a parenthesized expression.
private double evalExp6() throws ParserException
{
  double result;

  if(token.equals("(")) {
    getToken();
    result = evalExp2();
    if(!token.equals(")"))
      handleErr(UNBALPARENS);
    getToken();
  }
```

```
      else result = atom();

      return result;
    }

    // Get the value of a number.
    private double atom() throws ParserException
    {
      double result = 0.0;

      switch(tokType) {
        case NUMBER:
          try {
            result = Double.parseDouble(token);
          } catch (NumberFormatException exc) {
            handleErr(SYNTAX);
          }
          getToken();
          break;
        default:
          handleErr(SYNTAX);
          break;
      }
      return result;
    }

    // Handle an error.
    private void handleErr(int error) throws ParserException
    {
      String[] err = {
        "Syntax Error",
        "Unbalanced Parentheses",
        "No Expression Present",
        "Division by Zero"
      };

      throw new ParserException(err[error]);
    }

    // Obtain the next token.
    private void getToken()
    {
      tokType = NONE;
      token = "";
```

```java
    // Check for end of expression.
    if(expIdx == exp.length()) {
      token = EOE;
      return;
    }

    // Skip over white space.
    while(expIdx < exp.length() &&
      Character.isWhitespace(exp.charAt(expIdx))) ++expIdx;

    // Trailing whitespace ends expression.
    if(expIdx == exp.length()) {
      token = EOE;
      return;
    }

    if(isDelim(exp.charAt(expIdx))) { // is operator
      token += exp.charAt(expIdx);
      expIdx++;
      tokType = DELIMITER;
    }
    else if(Character.isLetter(exp.charAt(expIdx))) { // is variable
      while(!isDelim(exp.charAt(expIdx))) {
        token += exp.charAt(expIdx);
        expIdx++;
        if(expIdx >= exp.length()) break;
      }
      tokType = VARIABLE;
    }
    else if(Character.isDigit(exp.charAt(expIdx))) { // is number
      while(!isDelim(exp.charAt(expIdx))) {
        token += exp.charAt(expIdx);
        expIdx++;
        if(expIdx >= exp.length()) break;
      }
      tokType = NUMBER;
    }
    else { // unknown character terminates expression
      token = EOE;
      return;
    }
  }

  // Return true if c is a delimiter.
  private boolean isDelim(char c)
  {
```

```
    if((" +-/*%^=()".indexOf(c) != -1))
      return true;
    return false;
  }

}
```

Notice the **ParserException** class declared near the top of the code. This is the type of exception that will be thrown by the parser if it encounters an error while processing the expression. This exception will need to be handled by code that uses the parser.

The parser as it is shown can handle the following operators: +, −, *, /, %. In addition, it can handle integer exponentiation (^) and the unary minus. The parser can also deal with parentheses correctly.

To use the parser, first create an object of type **Parser**. Then call **evaluate( )**, passing the expression string that you want evaluated as an argument. The result is returned. Because **Parser** throws a **ParserException** on error, your application must handle such an exception. The following example demonstrates the parser:

```
// Demonstrate the parser.
import java.io.*;

class PDemo {
  public static void main(String args[])
    throws IOException
  {
    String expr;

    BufferedReader br = new
      BufferedReader(new InputStreamReader(System.in));
    Parser p = new Parser();

    System.out.println("Enter an empty expression to stop.");

    for(;;) {
      System.out.print("Enter expression: ");
      expr = br.readLine();
      if(expr.equals("")) break;
      try {
        System.out.println("Result: " + p.evaluate(expr));
        System.out.println();
      } catch (ParserException exc) {
        System.out.println(exc);
      }
    }
  }
}
```

Here is a sample run:

```
Enter an empty expression to stop.
Enter expression: 10-2*3
Result: 4.0

Enter expression: (10-2)*3
Result: 24.0

Enter expression: 10/3.5
Result: 2.857142857142857
```

Understanding the Parser

Let's now take a detailed look at **Parser**. The string containing the expression to be evaluated is referred to by **exp**. This field is set each time **evaluate( )** is called. It is important to remember that the parser evaluates expressions that are contained in standard Java strings. For example, the following strings contain expressions that the parser can evaluate:

> "10 − 5"
> "2 * 3.3 / (3.1416 * 3.3)"

The current index into **exp** is stored in **expIdx**. When parsing begins execution, **expIdx** is set to zero. **expIdx** is incremented as the parser moves through the expression. The **token** field holds the current token, and **tokType** contains the token type.

The entry point to the parser is through **evaluate( )**, which must be called with a string containing the expression to be analyzed. The methods **evalExp2( )** through **evalExp6( )** along with **atom( )** form the recursive-descent parser. They implement an enhanced set of the expression production rules discussed earlier. The comments at the top of each method describe the function they perform. In the next version of the parser, a method called **evalExp1( )** will also be added.

The **handleErr( )** method handles syntax errors in the expression. The methods **getToken( )** and **isDelim( )** dissect the expression into its component parts, as described earlier. The parser uses **getToken( )** to obtain tokens from the expression, beginning at the beginning of the expression and working to the end. Based on the type of token obtained, different actions are taken.

To understand exactly how the parser evaluates an expression, work through the following expression:

> 10 − 3 * 2

When **evaluate( )**, the entry point into the parser, is called, it gets the first token. If the token is **EOE**, then **evaluate( )** has been called with a null string, and the **NOEXP** error is generated. However, in this example, the token contains the number **10**. Next, **evalExp2( )** is called. **evalExp2( )** then calls **evalExp3( )**, and **evalExp3( )** calls **evalExp4( )**, which in turn calls **evalExp5( )**. Then **evalExp5( )** checks whether the token is a unary plus or minus, which in this case, it is not, so **evalExp6( )** is called. At this point **evalExp6( )** either recursively calls **evalExp2( )** (in the case of a parenthesized expression) or **atom( )** to find the value of a number. Since the token is not a left parentheses, **atom( )** is executed and the value 10 is returned. Next, another token is retrieved, and the methods begin to return up the chain. At this point, the token is –, and the methods return up to **evalExp2( )**.

What happens next is very important. Because the token is –, it is saved in **op**. The parser then gets the next token, which is **3**, and the descent down the chain begins again. As before, **atom( )** is entered. The value 3 is returned in **result** and the token * is read. This causes a return back up the chain to **evalExp3( )**, where the final token 2 is read. At this point, the first arithmetic operation occurs—the multiplication of 2 and 3. The result is returned to **evalExp2( )** and the subtraction is performed. The subtraction yields the answer 4. Although the process may at first seem complicated, work through some other examples to verify that it functions correctly every time.

If an error occurs while parsing, the **handleErr( )** method is called. This method throws a **ParserException** that describes the error. This exception is thrown out of **evalutate( )** and must be handled by code that uses the parser.

This parser would be suitable for use by a simple desktop calculator, as is illustrated by the previous program. Before it could be used in a computer language, a database, or in a sophisticated calculator, it needs the ability to handle variables. This is the subject of the next section.

Adding Variables to the Parser

All programming languages, many calculators, and spreadsheets use variables to store values for later use. Before the parser can be used for such applications, it needs to be expanded to include variables. To accomplish this, you need to add several things to the parser. First, of course, are the variables themselves. As stated earlier, we will use the letters **A** through **Z** for variables. The variables are stored in an array inside the **Parser** class. Each variable uses one array location in a 26-element array of **double**s. Therefore, add the following field to the **Parser** class:

```
// Array for variables.
private double vars[] = new double[26];
```

Each element in the array is automatically initialized to zero when a **Parser** object is instantiated.

You will also need a method to look up the value of a given variable. Because the variables are named **A** through **Z**, they can easily be used to index the array **vars** by subtracting the ASCII value for **A** from the variable name. The method **findVar( )**, shown here, accomplishes this:

```
 // Return the value of a variable.
private double findVar(String vname) throws ParserException
{
  if(!Character.isLetter(vname.charAt(0))){
    handleErr(SYNTAX);
```

```
    return 0.0;
  }
  return vars[Character.toUpperCase(vname.charAt(0))-'A'];
}
```

As this method is written, it will actually accept long variable names, such as **A12** or **test**, but only the first letter is significant. You can change this feature to fit your needs.

You must also modify the **atom( )** method to handle both numbers and variables. The new version is shown here:

```
// Get the value of a number or variable.
private double atom() throws ParserException
{
  double result = 0.0;

  switch(tokType) {
    case NUMBER:
      try {
        result = Double.parseDouble(token);
      } catch (NumberFormatException exc) {
        handleErr(SYNTAX);
      }
      getToken();
      break;
    case VARIABLE:
      result = findVar(token);
      getToken();
      break;
    default:
      handleErr(SYNTAX);
      break;
  }
  return result;
}
```

Technically, these additions are all that is needed for the parser to use variables correctly; however, there is no way for these variables to be assigned a value. To enable a variable to be given a value, the parser needs to be able to handle the assignment operator, which is =. To implement assignment, we will add another method, called **evalExp1( )**, to the **Parser** class. This method will now begin the recursive-descent chain. This means that it, not **evalExp2( )**, must be called by **evaluate( )** to begin parsing the expression. The **evalExp1( )** method is shown here:

```
// Process an assignment.
private double evalExp1() throws ParserException
{
```

```
  double result;
  int varIdx;
  int ttokType;
  String temptoken;

  if(tokType == VARIABLE) {
    // save old token
    temptoken = new String(token);
    ttokType = tokType;

    // Compute the index of the variable.
    varIdx = Character.toUpperCase(token.charAt(0)) - 'A';

    getToken();
    if(!token.equals("=")) {
      putBack(); // return current token
      // restore old token -- not an assignment
      token = new String(temptoken);
      tokType = ttokType;
    }
    else {
      getToken(); // get next part of exp
      result = evalExp2();
      vars[varIdx] = result;
      return result;
    }
  }

  return evalExp2();
}
```

The **evalExp1( )** method needs to look ahead to determine whether an assignment is actually being made. This is because a variable name always precedes an assignment, but a variable name alone does not guarantee that an assignment expression follows. That is, the parser knows that A = 100 is an assignment, but it is also smart enough to know that A/10 is not. To accomplish this, **evalExp1( )** reads the next token from the input stream. If it is not an equal sign, the token is returned to the input stream for later use by calling **putBack( )**, shown here:

```
// Return a token to the input stream.
private void putBack()
{
  if(token == EOE) return;
  for(int i=0; i < token.length(); i++) expIdx--;
}
```

After making all the necessary changes, the parser will now look like this:

```
/*
   This module contains the recursive descent
   parser that uses variables.
*/

// Exception class for parser errors.
class ParserException extends Exception {
  String errStr; // describes the error

  public ParserException(String str) {
    errStr = str;
  }

  public String toString() {
    return errStr;
  }
}

class Parser {
  // These are the token types.
  final int NONE = 0;
  final int DELIMITER = 1;
  final int VARIABLE = 2;
  final int NUMBER = 3;

  // These are the types of syntax errors.
  final int SYNTAX = 0;
  final int UNBALPARENS = 1;
  final int NOEXP = 2;
  final int DIVBYZERO = 3;

   // This token indicates end-of-expression.
  final String EOE = "\0";

  private String exp;    // refers to expression string
  private int expIdx;    // current index into the expression
  private String token;  // holds current token
  private int tokType;   // holds token's type

  // Array for variables.
  private double vars[] = new double[26];

  // Parser entry point.
```

```java
public double evaluate(String expstr) throws ParserException
{
  double result;
  exp = expstr;
  expIdx = 0;

  getToken();
  if(token.equals(EOE))
    handleErr(NOEXP); // no expression present

  // Parse and evaluate the expression.
  result = evalExp1();

  if(!token.equals(EOE)) // last token must be EOE
    handleErr(SYNTAX);

  return result;
}

// Process an assignment.
private double evalExp1() throws ParserException
{
  double result;
  int varIdx;
  int ttokType;
  String temptoken;

  if(tokType == VARIABLE) {
    // save old token
    temptoken = new String(token);
    ttokType = tokType;

    // Compute the index of the variable.
    varIdx = Character.toUpperCase(token.charAt(0)) - 'A';

    getToken();
    if(!token.equals("=")) {
      putBack(); // return current token
      // restore old token -- not an assignment
      token = new String(temptoken);
      tokType = ttokType;
    }
    else {
      getToken(); // get next part of exp
      result = evalExp2();
```

```
      vars[varIdx] = result;
      return result;
    }
  }

  return evalExp2();
}

// Add or subtract two terms.
private double evalExp2() throws ParserException
{
  char op;
  double result;
  double partialResult;

  result = evalExp3();

  while((op = token.charAt(0)) == '+' || op == '-') {
    getToken();
    partialResult = evalExp3();
    switch(op) {
      case '-':
        result = result - partialResult;
        break;
      case '+':
        result = result + partialResult;
        break;
    }
  }
  return result;
}

// Multiply or divide two factors.
private double evalExp3() throws ParserException
{
  char op;
  double result;
  double partialResult;

  result = evalExp4();

  while((op = token.charAt(0)) == '*' ||
        op == '/' || op == '%') {
    getToken();
    partialResult = evalExp4();
```

```
    switch(op) {
      case '*':
        result = result * partialResult;
        break;
      case '/':
        if(partialResult == 0.0)
          handleErr(DIVBYZERO);
        result = result / partialResult;
        break;
      case '%':
        if(partialResult == 0.0)
          handleErr(DIVBYZERO);
        result = result % partialResult;
        break;
    }
  }
  return result;
}

// Process an exponent.
private double evalExp4() throws ParserException
{
  double result;
  double partialResult;
  double ex;
  int t;

  result = evalExp5();

  if(token.equals("^")) {
    getToken();
    partialResult = evalExp4();
    ex = result;
    if(partialResult == 0.0) {
      result = 1.0;
    } else
      for(t=(int)partialResult-1; t > 0; t--)
        result = result * ex;
  }
  return result;
}

// Evaluate a unary + or -.
private double evalExp5() throws ParserException
{
```

```
    double result;
    String  op;

    op = "";
    if((tokType == DELIMITER) &&
        token.equals("+") || token.equals("-")) {
      op = token;
      getToken();
    }
    result = evalExp6();

    if(op.equals("-")) result = -result;

    return result;
  }

  // Process a parenthesized expression.
  private double evalExp6() throws ParserException
  {
    double result;

    if(token.equals("(")) {
      getToken();
      result = evalExp2();
      if(!token.equals(")"))
        handleErr(UNBALPARENS);
      getToken();
    }
    else result = atom();

    return result;
  }

  // Get the value of a number or variable.
  private double atom() throws ParserException
  {
    double result = 0.0;

    switch(tokType) {
      case NUMBER:
        try {
          result = Double.parseDouble(token);
        } catch (NumberFormatException exc) {
          handleErr(SYNTAX);
        }
```

```
        getToken();
        break;
      case VARIABLE:
        result = findVar(token);
        getToken();
        break;
      default:
        handleErr(SYNTAX);
        break;
    }
    return result;
}

  // Return the value of a variable.
  private double findVar(String vname) throws ParserException
  {
    if(!Character.isLetter(vname.charAt(0))){
      handleErr(SYNTAX);
      return 0.0;
    }
    return vars[Character.toUpperCase(vname.charAt(0))-'A'];
  }

  // Return a token to the input stream.
  private void putBack()
  {
    if(token == EOE) return;
    for(int i=0; i < token.length(); i++) expIdx--;
  }

  // Handle an error.
  private void handleErr(int error) throws ParserException
  {
    String[] err = {
      "Syntax Error",
      "Unbalanced Parentheses",
      "No Expression Present",
      "Division by Zero"
    };

    throw new ParserException(err[error]);
  }

  // Obtain the next token.
  private void getToken()
```

```
{
  tokType = NONE;
  token = "";

  // Check for end of expression.
  if(expIdx == exp.length()) {
    token = EOE;
    return;
  }

  // Skip over white space.
  while(expIdx < exp.length() &&
    Character.isWhitespace(exp.charAt(expIdx))) ++expIdx;

  // Trailing whitespace ends expression.
  if(expIdx == exp.length()) {
    token = EOE;
    return;
  }

  if(isDelim(exp.charAt(expIdx))) { // is operator
    token += exp.charAt(expIdx);
    expIdx++;
    tokType = DELIMITER;
  }
  else if(Character.isLetter(exp.charAt(expIdx))) { // is variable
    while(!isDelim(exp.charAt(expIdx))) {
      token += exp.charAt(expIdx);
      expIdx++;
      if(expIdx >= exp.length()) break;
    }
    tokType = VARIABLE;
  }
  else if(Character.isDigit(exp.charAt(expIdx))) { // is number
    while(!isDelim(exp.charAt(expIdx))) {
      token += exp.charAt(expIdx);
      expIdx++;
      if(expIdx >= exp.length()) break;
    }
    tokType = NUMBER;
  }
  else { // unknown character terminates expression
    token = EOE;
    return;
```

```
    }
  }

  // Return true if c is a delimiter.
  private boolean isDelim(char c)
  {
    if((" +-/*%^=()".indexOf(c) != -1))
      return true;
    return false;
  }
}
```

To try the enhanced parser, you can use the same program that you used for the simple parser. With the enhanced parser, you can now enter expressions like

    A = 10/4
    A – B
    C = A * (F – 21)

Syntax Checking in a Recursive-Descent Parser

In expression parsing, a syntax error is simply a situation in which the input expression does not conform to the strict rules required by the parser. Most of the time, this is caused by human error, usually typing mistakes. For example, the following expressions are not valid for the parsers in this chapter:

    10 ** 8
    ((10 – 5) * 9
    /8

The first contains two operators in a row, the second has unbalanced parentheses, and the last has a division sign at the start of an expression. None of these conditions is allowed by the parser. Because syntax errors can cause the parser to give erroneous results, you need to guard against them.

In the parser, the **handleErr( )** method is called when an error is detected. Unlike some other types of parsers, the recursive-descent method makes syntax checking easy because, for the most part, it occurs in **atom( )**, **findVar( )**, or **evalExp6( )**, where parentheses are checked.

When **handleErr( )** is called, it throws a **ParserException** that contains a description of the error. This exception is not caught by **Parser**, but thrown to the calling code. Thus, the parser immediately stops when an error is encountered. You can, of course, change this behavior to suit your own needs.

One thing you might want to do is expand the information contained in a **ParserException** object. As it is currently written, this class stores only a string describing the error. You might want to add the error code itself, the index in the expression string at which point the error occurred, or other information.

A Calculator Applet

The parser is extremely simple to use and can be added to nearly any application. To understand just how easy it is to utilize the parser consider the following example. In only a few lines of code it creates a fully functional calculator applet. The calculator uses two text fields. The first contains the expression to be evaluated. The second displays the result. The result text field is read-only. Error messages are displayed on the status line. Sample output (using the Applet Viewer) is shown in Figure 2-1.

```java
// A simple calculator applet.
import java.awt.*;
import java.awt.event.*;
import java.applet.*;
/*
  <applet code="Calc" width=200 height=150>
  </applet>
*/

public class Calc extends Applet
  implements ActionListener {

  TextField expText, resText;
  Parser p;

  public void init() {
    Label heading = new
          Label("Expression Calculator ", Label.CENTER);

    Label explab = new Label("Expression ", Label.CENTER);
    Label reslab = new Label("Result      ", Label.CENTER);
    expText = new TextField(24);
    resText = new TextField(24);

    resText.setEditable(false); // result field for display only

    add(heading);
    add(explab);
    add(expText);
    add(reslab);
    add(resText);

    /* Register expression text field
       to receive action events. */
    expText.addActionListener(this);

    // create parser
```

```
    p = new Parser();
  }

  // User pressed Enter.
  public void actionPerformed(ActionEvent ae) {
    repaint();
  }

  public void paint(Graphics g) {
    double result = 0.0;
    String expstr = expText.getText();

    try {
      if(expstr.length() != 0)
        result = p.evaluate(expstr);

// To clear expression after ENTER is pressed
// use the foliing line:
//    expText.setText("");

      resText.setText(Double.toString(result));

      showStatus(""); // erase any previous error message
    } catch (ParserException exc) {
      showStatus(exc.toString());
      resText.setText("");
    }
  }
}
```

Calc begins by declaring three instance variables. The first two are **expText** and **resText**, which hold references to the expression and result text field components. A reference to the parser is held in **p**.

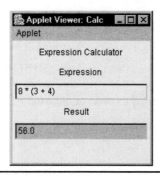

Figure 2-1   *A simple yet effective calculator applet*

Inside **init( )**, the text fields are created and added to the applet. An action listener is registered for **expText**, which is the applet itself. An action event is generated by a text field whenever the user presses ENTER. Because the result text field, **resText**, is for display purposes only, it is marked as read-only by calling **setEditable(false)**. This causes it to be grayed, and it will not respond to user input. Finally, a **Parser** instance is instantiated and assigned to **p**.

To use the calculator, simply enter an expression and then press ENTER. This causes an **ActionEvent** to be generated, which is handled by the **actionPerformed( )** method. This causes **repaint( )** to be called, which eventually leads to **paint( )** being called. Inside **paint( )**, the parser is executed to compute the value of the expression and the result is displayed. Notice that errors are displayed on the status line.

Some Things to Try

The expression parsers shown in this chapter are quite useful in a variety of applications because they enable you to offer expanded functionality without significant effort on your part. Consider the situation in which your program requests that the user enter a numeric value. For example, an application might ask the user to enter the number of copies of a document to print. Normally, you would simply display a text field, wait for input, and then convert that text into its internal numeric format. This simple approach would allow the user to enter a value, such as 100. However, what if the user wanted to print 72 copies for each of 9 departments? The user would need to manually compute that product and then enter the value 648 into the text field. However, if you use the parser to compute the value obtained from the text field, then the user could enter 9*72, and no manual computation would be required. The ability to parse and evaluate a numeric expression can add a sophisticated, professional feel to even the simplest application. Try using the parser to handle numeric input for one of your applications.

As mentioned early on in this chapter, only minimal error checking is performed by the parser. You might want to add detailed error reporting. For example, you could highlight the point in the expression at which an error was detected. This would allow the user to find and correct a syntax error.

As the parser now stands it can evaluate only numeric expressions. However, with a few additions, it is possible to evaluate other types of expressions, such as strings, spatial coordinates, or complex numbers. For example, to allow the parser to evaluate strings, you must make the following changes:

1. Define a new token type called **STRING**.
2. Enhance **getToken( )** so that it recognizes strings.
3. Add a new case inside **atom( )** that handles **STRING** tokens.

After implementing these steps, the parser could handle string expressions like these:

```
a = "one"
b = "two"
c = a + b
```

The result in **c** should be the concatenation of **a** and **b**, or "onetwo".

CHAPTER 3

Implementing Language Interpreters in Java

by Herb Schildt

Have you ever wanted to create your own computer language? If you're like most programmers, you probably have. Frankly, the idea of being able to create, control, enhance, and modify your own computer language is very appealing. However, few programmers realize how easy, and enjoyable, it can be. Be assured that the development of a full-featured compiler, such as Java, is a major undertaking, but the creation of a language interpreter is a much simpler task.

Although both interpreters and compilers take as input the source code for a program, what they do with that source code differs significantly. A compiler converts the source code of a program into an executable form. Often, as is the case with a language like C++, this executable form consists of actual CPU instructions that are directly executed by the computer. In other cases, the output of a compiler is a portable intermediate form, which is then executed by a runtime system. This is the way Java works. In Java, this intermediate code is called *bytecode*.

An interpreter works in a completely different way. It reads the source code to a program, executing each statement as it is encountered. Thus, an interpreter does not translate the source code into object code. Instead, the interpreter directly executes the program. Although program execution via an interpreter is slower than when the same program is executed in its compiled form, interpreters are still commonly used in programming for the following reasons.

First, they can provide a truly interactive environment in which program execution can be paused and resumed through user interaction. Such an interactive environment is helpful in robotics, for example. Second, because of the nature of language interpreters, they are especially well suited for interactive debugging. Third, interpreters are excellent for "script languages," such as query languages for databases. Fourth, they allow the same program to run on a variety of different platforms. Only the interpreter's runtime package must be implemented for each new environment.

Sometimes the term *interpreter* is used in situations other than those just described. For example, the original Java runtime system was called a *bytecode interpreter*. This is *not* the same type of interpreter developed in this chapter. The Java runtime system provides an execution environment for bytecode, which is a highly optimized set of portable machine instructions. Thus, the Java runtime system does not operate on source code, but on portable machine code. This is why the Java runtime system is called the Java Virtual Machine.

In addition to being an interesting and useful piece of code, the interpreter developed in this chapter serves a second purpose: it demonstrates the streamlined elegance of the Java language. Like the parser in Chapter 2, the language interpreter is a "pure code" example. It is also a fairly sophisticated program. The ease by which the interpreter can be implemented in Java gives testimony to Java's versatility. Moreover, the transparency of the code shows the expressive power of the Java syntax and libraries.

What Computer Language to Interpret?

Before we can build an interpreter, it is necessary to choose the language that we want to interpret. Although Java might seem an obvious choice, it is too large and sophisticated a language. The source code for an interpreter for even a small subset of the Java language would be far too big to fit into a chapter of this book! Moreover, you won't normally need to write an interpreter for a language as powerful as Java. Most likely, you will be writing interpreters for relatively simple languages. Thus, a better choice for the interpreter is a compact language that is readily adapted to interpretation. A language that fits these criteria is the original version of BASIC, and the interpreter developed in this chapter will accept a subset of this language. This subset is hereafter referred to as *Small BASIC*.

A BASIC-like language was chosen for three reasons. First, BASIC was originally designed to be interpreted. As such, it is relatively easy to implement an interpreter for BASIC. For example, the original version of BASIC did not support local variables, recursive methods, blocks, classes, overloading, and so on—all of which increase the complexity of the language. However, the same principles used to interpret a subset of BASIC will also apply to other languages, and you can use the code developed here as a starting point. The second reason for selecting BASIC is that a reasonable subset can be implemented in a relatively small amount of code. Finally, the original BASIC syntax is easy to master, requiring nearly no time to learn. Thus, even if you have no familiarity with traditional BASIC, you will have no trouble using Small BASIC.

The following example of a Small BASIC program illustrates just how easy the language is. Even if you have never seen a traditional-style BASIC program before, you will probably find its operation clear.

```
PRINT "A Simple Small BASIC Program"

FOR X = 1 TO 10
   GOSUB 100
NEXT

END

100 PRINT X
   RETURN
```

The program produces the following output:

```
A Simple Small BASIC Program
1.0
2.0
3.0
4.0
5.0
6.0
7.0
8.0
9.0
10.0
```

Although the meanings of the Small BASIC keywords are nearly intuitive, each is also fully explained later in this chapter.

One last point: Small BASIC is patterned after the original version of BASIC from several years ago, not Visual Basic. Visual Basic has very little in common with the original BASIC language. Of course, once you understand how the interpreter works, you can change it to interpret whatever language or variant you desire.

An Overview of the Interpreter

At the outset it is necessary to reemphasize that the interpreter developed in this chapter is a *source code interpreter*. This means that it executes a program by reading its source code one statement at a time, performing each specified operation as it goes. This differs from a *pseudo-code interpreter*, such as the original Java runtime system that interprets bytecode. The difference is that a source code interpreter operates directly on the source code of the program. A pseudo-code interpreter executes a program after it has been converted by a compiler into a machine-independent, intermediate code. Source code interpreters are easier to create and don't require a separate compilation stage.

The Small BASIC interpreter contains two major subsystems: the expression parser, which handles numeric expressions, and the interpreter, which actually executes the program. The expression parser is adapted from the one shown in Chapter 2. As it is used here, it parses a numeric expression that is contained within a larger program, rather than just parsing a self-contained expression as it did in Chapter 2.

Both the interpreter and the parser subsystems are contained within a single interpreter class, called **SBasic**. Although it would in theory have been possible to use two separate classes, one for the interpreter and one for the expression parser, it was more efficient to combine both into a single class. The reason for this is that the expression parser and the interpreter code are highly intertwined. For example, both operate on the same character array that holds the program. Separating them into two classes would have added considerable overhead, a loss of performance, and duplication of functionality. Furthermore, because parsing an expression is simply a part of the larger task of interpreting a program, it makes sense to have the entire mechanism contained within a single class.

The interpreter works by reading the source code of a program one token at a time. When it encounters a keyword, it does whatever that keyword requests. For example, when the interpreter reads PRINT, it prints the value of the expression that follows. When it reads GOSUB, it executes the specified subroutine. This process continues until the end of the program is reached. Thus, the interpreter simply does what the program tells it to do!

The Small BASIC Interpreter

The code for the Small BASIC interpreter is fairly long—longer than one would normally put in a chapter of a book. However, don't be intimidated by its size. Despite its length, the interpreter is conceptually simple, and once you grasp its general mode of operation, each part is easy to understand.

The entire code for the Small BASIC interpreter is shown next. The remainder of this chapter will explain how it works, and how to use it.

```java
// A Small BASIC Interpreter.

import java.io.*;
import java.util.*;

// Exception class for interpreter errors.
class InterpreterException extends Exception {
  String errStr; // describes the error

  public InterpreterException(String str) {
    errStr = str;
  }

  public String toString() {
    return errStr;
  }
}

// The Small BASIC interpreter.
class SBasic {
  final int PROG_SIZE = 10000; // maximum program size

  // These are the token types.
  final int NONE = 0;
  final int DELIMITER = 1;
  final int VARIABLE = 2;
  final int NUMBER = 3;
  final int COMMAND = 4;
  final int QUOTEDSTR = 5;

  // These are the types of errors.
  final int SYNTAX = 0;
  final int UNBALPARENS = 1;
  final int NOEXP = 2;
  final int DIVBYZERO = 3;
  final int EQUALEXPECTED = 4;
  final int NOTVAR = 5;
  final int LABELTABLEFULL = 6;
  final int DUPLABEL = 7;
  final int UNDEFLABEL = 8;
  final int THENEXPECTED = 9;
  final int TOEXPECTED = 10;
  final int NEXTWITHOUTFOR = 11;
  final int RETURNWITHOUTGOSUB = 12;
  final int MISSINGQUOTE = 13;
```

```
final int FILENOTFOUND = 14;
final int FILEIOERROR = 15;
final int INPUTIOERROR = 16;

// Internal representation of the Small BASIC keywords.
final int UNKNCOM = 0;
final int PRINT = 1;
final int INPUT = 2;
final int IF = 3;
final int THEN = 4;
final int FOR = 5;
final int NEXT = 6;
final int TO = 7;
final int GOTO = 8;
final int GOSUB = 9;
final int RETURN = 10;
final int END = 11;
final int EOL = 12;

// This token indicates end-of-program.
final String EOP = "\0";

// Codes for double-operators, such as <=.
final char LE = 1;
final char GE = 2;
final char NE = 3;

// Array for variables.
private double vars[];

// This class links keywords with their keyword tokens.
class Keyword {
  String keyword; // string form
  int keywordTok; // internal representation

  Keyword(String str, int t) {
    keyword = str;
    keywordTok = t;
  }
}

/* Table of keywords with their internal representation.
   All keywords must be entered lowercase. */
Keyword kwTable[] = {
  new Keyword("print", PRINT), // in this table.
```

```java
  new Keyword("input", INPUT),
  new Keyword("if", IF),
  new Keyword("then", THEN),
  new Keyword("goto", GOTO),
  new Keyword("for", FOR),
  new Keyword("next", NEXT),
  new Keyword("to", TO),
  new Keyword("gosub", GOSUB),
  new Keyword("return", RETURN),
  new Keyword("end", END)
};

private char[] prog; // refers to program array
private int progIdx; // current index into program

private String token; // holds current token
private int tokType;  // holds token's type

private int kwToken; // internal representation of a keyword

// Support for FOR loops.
class ForInfo {
  int var; // counter variable
  double target; // target value
  int loc; // index in source code to loop to
}

// Stack for FOR loops.
private Stack fStack;

// Defines label table entries.
class Label {
  String name; // label
  int loc; // index of label's location in source file
  public Label(String n, int i) {
    name = n;
    loc = i;
  }
}

// A map for labels.
private TreeMap labelTable;

// Stack for gosubs.
private Stack gStack;
```

```
// Relational operators.
char rops[] = {
  GE, NE, LE, '<', '>', '=', 0
};

/* Create a string containing the relational
   operators in order to make checking for
   them more convenient. */
String relops = new String(rops);

// Constructor for SBasic.
public SBasic(String progName)
    throws InterpreterException {

  char tempbuf[] = new char[PROG_SIZE];
  int size;

  // Load the program to execute.
  size = loadProgram(tempbuf, progName);

  if(size != -1) {
    // Create a properly sized array to hold the program.
    prog = new char[size];

    // Copy the program into program array.
    System.arraycopy(tempbuf, 0, prog, 0, size);
  }
}

// Load a program.
private int loadProgram(char[] p, String fname)
  throws InterpreterException
{
  int size = 0;

  try {
    FileReader fr = new FileReader(fname);

    BufferedReader br = new BufferedReader(fr);

    size = br.read(p, 0, PROG_SIZE);

    fr.close();
  } catch(FileNotFoundException exc) {
    handleErr(FILENOTFOUND);
```

```java
    } catch(IOException exc) {
      handleErr(FILEIOERROR);
    }

    // If file ends with an EOF mark, back up.
    if(p[size-1] == (char) 26) size--;

    return size; // return size of program
  }

  // Execute the program.
  public void run() throws InterpreterException {

    // Initialize for new program run.
    vars = new double[26];
    fStack = new Stack();
    labelTable = new TreeMap();
    gStack = new Stack();
    progIdx = 0;

    scanLabels(); // find the labels in the program

    sbInterp(); // execute

  }

  // Entry point for the Small BASIC interpreter.
  private void sbInterp() throws InterpreterException
  {

    // This is the interpreter's main loop.
    do {
      getToken();
      // Check for assignment statement.
      if(tokType==VARIABLE) {
        putBack(); // return the var to the input stream
        assignment(); // handle assignment statement
      }
      else // is keyword
        switch(kwToken) {
          case PRINT:
            print();
            break;
          case GOTO:
            execGoto();
```

```
              break;
          case IF:
            execIf();
            break;
          case FOR:
            execFor();
            break;
          case NEXT:
            next();
            break;
          case INPUT:
            input();
            break;
          case GOSUB:
            gosub();
            break;
          case RETURN:
            greturn();
            break;
          case END:
            return;
      }
  } while (!token.equals(EOP));
}

// Find all labels.
private void scanLabels() throws InterpreterException
{
  int i;
  Object result;

  // See if the first token in the file is a label.
  getToken();
  if(tokType==NUMBER)
    labelTable.put(token, new Integer(progIdx));

  findEOL();

  do {
    getToken();
    if(tokType==NUMBER) {// must be a line number
      result = labelTable.put(token,
                              new Integer(progIdx));
      if(result != null)
        handleErr(DUPLABEL);
```

```
    }

    // If not on a blank line, find next line.
    if(kwToken != EOL) findEOL();
  } while(!token.equals(EOP));
  progIdx = 0; // reset index to start of program
}

// Find the start of the next line.
private void findEOL()
{
  while(progIdx < prog.length &&
        prog[progIdx] != '\n') ++progIdx;
  if(progIdx < prog.length) progIdx++;
}

// Assign a variable a value.
private void assignment() throws InterpreterException
{
  int var;
  double value;
  char vname;

  // Get the variable name.
  getToken();
  vname = token.charAt(0);

  if(!Character.isLetter(vname)) {
    handleErr(NOTVAR);
    return;
  }

  // Convert to index into variable table.
  var = (int) Character.toUpperCase(vname) - 'A';

  // Get the equal sign.
  getToken();
  if(!token.equals("=")) {
    handleErr(EQUALEXPECTED);
    return;
  }

  // Get the value to assign.
  value = evaluate();
```

```
    // Assign the value.
    vars[var] = value;
}

// Execute a simple version of the PRINT statement.
private void print() throws InterpreterException
{
  double result;
  int len=0, spaces;
  String lastDelim = "";

  do {
    getToken(); // get next list item
    if(kwToken==EOL || token.equals(EOP)) break;

    if(tokType==QUOTEDSTR) { // is string
      System.out.print(token);
      len += token.length();
      getToken();
    }
    else { // is expression
      putBack();
      result = evaluate();
      getToken();
      System.out.print(result);

      // Add length of output to running total.
      Double t = new Double(result);
      len += t.toString().length(); // save length
    }
    lastDelim = token;

    // If comma, move to next tab stop.
    if(lastDelim.equals(",")) {
      // compute number of spaces to move to next tab
      spaces = 8 - (len % 8);
      len += spaces; // add in the tabbing position
      while(spaces != 0) {
        System.out.print(" ");
        spaces--;
      }
    }
    else if(token.equals(";")) {
      System.out.print(" ");
      len++;
```

```
    }
    else if(kwToken != EOL && !token.equals(EOP))
      handleErr(SYNTAX);
  } while (lastDelim.equals(";") || lastDelim.equals(","));

  if(kwToken==EOL || token.equals(EOP)) {
    if(!lastDelim.equals(";") && !lastDelim.equals(","))
      System.out.println();
  }
  else handleErr(SYNTAX);
}

// Execute a GOTO statement.
private void execGoto() throws InterpreterException
{
  Integer loc;

  getToken(); // get label to go to

  // Find the location of the label.
  loc = (Integer) labelTable.get(token);

  if(loc == null)
    handleErr(UNDEFLABEL); // label not defined
  else // start program running at that loc
    progIdx = loc.intValue();
}

// Execute an IF statement.
private void execIf() throws InterpreterException
{
  double result;

  result = evaluate(); // get value of expression

  /* If the result is true (non-zero),
     process target of IF. Otherwise move on
     to next line in the program. */
  if(result != 0.0) {
    getToken();
    if(kwToken != THEN) {
      handleErr(THENEXPECTED);
      return;
    } // else, target statement will be executed
  }
```

```
      else findEOL(); // find start of next line
  }

  // Execute a FOR loop.
  private void execFor() throws InterpreterException
  {
    ForInfo stckvar = new ForInfo();
    double value;
    char vname;

    getToken(); // read the control variable
    vname = token.charAt(0);
    if(!Character.isLetter(vname)) {
      handleErr(NOTVAR);
      return;
    }

    // Save index of control var.
    stckvar.var = Character.toUpperCase(vname) - 'A';

    getToken(); // read the equal sign
    if(token.charAt(0) != '=') {
      handleErr(EQUALEXPECTED);
      return;
    }

    value = evaluate(); // get initial value

    vars[stckvar.var] = value;

    getToken(); // read and discard the TO
    if(kwToken != TO) handleErr(TOEXPECTED);

    stckvar.target = evaluate(); // get target value

    /* If loop can execute at least once,
       push info on stack. */
    if(value >= vars[stckvar.var]) {
      stckvar.loc = progIdx;
      fStack.push(stckvar);
    }
    else // otherwise, skip loop code altogether
      while(kwToken != NEXT) getToken();
  }
```

```java
// Execute a NEXT statement.
private void next() throws InterpreterException
{
  ForInfo stckvar;

  try {
    // Retrieve info for this For loop.
    stckvar = (ForInfo) fStack.pop();
    vars[stckvar.var]++; // increment control var

    // If done, return.
    if(vars[stckvar.var] > stckvar.target) return;

    // Otherwise, restore the info.
    fStack.push(stckvar);
    progIdx = stckvar.loc;  // loop
  } catch(EmptyStackException exc) {
    handleErr(NEXTWITHOUTFOR);
  }
}

// Execute a simple form of INPUT.
private void input() throws InterpreterException
{
  int var;
  double val = 0.0;
  String str;

  BufferedReader br = new
    BufferedReader(new InputStreamReader(System.in));

  getToken(); // see if prompt string is present
  if(tokType == QUOTEDSTR) {
    // if so, print it and check for comma
    System.out.print(token);
    getToken();
    if(!token.equals(",")) handleErr(SYNTAX);
    getToken();
  }
  else System.out.print("? "); // otherwise, prompt with ?

  // get the input var
  var = Character.toUpperCase(token.charAt(0)) - 'A';

  try {
```

```
    str = br.readLine();
    val = Double.parseDouble(str); // read the value
  } catch (IOException exc) {
    handleErr(INPUTIOERROR);
  } catch (NumberFormatException exc) {
    /* You might want to handle this error
       differently than the other interpreter
       errors. */
    System.out.println("Invalid input.");
  }

  vars[var] = val; // store it
}


// Execute a GOSUB.
private void gosub() throws InterpreterException
{
  Integer loc;

  getToken();

  // Find the label to call.
  loc = (Integer) labelTable.get(token);

  if(loc == null)
    handleErr(UNDEFLABEL); // label not defined
  else {
    // Save place to return to.
    gStack.push(new Integer(progIdx));

    // Start program running at that loc.
    progIdx = loc.intValue();
  }
}


// Return from GOSUB.
private void greturn() throws InterpreterException
{
  Integer t;

  try {
    // Restore program index.
    t = (Integer) gStack.pop();
    progIdx = t.intValue();
  } catch(EmptyStackException exc) {
```

```
    handleErr(RETURNWITHOUTGOSUB);
  }

}

// *************** Expression Parser ***************

// Parser entry point.
private double evaluate() throws InterpreterException
{
  double result = 0.0;

  getToken();
  if(token.equals(EOP))
    handleErr(NOEXP); // no expression present

  // Parse and evaluate the expression.
  result = evalExp1();

  putBack();

  return result;
}

// Process relational operators.
private double evalExp1() throws InterpreterException
{
  double l_temp, r_temp, result;
  char op;

  result = evalExp2();
  // If at end of program, return.
  if(token.equals(EOP)) return result;

  op = token.charAt(0);

  if(isRelop(op)) {
    l_temp = result;
    getToken();
    r_temp = evalExp1();
    switch(op) { // perform the relational operation
      case '<':
        if(l_temp < r_temp) result = 1.0;
        else result = 0.0;
        break;
```

```
      case LE:
        if(l_temp <= r_temp) result = 1.0;
        else result = 0.0;
        break;
      case '>':
        if(l_temp > r_temp) result = 1.0;
        else result = 0.0;
        break;
      case GE:
        if(l_temp >= r_temp) result = 1.0;
        else result = 0.0;
        break;
      case '=':
        if(l_temp == r_temp) result = 1.0;
        else result = 0.0;
        break;
      case NE:
        if(l_temp != r_temp) result = 1.0;
        else result = 0.0;
        break;
    }
  }
  return result;
}

// Add or subtract two terms.
private double evalExp2() throws InterpreterException
{
  char op;
  double result;
  double partialResult;

  result = evalExp3();

  while((op = token.charAt(0)) == '+' || op == '-') {
    getToken();
    partialResult = evalExp3();
    switch(op) {
      case '-':
        result = result - partialResult;
        break;
      case '+':
        result = result + partialResult;
        break;
    }
```

```
  }
  return result;
}


// Multiply or divide two factors.
private double evalExp3() throws InterpreterException
{
  char op;
  double result;
  double partialResult;

  result = evalExp4();

  while((op = token.charAt(0)) == '*' ||
        op == '/' || op == '%') {
    getToken();
    partialResult = evalExp4();
    switch(op) {
      case '*':
        result = result * partialResult;
        break;
      case '/':
        if(partialResult == 0.0)
          handleErr(DIVBYZERO);
        result = result / partialResult;
        break;
      case '%':
        if(partialResult == 0.0)
          handleErr(DIVBYZERO);
        result = result % partialResult;
        break;
    }
  }
  return result;
}


// Process an exponent.
private double evalExp4() throws InterpreterException
{
  double result;
  double partialResult;
  double ex;
  int t;

  result = evalExp5();
```

```
      if(token.equals("^")) {
        getToken();
        partialResult = evalExp4();
        ex = result;
        if(partialResult == 0.0) {
          result = 1.0;
        } else
          for(t=(int)partialResult-1; t > 0; t--)
            result = result * ex;
      }
      return result;
    }

    // Evaluate a unary + or -.
    private double evalExp5() throws InterpreterException
    {
      double result;
      String  op;

      op = "";
      if((tokType == DELIMITER) &&
          token.equals("+") || token.equals("-")) {
        op = token;
        getToken();
      }
      result = evalExp6();

      if(op.equals("-")) result = -result;

      return result;
    }

    // Process a parenthesized expression.
    private double evalExp6() throws InterpreterException
    {
      double result;

      if(token.equals("(")) {
        getToken();
        result = evalExp2();
        if(!token.equals(")"))
          handleErr(UNBALPARENS);
        getToken();
      }
      else result = atom();
```

```java
    return result;
}


// Get the value of a number or variable.
private double atom() throws InterpreterException
{
  double result = 0.0;

  switch(tokType) {
    case NUMBER:
      try {
        result = Double.parseDouble(token);
      } catch (NumberFormatException exc) {
        handleErr(SYNTAX);
      }
      getToken();
      break;
    case VARIABLE:
      result = findVar(token);
      getToken();
      break;
    default:
      handleErr(SYNTAX);
      break;
  }
  return result;
}


 // Return the value of a variable.
private double findVar(String vname)
  throws InterpreterException
{
  if(!Character.isLetter(vname.charAt(0))){
    handleErr(SYNTAX);
    return 0.0;
  }
  return vars[Character.toUpperCase(vname.charAt(0))-'A'];
}


// Return a token to the input stream.
private void putBack()
{
  if(token == EOP) return;
  for(int i=0; i < token.length(); i++) progIdx--;
}
```

```java
// Handle an error.
private void handleErr(int error)
  throws InterpreterException
{
  String[] err = {
    "Syntax Error",
    "Unbalanced Parentheses",
    "No Expression Present",
    "Division by Zero",
    "Equal sign expected",
    "Not a variable",
    "Label table full",
    "Duplicate label",
    "Undefined label",
    "THEN expected",
    "TO expected",
    "NEXT without FOR",
    "RETURN without GOSUB",
    "Closing quotes needed",
    "File not found",
    "I/O error while loading file",
    "I/O error on INPUT statement"
  };

  throw new InterpreterException(err[error]);
}

// Obtain the next token.
private void getToken() throws InterpreterException
{
  char ch;

  tokType = NONE;
  token = "";
  kwToken = UNKNCOM;

  // Check for end of program.
  if(progIdx == prog.length) {
    token = EOP;
    return;
  }

  // Skip over white space.
  while(progIdx < prog.length &&
        isSpaceOrTab(prog[progIdx])) progIdx++;
```

```java
// Trailing whitespace ends program.
if(progIdx == prog.length) {
  token = EOP;
  tokType = DELIMITER;
  return;
}


if(prog[progIdx] == '\r') { // handle crlf
  progIdx += 2;
  kwToken = EOL;
  token = "\r\n";
  return;
}


// Check for relational operator.
ch = prog[progIdx];
if(ch == '<' || ch == '>') {
  if(progIdx+1 == prog.length) handleErr(SYNTAX);

  switch(ch) {
    case '<':
      if(prog[progIdx+1] == '>') {
        progIdx += 2;;
        token = String.valueOf(NE);
      }
      else if(prog[progIdx+1] == '=') {
        progIdx += 2;
        token = String.valueOf(LE);
      }
      else {
        progIdx++;
        token = "<";
      }
      break;
    case '>':
      if(prog[progIdx+1] == '=') {
        progIdx += 2;;
        token = String.valueOf(GE);
      }
      else {
        progIdx++;
        token = ">";
      }
      break;
  }
```

```
    tokType = DELIMITER;
    return;
}

if(isDelim(prog[progIdx])) {
  // Is an operator.
  token += prog[progIdx];
  progIdx++;
  tokType = DELIMITER;
}
else if(Character.isLetter(prog[progIdx])) {
  // Is a variable or keyword.
  while(!isDelim(prog[progIdx])) {
    token += prog[progIdx];
    progIdx++;
    if(progIdx >= prog.length) break;
  }

  kwToken = lookUp(token);
  if(kwToken==UNKNCOM) tokType = VARIABLE;
  else tokType = COMMAND;
}
else if(Character.isDigit(prog[progIdx])) {
  // Is a number.
  while(!isDelim(prog[progIdx])) {
    token += prog[progIdx];
    progIdx++;
    if(progIdx >= prog.length) break;
  }
  tokType = NUMBER;
}
else if(prog[progIdx] == '"') {
  // Is a quoted string.
  progIdx++;
  ch = prog[progIdx];
  while(ch !='"' && ch != '\r') {
    token += ch;
    progIdx++;
    ch = prog[progIdx];
  }
  if(ch == '\r') handleErr(MISSINGQUOTE);
  progIdx++;
  tokType = QUOTEDSTR;
```

```java
    }
    else { // unknown character terminates program
      token = EOP;
      return;
    }
  }


  // Return true if c is a delimiter.
  private boolean isDelim(char c)
  {
    if((" \r,;<>+-/*%^=()".indexOf(c) != -1))
      return true;
    return false;
  }


  // Return true if c is a space or a tab.
  boolean isSpaceOrTab(char c)
  {
    if(c == ' ' || c =='\t') return true;
    return false;
  }


  // Return true if c is a relational operator.
  boolean isRelop(char c) {
    if(relops.indexOf(c) != -1) return true;
    return false;
  }


  /* Look up a token's internal representation in the
     token table. */
  private int lookUp(String s)
  {
    int i;

    // Convert to lowercase.
    s = s.toLowerCase();

    // See if token is in table.
    for(i=0; i < kwTable.length; i++)
      if(kwTable[i].keyword.equals(s))
        return kwTable[i].keywordTok;
    return UNKNCOM; // unknown keyword
  }
}
```

The Small BASIC Expression Parser

At the core of the interpreter is the expression parser. As mentioned, the parser used by Small BASIC is adapted from the one shown in Chapter 2. If you have not yet read Chapter 2, do so now because it provides the detailed description of the parser. Although its fundamental operation is unchanged, a special version of the parser is required for Small BASIC.

Many of the changes to the parser allow it to handle the syntax of the Small BASIC language. For example, the parser must be able to recognize the keywords of the language, it must not treat the equal sign (=) as an operator, and it must evaluate relational operators. The **getToken( )** method is substantially enhanced to handle the expanded demands placed on it.

Other differences between the parser in Chapter 2 and the one used here are caused by efficiency considerations. For example, in Chapter 2, a reference to the expression was passed to the parser. In the Small BASIC version, a reference to the program being interpreted is held in an instance variable shared by both the interpreter and the parser. Thus, the overhead associated with passing the reference is avoided. Because interpreters are slow by nature, these types of efficiency enhancements are important.

Another change in the parser is caused by the fact that the Small BASIC version operates on an array of characters rather than on a string. Recall that the parser developed in Chapter 2 was passed a string containing the expression to evaluate. The reason for the change is efficiency. As you know, a program is stored in a normal text file, which is a sequence of characters, not a string. Thus, when the interpreter loads the file prior to execution, it reads the file into a character array. Although it would have been possible to convert this array into a string, to do so would introduce a needless inefficiency.

Since the Small BASIC expression parser uses the same techniques as described in Chapter 2, you will have no trouble following its operation and we will not examine it in detail here. However, before moving on to the interpreter, a few general comments are in order. We will begin by explaining precisely what an expression is as it relates to Small BASIC.

Small BASIC Expressions

As they apply to the small BASIC interpreter developed in this chapter, expressions are comprised of the following items:

▶ Integers
▶ The operators + − / * ^ = ( ) < > >= <= <>
▶ Variables

In Small BASIC, the ^ indicates exponentiation. The = is used for both assignments and for equality. However, relative to BASIC expressions, it is only an operator when used in a relational expression. (In standard BASIC, assignment is a statement and not an operation.) Not equal is denoted as < >. These items can be combined in expressions according to the rules of algebra. Here are some examples:

```
7 − 8
(100 − 5) * 14/6
a + b − c
10 ^ 5
A < B
```

The precedence of the operators is shown here:

Highest	( )
	unary + −
	∧
	* /
	+ −
Lowest	< > <= >= <> =

Operators of equal precedence evaluate from left to right.

Small BASIC makes the following assumptions:

▶ All variables are single letters; this means that 26 variables, the letters A through Z, are available for use.

▶ The variables are not case sensitive; 'a' and 'A' will be treated as the same variable.

▶ All numbers are **double**s.

▶ No string variables are supported, although quoted string constants can be used for writing messages to the screen.

These assumptions are built in to the parser.

Small BASIC Tokens

At the core of the Small BASIC parser is the **getToken( )** method. This method is an expanded version of the one shown in Chapter 2. The changes allow it to tokenize not just numeric expressions, but also other elements of the Small BASIC language, such as keywords and strings.

In Small BASIC, each keyword token has two formats: external and internal. The external format is the text form that you use when writing a program. For example, "PRINT" is the external form of the PRINT keyword. Although it is possible for an interpreter to be designed in such a way that each token is used in its external string form, this is seldom (if ever) done because it is inefficient. Instead, Small BASIC operates on the internal format of a token, which is simply an integer value. For example, the PRINT command is represented by 1; the INPUT command by 2; and so on. The advantage of the internal representation is that much faster code can be written using integers rather than strings. It is the job of **getToken( )** to convert the token from its external format into its internal format.

The Small BASIC **getToken( )** method is shown here. It progresses through the program one character at a time.

```
// Obtain the next token.
private void getToken() throws InterpreterException
{
  char ch;

  tokType = NONE;
  token = "";
  kwToken = UNKNCOM;

  // Check for end of program.
  if(progIdx == prog.length) {
    token = EOP;
    return;
  }

  // Skip over white space.
  while(progIdx < prog.length &&
        isSpaceOrTab(prog[progIdx])) progIdx++;

  // Trailing whitespace ends program.
  if(progIdx == prog.length) {
    token = EOP;
    tokType = DELIMITER;
    return;
  }

  if(prog[progIdx] == '\r') { // handle crlf
    progIdx += 2;
    kwToken = EOL;
    token = "\r\n";
    return;
  }

  // Check for relational operator.
  ch = prog[progIdx];
  if(ch == '<' || ch == '>') {
    if(progIdx+1 == prog.length) handleErr(SYNTAX);

    switch(ch) {
      case '<':
        if(prog[progIdx+1] == '>') {
          progIdx += 2;;
```

```
          token = String.valueOf(NE);
        }
        else if(prog[progIdx+1] == '=') {
          progIdx += 2;
          token = String.valueOf(LE);
        }
        else {
          progIdx++;
          token = "<";
        }
        break;
      case '>':
        if(prog[progIdx+1] == '=') {
          progIdx += 2;;
          token = String.valueOf(GE);
        }
        else {
          progIdx++;
          token = ">";
        }
        break;
    }
    tokType = DELIMITER;
    return;
  }

  if(isDelim(prog[progIdx])) {
    // Is an operator.
    token += prog[progIdx];
    progIdx++;
    tokType = DELIMITER;
  }
  else if(Character.isLetter(prog[progIdx])) {
    // Is variable or keyword.
    while(!isDelim(prog[progIdx])) {
      token += prog[progIdx];
      progIdx++;
      if(progIdx >= prog.length) break;
    }

    kwToken = lookUp(token);
    if(kwToken==UNKNCOM) tokType = VARIABLE;
    else tokType = COMMAND;
  }
  else if(Character.isDigit(prog[progIdx])) {
```

```
    // Is a number.
    while(!isDelim(prog[progIdx])) {
      token += prog[progIdx];
      progIdx++;
      if(progIdx >= prog.length) break;
    }
    tokType = NUMBER;
  }
  else if(prog[progIdx] == '"') {
    // Is a quoted string.
    progIdx++;
    ch = prog[progIdx];
    while(ch !='"' && ch != '\r') {
      token += ch;
      progIdx++;
      ch = prog[progIdx];
    }
    if(ch == '\r') handleErr(MISSINGQUOTE);
    progIdx++;
    tokType = QUOTEDSTR;
  }
  else { // unknown character terminates program
    token = EOP;
    return;
  }
}
```

SBasic defines the following instance variables that are used extensively by **getToken( )** and the rest of the interpreter code:

```
private char[] prog; // refers to program array
private int progIdx; // current index into program

private String token; // holds current token
private int tokType;  // holds token's type

private int kwToken; // internal representation of a keyword
```

The program is stored in a character array that is referred to by **prog**. The specific location at which the interpreter is operating is stored in **progIdx**. The string version of the token is held in **token**. The token type is stored in **tokType**. The internal representation of a token representing a keyword is stored in **kwToken**.

The Small BASIC parser recognizes five token types: **DELIMITER**, **VARIABLE**, **NUMBER**, **COMMAND**, and **QUOTESTR**. **DELIMITER** is used both for operators and parentheses. **VARIABLE** is used when a variable is encountered. **NUMBER** is for numbers. The **COMMAND** type is assigned when a BASIC keyword is found. Tokens of type **COMMAND** require that an action be taken by the interpreter. Type **QUOTESTR** is for quoted strings.

Look closely at **getToken( )**. If the end of the program has been reached, then **token** is assigned **EOP** and the method returns. Otherwise, leading spaces are skipped with the help of the method **isSpaceOrTab( )**, which returns true if its argument is a space or tab. It is not possible to use Java's **Character.isWhitespace( )** method (which returns true for any whitespace character) for this determination because BASIC recognizes the newline character as a terminator. Thus, for Small BASIC, white space is limited to just spaces and tabs. Assuming that trailing spaces don't end the program, once the spaces have been skipped, **prog[progIdx]** will be referring to either a number, a variable, a keyword, a carriage-return/linefeed sequence, an operator, or a quoted string.

If the next character is a carriage return, **kwToken** is set equal to **EOL**, a carriage return/line feed sequence is stored in **token**, and **DELIMITER** is put into **tokType**.

Otherwise, **getToken( )** checks for relational operators, which might be two-character operators, such as <=. **getToken( )** converts two-character operators into their internal, one-character representation. The values **NE**, **GE**, and **LE** are defined as **final** values within **SBasic**. Next, **getToken( )** checks for the other operators. If any type of operator is found, it is returned as a string in **token** and the type of **DELIMITER** is placed in **tokType**.

If the next character is not an operator, **getToken( )** checks to see if it is a letter. If it is, then the token will be either a variable, such as A or X, or a keyword, such as **PRINT**. The **lookUp( )** method checks to see if it is a keyword. If it is, **lookUp( )** returns the appropriate internal representation of the keyword. If it is not a keyword, then the token is assumed to be a variable.

Otherwise, if the next character is a digit, then **getToken( )** reads a number. If, instead, the next character is a quotation mark, then a quoted string is read. Finally, if the next character is none of the above, it is assumed that the end of the expression has been reached.

The rest of the parser works essentially the same as it did in Chapter 2 with the exception of **evalExp1( )**. In Chapter 2 **evalExp1( )** was used to handle the assignment operator. However, in traditional BASIC, assignment is a statement, not an operation. Therefore, **evalExp1( )** is not used for assignment when parsing expressions found in Small BASIC programs. Instead, it is used to evaluate the relational operators. If you use the interpreter to experiment with other types of languages, then you may need to add a method called **evalExp0( )**, which would be used to handle assignment as an operator.

One other important difference between the parser in Chapter 2 and the one used here is that in Chapter 2, the end of the string that held the expression indicated the end of the expression. In this version, the end of the expression is signaled by the end of the line or anything else that is not a valid part of an expression, such as a keyword.

The Small BASIC parser recognizes only the variables A through Z. Although it will accept long variable names, only the first letter is significant. You can modify it to enforce single-letter variable names if you like.

The Interpreter

The interpreter portion of **SBasic** is the code that actually executes a program. In general, it is quite easy to interpret a Small BASIC program because each statement (except for assignment) begins with a keyword. Thus, the interpreter works by obtaining the keyword at the start of each line and then doing what that keyword specifies. This process repeats until the entire program has been interpreted. The remainder of this section examines each part of the interpreter in detail.

The InterpreterException Class

At the start of the interpreter file, you will find the class **InterpreterException**. This is the type of exception that the interpreter will throw if an error occurs. Code that uses **SBasic** must handle this exception. Exceptions can be caused by syntax errors, by I/O errors, and by errors in numeric expressions.

The SBasic Constructor

The constructor for **SBasic** is shown here:

```
// Constructor for SBasic.
public SBasic(String progName)
    throws InterpreterException {

  char tempbuf[] = new char[PROG_SIZE];
  int size;

  // Load the program to execute.
  size = loadProgram(tempbuf, progName);

  if(size != -1) {
    // Create a properly sized array to hold the program.
    prog = new char[size];

    // Copy the program into program array.
    System.arraycopy(tempbuf, 0, prog, 0, size);
  }
}
```

The constructor is passed the name of the Small BASIC file that you want to interpret. It then creates a temporary buffer into which this file will be read. The size of this buffer is specified by **PROG_SIZE**, which is arbitrarily set to 10,000. This is the size of the largest program that **SBasic** can interpret. You can change this size if you want.

Next, the constructor calls **loadProgram( )**, which actually reads the program and returns its size, in characters, or –1 on failure. Then, a new array that is precisely the size of the program is created and a reference to it assigned to **prog**. Finally, the program is copied into this array. Thus, the size of the array referred to by **prog** will be exactly the same as the size of the program.

The **loadProgram( )** method is shown here:

```java
// Load a program.
private int loadProgram(char[] p, String fname)
  throws InterpreterException
{
  int size = 0;

  try {
    FileReader fr = new FileReader(fname);

    BufferedReader br = new BufferedReader(fr);

    size = br.read(p, 0, PROG_SIZE);

    fr.close();
  } catch(FileNotFoundException exc) {
    handleErr(FILENOTFOUND);
  } catch(IOException exc) {
    handleErr(FILEIOERROR);
  }

  // If file ends with an EOF mark, back up.
  if(p[size-1] == (char) 26) size--;

  return size; // return size of program
}
```

Most of this method is easily understandable, but pay special attention to these lines:

```java
// If file ends with an EOF mark, back up.
if(p[size-1] == (char) 26) size--;
```

As the comment indicates, this line discards a trailing EOF mark that might end the file. As you may know, some text editors append an end-of-file marker (which is usually the value 26). Others do not. **loadProgram( )** handles both cases by removing the mark if it is present.

The Keywords

The subset of BASIC that Small BASIC interprets is represented by these keywords:

PRINT	INPUT	IF
THEN	FOR	NEXT
TO	GOTO	GOSUB
RETURN	END	

The internal representation of these keywords plus **EOL**, for end of line, are declared as **final** values in **SBasic**, as shown here:

```
// Internal representation of the Small BASIC keywords.
final int UNKNCOM = 0;
final int PRINT = 1;
final int INPUT = 2;
final int IF = 3;
final int THEN = 4;
final int FOR = 5;
final int NEXT = 6;
final int TO = 7;
final int GOTO = 8;
final int GOSUB = 9;
final int RETURN = 10;
final int END = 11;
final int EOL = 12;
```

Notice **UNKNCOM**. This value is used by the **lookUp( )** method to indicate an unknown keyword.

To facilitate the conversion of a keyword's external representation into its internal representation, both the external and internal forms are held in a table called **kwTable** comprised of **Keyword** objects. Both are shown here:

```
// This class links keywords with their keyword tokens.
class Keyword {
  String keyword; // string form
  int keywordTok; // internal representation

  Keyword(String str, int t) {
    keyword = str;
    keywordTok = t;
  }
}

/* Table of keywords with their internal representation.
```

```
   All keywords must be entered lowercase. */
Keyword kwTable[] = {
  new Keyword("print", PRINT), // in this table.
  new Keyword("input", INPUT),
  new Keyword("if", IF),
  new Keyword("then", THEN),
  new Keyword("goto", GOTO),
  new Keyword("for", FOR),
  new Keyword("next", NEXT),
  new Keyword("to", TO),
  new Keyword("gosub", GOSUB),
  new Keyword("return", RETURN),
  new Keyword("end", END)
};
```

The **lookUp( )** method, shown next, uses **kwTable** to convert a token to its internal representation. If no match is found, **UNKNCOM** is returned.

```
/* Look up a token's internal representation in the
   token table. */
private int lookUp(String s)
{
  int i;

  // Convert to lowercase.
  s = s.toLowerCase();

  // See if token is in table.
  for(i=0; i < kwTable.length; i++)
    if(kwTable[i].keyword.equals(s))
      return kwTable[i].keywordTok;
  return UNKNCOM; // unknown keyword
}
```

The run( ) Method

After an **SBasic** object has been created, the program that it encapsulates is executed by calling **run( )**, shown here:

```
// Execute the program.
public void run() throws InterpreterException {

  // Initialize for new program run.
  vars = new double[26];
  fStack = new Stack();
  labelTable = new TreeMap();
```

```
    gStack = new Stack();
    progIdx = 0;

    scanLabels(); // find the labels in the program

    sbInterp(); // execute
}
```

The **run( )** method begins by allocating the array that holds the values of the variables, a stack for FOR loops, a tree map for labels, and a stack for GOSUBs. Next, **progIdx**, which holds the location of the program that is currently being interpreted, is set to 0. These fields are set each time **run( )** is called, thus enabling repeated execution of the same program.

Next, **scanLabels( )** is called, which scans the program, looking for labels. When one is found, the label and its location are stored in the **labelTable** map. By finding all labels prior to execution, the execution speed of the program is improved.

Finally, **sbInterp( )** is called to begin execution of the program.

The sbInterp( ) Method

The **sbInterp( )** method begins and controls the execution of a Small BASIC program. This method is shown here:

```
// Entry point for the Small BASIC interpreter.
private void sbInterp() throws InterpreterException
{

  // This is the interpreter's main loop.
  do {
    getToken();
    // Check for assignment statement.
    if(tokType==VARIABLE) {
      putBack(); // return the var to the input stream
      assignment(); // handle assignment statement
    }
    else // is keyword
      switch(kwToken) {
        case PRINT:
          print();
          break;
        case GOTO:
          execGoto();
          break;
        case IF:
          execIf();
          break;
```

```
        case FOR:
          execFor();
          break;
        case NEXT:
          next();
          break;
        case INPUT:
          input();
          break;
        case GOSUB:
          gosub();
          break;
        case RETURN:
          greturn();
          break;
        case END:
          return;
      }
  } while (!token.equals(EOP));
}
```

All interpreters are driven by a top-level loop that reads the next token from the program and selects the appropriate action to process it. The Small BASIC interpreter is no exception. This main loop is contained in **sbInterp( )**. It works like this. First, a token is read from the program. Assuming no syntax errors are found, if the token is a variable, then an assignment is taking place. Otherwise, the token must be either a line number (which is ignored) or a keyword. If it is a keyword, the appropriate **case** statement is selected based on the value of **kwToken**, which contains the internal representation of the keyword. Each keyword is handled by its own method and is described in turn by the sections that follow.

Assignment

In traditional BASIC, assignment is a statement, not an operation, and this is the way it is treated by Small BASIC, too. The general form of a BASIC assignment statement is

>   *var-name* = *expression*

The assignment statement is interpreted using the **assignment( )** method shown here:

```
// Assign a variable a value.
private void assignment() throws InterpreterException
{
  int var;
  double value;
  char vname;
```

```
    // Get the variable name.
    getToken();
    vname = token.charAt(0);

    if(!Character.isLetter(vname)) {
      handleErr(NOTVAR);
      return;
    }

    // Convert to index into variable table.
    var = (int) Character.toUpperCase(vname) - 'A';

    // Get the equal sign.
    getToken();
    if(!token.equals("=")) {
      handleErr(EQUALEXPECTED);
      return;
    }

    // Get the value to assign.
    value = evaluate();

    // Assign the value.
    vars[var] = value;
}
```

The first thing **assignment( )** does is read a token from the program. This will be the variable that will have its value assigned. If it is not a valid variable, an error will be reported. Next, the equal sign is read. Then, **evaluate( )** is called to obtain the value to assign to the variable. Finally, the value is assigned to the variable. The method is surprisingly simple and uncluttered because the expression parser and the **getToken( )** method do much of the "messy" work.

The PRINT Statement

In BASIC, the PRINT statement is actually quite powerful and flexible. While it is beyond the scope of this chapter to create a method that supports all the functionality of the PRINT statement, the one defined by Small BASIC supports its most important features. The general form of the PRINT statement is

PRINT *arg-list*

where *arg-list* is a comma- or semicolon-separated list of expressions or quoted strings. The **print( )** method, shown here, interprets the PRINT statement:

```
// Execute a simple version of the PRINT statement.
private void print() throws InterpreterException
```

```
{
  double result;
  int len=0, spaces;
  String lastDelim = "";

  do {
    getToken(); // get next list item
    if(kwToken==EOL || token.equals(EOP)) break;

    if(tokType==QUOTEDSTR) { // is string
      System.out.print(token);
      len += token.length();
      getToken();
    }
    else { // is expression
      putBack();
      result = evaluate();
      getToken();
      System.out.print(result);

      // Add length of output to running total.
      Double t = new Double(result);
      len += t.toString().length(); // save length
    }
    lastDelim = token;

    // If comma, move to next tab stop.
    if(lastDelim.equals(",")) {
      // compute number of spaces to move to next tab
      spaces = 8 - (len % 8);
      len += spaces; // add in the tabbing position
      while(spaces != 0) {
        System.out.print(" ");
        spaces--;
      }
    }
    else if(token.equals(";")) {
      System.out.print(" ");
      len++;
    }
    else if(kwToken != EOL && !token.equals(EOP))
      handleErr(SYNTAX);
  } while (lastDelim.equals(";") || lastDelim.equals(","));

  if(kwToken==EOL || token.equals(EOP)) {
```

```
     if(!lastDelim.equals(";") && !lastDelim.equals(","))
       System.out.println();
   }
   else handleErr(SYNTAX);
}
```

The PRINT statement can be used to print a list of variables and quoted strings on the screen. If one item is separated from the next by a semicolon, then one space is printed between them. If two items are separated by a comma, then the second item will be displayed beginning with the next tab position. If the list ends in a comma or semicolon, then no newline is issued. Here are some examples of valid PRINT statements:

```
PRINT X; Y; "THIS IS A STRING"
PRINT 10 / 4
PRINT
```

The last example simply prints a new line.

The operation of **print( )** is straightforward. However, notice that **print( )** makes use of the **putBack( )** method to return a token to the input stream. The reason for this is that **print( )** must look ahead to see whether the next item to be printed is a quoted string or a numeric expression. If it is an expression, then the first term in the expression must be returned to the input stream so that the expression parser can correctly compute the value of the expression.

The INPUT Statement

In BASIC, the INPUT statement is used to read a value from the keyboard and assign that value to a variable. It has two general forms. The first is

INPUT *var*

which displays a question mark and waits for input. The second is

INPUT "*prompt-string*", *var*

which displays a prompting message and waits for input. In both cases, the value entered by the user is stored in *var*. For example,

```
INPUT "Enter width: ", w
```

displays **Enter width:** and stores the value entered by the user in **w**.

The method **input( )**, shown here, implements the INPUT statement.

```
// Execute a simple form of INPUT.
private void input() throws InterpreterException
{
  int var;
```

```
double val = 0.0;
String str;

BufferedReader br = new
  BufferedReader(new InputStreamReader(System.in));

getToken(); // see if prompt string is present
if(tokType == QUOTEDSTR) {
  // if so, print it and check for comma
  System.out.print(token);
  getToken();
  if(!token.equals(",")) handleErr(SYNTAX);
  getToken();
}
else System.out.print("? "); // otherwise, prompt with ?

// get the input var
var = Character.toUpperCase(token.charAt(0)) - 'A';

try {
  str = br.readLine(); // read the value
  val = Double.parseDouble(str);
} catch (IOException exc) {
  handleErr(INPUTIOERROR);
} catch (NumberFormatException exc) {
  /* You might want to handle this error
     differently than the other interpreter
     errors. */
  System.out.println("Invalid input.");
}

vars[var] = val; // store it
}
```

The operation of this method is straightforward and should be clear after reading the comments. Briefly, a **BufferedReader** is created to read keyboard input. The next token is obtained, which will be either a prompting string or the name of the variable receiving input. If it is a prompting string, the string is displayed and **getToken( )** is again called to obtain the name of the variable. Next, numeric input is read and converted to a **double** value. This value is then assigned to the variable.

The GOTO Statement

In traditional BASIC, the most important form of program control is the GOTO. The object of a GOTO must be a line number. In Small BASIC, this traditional approach is preserved.

As you may know, early versions of BASIC required that every line in a program start with a line number. However, Small BASIC does not require a line number for each line; one is needed only if that line will be the target of a GOTO. Thus, in Small BASIC, line numbers are simply labels. The general form of the GOTO is

GOTO *line-number*

When a GOTO statement is encountered, execution branches to the specified line number.

The main complexity associated with the GOTO is that both forward and backward jumps must be allowed. To satisfy this constraint in an efficient manner requires that the entire program be scanned prior to execution and the location of each label be placed in a table. Then, each time a GOTO is executed, the location of the target line can be obtained from the table and program control transferred to that point.

A **TreeMap** collection makes an ideal data structure to hold the labels and locations because maps link a key with a value. In this case, the key is the label and the value is the index of the label within the program. The map that holds label/index pairs is referred to by **labelTable**, which is an instance variable declared as shown here:

```
// A map for labels.
private TreeMap labelTable;
```

The method that scans the program and puts each label's location in the table is called **scanLabels( )**. This method is called by **run( )** just before the program is interpreted. It is shown here along with **findEOL( )**, which is used to find the end of a line in the program:

```
// Find all labels.
private void scanLabels() throws InterpreterException
{
  int i;
  Object result;

  // See if the first token in the file is a label.
  getToken();
  if(tokType==NUMBER)
    labelTable.put(token, new Integer(progIdx));

  findEOL();

  do {
    getToken();
    if(tokType==NUMBER) { // must be a line number
      result = labelTable.put(token,
                              new Integer(progIdx));
      if(result != null)
        handleErr(DUPLABEL);
    }

    // If not on a blank line, find next line.
```

```
    if(kwToken != EOL) findEOL();
  } while(!token.equals(EOP));
  progIdx = 0; // reset index to start of program
}


// Find the start of the next line.
private void findEOL()
{
  while(progIdx < prog.length &&
        prog[progIdx] != '\n') ++progIdx;
  if(progIdx < prog.length) progIdx++;
}
```

The **scanLabels( )** method works by checking the first token of each line. If the token is a number, then it is assumed to be a line number (i.e., a label). When a label is found, it is stored by calling **put( )** on **labelTable**. The **put( )** method of **TreeMap** returns a reference to the previous mapping of the key, or null if there was not a previous mapping. Thus, if the return value is not null, then the label has already been stored in the map. This causes an error because no two labels in a program can be the same.

When a GOTO is encountered in a program, the **execGoto( )** method, shown here, is executed:

```
// Execute a GOTO statement.
private void execGoto() throws InterpreterException
{
  Integer loc;

  getToken(); // get label to go to

  // Find the location of the label.
  loc = (Integer) labelTable.get(token);

  if(loc == null)
    handleErr(UNDEFLABEL); // label not defined
  else // start program running at that loc
    progIdx = loc.intValue();
}
```

First, the location associated with the target label is obtained by this line:

```
loc = (Integer) labelTable.get(token);
```

For **TreeMap**, the **get( )** method returns the value associated with the key. As explained, the key is the label and the value is the index in the program of the label. If the label is not found, a null reference is returned. If the label is found, the value is assigned to **progIdx** and the method returns. This causes execution to resume at the new value of **progIdx**. (Remember, **progIdx** is the index at which the program is currently being executed.) If the label is not found, an error occurs.

The IF Statement

The Small BASIC interpreter executes a simple form of the IF statement. In Small BASIC, no ELSE is allowed. (However, you will find it easy to add the ELSE once you understand the operation of the IF.) The IF statement takes this general form:

IF *expression rel-op expression* THEN *statement*

Here, *rel-op* must be one of the relational operators. For example, **X < 10** is a valid expression for the IF. The statement that follows the THEN is executed only if the relational expression is true. The **execIf( )** method, shown here, executes the IF statement:

```
// Execute an IF statement.
private void execIf() throws InterpreterException
{
  double result;

  result = evaluate(); // get value of expression

  /* If the result is true (non-zero),
     process target of IF. Otherwise move on
     to next line in the program. */
  if(result != 0.0) {
    getToken();
    if(kwToken != THEN) {
      handleErr(THENEXPECTED);
      return;
    } // else, target statement will be executed
  }
  else findEOL(); // find start of next line
}
```

The **execIf( )** method operates as follows. First, the value of the relational expression is computed. If the expression is true, the target of the THEN is executed; otherwise, **findEOL( )** finds the start of the next line. Notice that if the expression is true, the **execIf( )** simply returns. This causes the main loop to iterate and the next token to be read. Since the target of an IF is a statement, returning to the main loop causes the target statement to be executed as if it were on its own line. If the expression is false, then the start of the next line is found before execution returns to the main loop.

The FOR Loop

The implementation of the FOR loop presents a challenging problem that lends itself to a rather elegant solution. The general form of the FOR loop is

FOR *control-var* = *initial-value* TO *target-value*
   statements to be repeated
NEXT

The Small BASIC version of the FOR allows only positively running loops that increment the control variable by one each iteration. The STEP command is not supported.

In BASIC, as in Java, loops may be nested to several levels. The main challenge presented by this is keeping the information associated with each loop straight. (That is, each NEXT must be associated with the proper FOR.) The solution to this problem is to implement the FOR loop using a stack-based mechanism. At the top of the loop, information about the status of the control variable, the target value, and the location of the top of the loop in the program is pushed onto a stack. Each time the NEXT is encountered, this information is popped, the control variable is updated, and its value is checked against the target value. If the control value exceeds the target, the loop stops and execution continues with the line following the NEXT statement. Otherwise, the updated information is pushed back onto the stack and execution resumes at the top of the loop. Implementing a FOR loop in this way works not only for a single loop but also for nested loops because the innermost NEXT will always be associated with the innermost FOR. (The last information pushed onto the stack will be the first information popped.) Once an inner loop terminates, its information is popped from the stack and, if it exists, an outer loop's information comes to the top of the stack. Thus, each NEXT is automatically associated with its corresponding FOR.

A stack is used to hold the loop information. For this purpose Small BASIC uses one of Java's collection classes: **Stack**. The loop information is contained in an object of the **ForInfo** class. The stack is referred to by the **fStack** instance variable. These are shown here:

```
// Support for FOR loops.
class ForInfo {
  int var; // counter variable
  double target; // target value
  int loc; // index in source code to loop to
}


// Stack for FOR loops.
private Stack fStack;
```

Stack supports **push( )** and **pop( )**, which push an object onto the stack and pop an object from the stack, respectively.

Two methods, called **execFor( )** and **next( )**, handle the FOR and NEXT statements. They are shown here:

```
// Execute a FOR loop.
private void execFor() throws InterpreterException
{
  ForInfo stckvar = new ForInfo();
  double value;
  char vname;
```

```
  getToken(); // read the control variable
  vname = token.charAt(0);
  if(!Character.isLetter(vname)) {
    handleErr(NOTVAR);
    return;
  }

  // Save index of control var.
  stckvar.var = Character.toUpperCase(vname) - 'A';

  getToken(); // read the equal sign
  if(token.charAt(0) != '=') {
    handleErr(EQUALEXPECTED);
    return;
  }

  value = evaluate(); // get initial value

  vars[stckvar.var] = value;

  getToken(); // read and discard the TO
  if(kwToken != TO) handleErr(TOEXPECTED);

  stckvar.target = evaluate(); // get target value

  /* If loop can execute at least once,
     push info on stack. */
  if(value >= vars[stckvar.var]) {
    stckvar.loc = progIdx;
    fStack.push(stckvar);
  }
  else // otherwise, skip loop code altogether
    while(kwToken != NEXT) getToken();
}

// Execute a NEXT statement.
private void next() throws InterpreterException
{
  ForInfo stckvar;

  try {
    // Retrieve info for this For loop.
    stckvar = (ForInfo) fStack.pop();
    vars[stckvar.var]++; // increment control var
```

```
    // If done, return.
    if(vars[stckvar.var] > stckvar.target) return;

    // Otherwise, restore the info.
    fStack.push(stckvar);
    progIdx = stckvar.loc;   // loop
  } catch(EmptyStackException exc) {
    handleErr(NEXTWITHOUTFOR);
  }
}
```

You should be able to follow the operation of these methods by reading the comments. Briefly, **execFor( )** constructs a **ForInfo** object that contains the index of the loop control variable, the target value, and the current value of **progIdx**. It pushes this object onto **fStack**. Execution then continues until a NEXT is encountered. When this happens, **fStack** is popped and the target value is compared with the current value of the loop control variable. If the target value has not yet been reached, the loop repeats by assigning to **progIdx** the index stored in **loc**. This index is, of course, the location of the top of the loop. This causes execution to loop back to the FOR, and the process repeats. If the target value has been reached, execution simply continues on after the matching NEXT statement.

As the code stands, it does not prevent a GOTO out of a FOR loop. However, jumping out of a FOR loop will corrupt the FOR stack and should be avoided.

The stack-based solution to the FOR loop problem can be generalized. Although Small BASIC does not implement any other loop statements, you can apply the same sort of procedure to any type of loop, including the WHILE or DO/WHILE loops. Also, as you will see in the next section, the stack-based solution can be applied to any language element that can be nested, including calling subroutines.

The GOSUB

Although Small BASIC does not support true stand-alone subroutines, it does allow portions of a program to be called by using GOSUB. To return from a subroutine, use RETURN. The general form of a GOSUB and RETURN is

> GOSUB *line-num*
>
> .
> .
> .
> *line-num*
> *subroutine code*
> RETURN

Calling a subroutine, even the limited subroutines implemented in Small BASIC, requires the use of a stack. The reason for this is similar to that given for the FOR statement. It is to allow nested subroutine calls. Because it is possible to have one subroutine call another, a stack is necessary to ensure that a RETURN statement is associated with its proper GOSUB. The GOSUB stack is stored in another **Stack** object referred to through **gStack**, defined as shown here:

```
// Stack for gosubs.
private Stack gStack;
```

In **gStack** are stored indexes into the program. Each time a GOSUB is encountered, its index in the program is pushed onto **gStack**. Each time a RETURN statement is executed, the index of the location to return to is popped from the stack.

The **gosub( )** and **return( )** methods are shown here:

```
// Execute a GOSUB.
private void gosub() throws InterpreterException
{
  Integer loc;

  getToken();

  // Find the label to call.
  loc = (Integer) labelTable.get(token);

  if(loc == null)
    handleErr(UNDEFLABEL); // label not defined
  else {
    // Save place to return to.
    gStack.push(new Integer(progIdx));

    // Start program running at that loc.
    progIdx = loc.intValue();
  }
}

// Return from GOSUB.
private void greturn() throws InterpreterException
{
  Integer t;

  try {
    // Restore program index.
    t = (Integer) gStack.pop();
    progIdx = t.intValue();
  } catch(EmptyStackException exc) {
    handleErr(RETURNWITHOUTGOSUB);
  }
}
```

The GOSUB statement works like this. When a GOSUB is encountered, the target line number is looked up and stored in **loc**. Next, the current value of **progIdx** is pushed onto the GOSUB stack. (This is the point in the program that the subroutine will return to once it is finished.) Finally, the index stored in **loc** is assigned to **progIdx**. This causes program execution to jump to the start of the subroutine. When a RETURN is encountered, the GOSUB stack is popped and this value is assigned to **progIDx**, causing execution to continue on to the next line after the GOSUB statement.

Because return addresses are stored on the GOSUB stack, subroutines may be nested. The most recently called subroutine will be the one returned from when its RETURN statement is encountered. (That is, the return address of the most recently called subroutine will be on the top of the **gstack** stack.) This process allows GOSUBs to be nested to any depth.

The END Statement

The END keyword signifies the end of program execution. It is not always needed because the physical end of the program also causes program execution to stop. END is simply used to end the program before the end of the file has been reached. Its only action is to cause the **sbInterp( )** method to return, thus ending execution.

Using Small BASIC

To use **SBasic**, first create an **SBasic** object, specifying the name of the file that you want to interpret. Then call **run( )**. You must remember to catch any **InterpreterException**s that might be thrown.

The following program lets you run any Small BASIC program you want by specifying its name on the command line:

```
// Demonstrate the Small BASIC Interpreter.

class SBDemo {
  public static void main(String args[])
  {
    if(args.length != 1) {
      System.out.println("Usage: sbasic <filename>");
      return;
    }

    try {
      SBasic ob = new SBasic(args[0]);
      ob.run();
    } catch(InterpreterException exc) {
      System.out.println(exc);
    }
  }
}
```

Compile **SBDemo** like this:

```
javac SBasic.java SBDemo.java
```

Execute **SBDemo** with the name of a Small BASIC program as the first command-line parameter. For example, to interpret a program called TEST.BAS, use this command line:

```
java SBDemo TEST.BAS
```

Here is a short Small BASIC program you can try:

```
PRINT "This program converts gallons to liters."

100 GOSUB 200
   INPUT "Again? (1 or 0): ", x
   IF x = 1 THEN GOTO 100
   END

200 INPUT "Enter gallons: ", g
   l = g * 3.7854
   PRINT g; "gallons is"; l; "liters."
   RETURN
```

Here is sample output produced when this program is run:

```
This program converts gallons to liters.
Enter gallons: 10
10.0 gallons is 37.854 liters.
Again? (1 or 0): 1
Enter gallons: 4
4.0 gallons is 15.1416 liters.
Again? (1 or 0): 0
```

More Small BASIC Sample Programs

Here is a sampling of programs that Small BASIC will execute. Notice that both upper- and lowercase are supported. That is, Small BASIC is not case sensitive. Thus, keywords and variables can be entered in either case. In addition to the programs shown here, you will want to write several of your own. Also, try writing programs that have syntax errors and observe the way Small BASIC reports them.

The following program exercises all of the features supported by Small BASIC:

```
PRINT "This program demonstrates all features."
FOR X = 1 TO 100
PRINT X; X/2, X; X*X
NEXT
GOSUB 300
PRINT "hello"
```

```
INPUT H
IF H<11 THEN GOTO 200
PRINT 12-4/2
PRINT 100
200 A = 100/2
IF A>10 THEN PRINT "this is ok"
PRINT A
PRINT A+34
INPUT H
PRINT H
INPUT "this is a test ", y
PRINT H+Y
END
300 PRINT "this is a subroutine"
    RETURN
```

The next program demonstrates nested subroutines:

```
PRINT "This program demonstrates nested GOSUBs."
INPUT "enter a number: ", I
GOSUB 100

END

100 FOR T = 1 TO I
  X = X + I
  GOSUB 150
NEXT
RETURN

150 PRINT X;
    RETURN
```

The following program illustrates the INPUT statement:

```
PRINT "This program computes the volume of a cube."
INPUT "Enter length of first side ", l
INPUT "Enter length of second side ", w
INPUT "Enter length of third side ", d
t = l * w * d
PRINT "Volume is ", t
```

The next program illustrates nested FOR loops:

```
PRINT "This program demonstrates nested FOR loops."
FOR X = 1 TO 100
  FOR Y = 1 TO 10
```

```
     PRINT X; Y; X*Y
   NEXT
NEXT
```

The following program exercises all of the relational operators:

```
PRINT "This demonstrates all of the relational operators."
A = 10
B = 20
IF A = B THEN PRINT "A = B"
IF A <> B THEN PRINT "A <> B"
IF A < B THEN PRINT "A < B"
IF A > B THEN PRINT "A > B"
IF A >= B THEN PRINT "A >= B"
IF A <= B THEN PRINT "A <= B"
```

Enhancing and Expanding the Interpreter

It is quite easy to add statements to the Small BASIC interpreter. Just follow the general
format taken by the statements presented in the chapter. To add different variable types, you
will need to create a class that stores the type and the value of the variable, and then use an
array of these objects to store the variables.

Creating Your Own Computer Language

While enhancing or expanding Small BASIC is a good way to become more familiar with
its operation and with the way language interpreters work, you are not limited to the BASIC
language. You can use the same techniques described in this chapter to write an interpreter
for just about any computer language, including a simplified subset of Java. You can even
invent your own language that reflects your own programming style and personality. In fact,
the interpreter skeleton used by Small BASIC is a perfect "test bench" for any type of special
language feature you might want to experiment with. For example, to add a REPEAT/UNTIL
loop to the interpreter, you need to follow these steps:

1. Add REPEAT and UNTIL as keywords and define integer values for them.
2. Add REPEAT and UNTIL to the main loop **switch** statement.
3. Define **repeat( )** and **until( )** methods that process the REPEAT and UNTIL
    statements. (Use **execFor( )** and **next( )** as starting points.)

For those readers who enjoy a challenge, try creating a script language that automates
various computing tasks, such as copying or erasing files, compiling a program, and so on.
Then create an interpreter for that language. Such a language could provide an alternative
to using standard batch files. In essence, you could adapt the interpreter to support your own
proprietary batch processing scheme.

Creating a Download Manager in Java

by James Holmes

Have you ever had an Internet download interrupted before its completion, just to put you back at square one? If you connect to the Internet with a dialup connection, it's very likely that you've run into this all too common nuisance. Everything from call waiting disconnects to computer crashes can leave a download dead in its tracks. To say the least, restarting a download from scratch over and over can be a very time-consuming and frustrating experience.

A little-known fact is that many interrupted downloads can be resumed. This allows you to recommence downloading from the point at which a download terminates instead of having to begin anew. However, most of today's Internet browsers either don't make this feature readily available or make it overly cumbersome to use. Enter the Download Manager: a tool that manages Internet downloads for you and makes simple work of resuming interrupted downloads.

At the core of the Download Manager's usefulness is its ability to take advantage of downloading only specific portions of a file. In a classic download scenario, a whole file is downloaded from beginning to end. If the transmission of the file is interrupted for any reason, the progress made toward completing the downloading of the file is lost. On the contrary, the Download Manager can pick up from where an interruption occurs and then download only the file's remaining fragment. Not all downloads are created equal, though, and there are some that simply cannot be resurrected. Details on which files are and aren't resumable are explained in the following section.

Not only is the Download Manager a useful utility, it is an excellent illustration of the power and succinctness of Java's built-in APIs—especially as they apply to interfacing to the Internet. The previous two chapters showed the fundamental elegance of the Java language; this and the following three chapters demonstrate the ease with which Java programs can access the Internet. Because the Internet was a driving force behind the creation of Java, it should come as no surprise that Java's networking capabilities are unsurpassed. For example, attempting to create the Download Manager in another language, such as C++, would entail significantly more trouble and effort. Of course, that is the art of Java!

Understanding Internet Downloads

To understand and appreciate the Download Manager, it's necessary to shed some light on how Internet downloads really work.

Internet downloads in their simplest form are merely client/server transactions. The client, your browser, requests to download a file from a server on the Internet. The server then responds by sending the requested file to your browser. In order for clients to communicate with servers, they must have an established protocol for doing so. The most common protocols for downloading files are File Transfer Protocol (FTP) and Hypertext Transfer Protocol (HTTP). FTP is usually associated generically with exchanging files between computers, where as HTTP is usually associated specifically with transferring Web pages and their related files (i.e., graphics, sounds, and so on). Over time, as the World Wide Web has grown in popularity, HTTP has become the dominant protocol for downloading files from the Internet. FTP is definitely not extinct, though.

For brevity's sake, the Download Manager developed in this chapter will only support HTTP downloads. Nonetheless, adding support for FTP would be an excellent exercise for extending the code. HTTP downloads come in two forms: resumable (HTTP 1.1) and nonresumable (HTTP 1.0). The difference between these two forms lies in the way files can be requested from servers. With the antiquated HTTP 1.0, a client can only request that a server send it a file, whereas with HTTP 1.1 a client can request that a server send it a file or *only a specific portion of a file*. This is the feature the Download Manager is built on.

An Overview of the Download Manager

The Download Manager uses a simple yet effective GUI interface built with Java's Swing libraries. The Download Manager window is shown in Figure 4-1. The use of Swing gives the interface a crisp, modern look and feel.

The GUI maintains a list of downloads that are currently being managed. Each download in the list reports its URL, size of the file in bytes, progress as a percentage toward completion, and current status. The downloads can each be in one of the following different states: Downloading, Paused, Complete, Error, or Cancelled. The GUI also has controls for adding downloads to the list and for changing the state of each download in the list. When a download in the list is selected, depending on its current state, it can be paused, resumed, cancelled, or removed from the list altogether.

The Download Manager is broken into a few classes for natural separation of functional components. These are the **Download**, **DownloadsTableModel**, **ProgressRenderer**, and **DownloadManager** classes, respectively. The **DownloadManager** class is responsible for the GUI interface and makes use of the **DownloadsTableModel** and **ProgressRenderer** classes for displaying the current list of downloads. The **Download** class represents a "managed" download and is responsible for performing the actual downloading of a file. In the following sections, we'll walk through each of these classes in detail, highlighting their inner workings and explaining how they relate to each other.

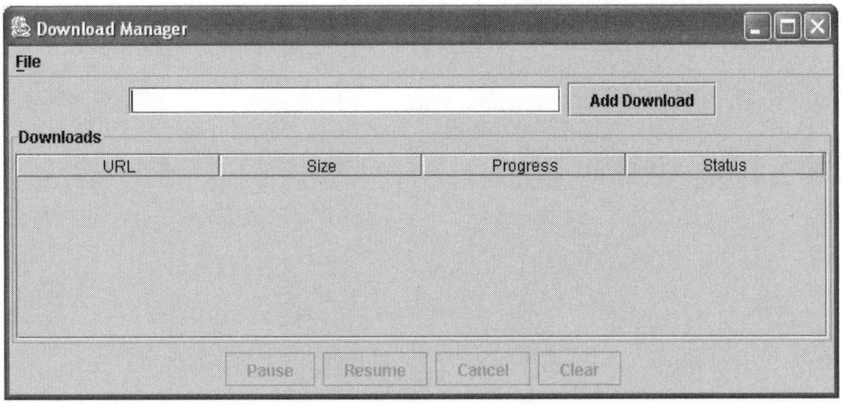

Figure 4-1   *The Download Manager GUI Interface*

The Download Class

The **Download** class is the workhorse of the Download Manager. Its primary purpose is to download a file and save that file's contents to disk. Each time a new download is added to the Download Manager, a new **Download** object is instantiated to handle the download.

The Download Manager has the ability to download multiple files at once. To achieve this, it's necessary for each of the simultaneous downloads to run independently. It's also necessary for each individual download to manage its own state so that it can be reflected in the GUI. This is accomplished with the **Download** class.

The entire code for **Download** is shown here. Notice that it extends **Observable** and implements **Runnable**. Each part is examined in detail in the sections that follow.

```java
import java.io.*;
import java.net.*;
import java.util.*;

// This class downloads a file from a URL.
class Download extends Observable implements Runnable {
  // Max size of download buffer.
  private static final int MAX_BUFFER_SIZE = 1024;

  // These are the status names.
  public static final String STATUSES[] = {"Downloading",
    "Paused", "Complete", "Cancelled", "Error"};

  // These are the status codes.
  public static final int DOWNLOADING = 0;
  public static final int PAUSED = 1;
  public static final int COMPLETE = 2;
  public static final int CANCELLED = 3;
  public static final int ERROR = 4;

  private URL url; // download URL
  private int size; // size of download in bytes
  private int downloaded; // number of bytes downloaded
  private int status; // current status of download

  // Constructor for Download.
  public Download(URL url) {
    this.url = url;
    size = -1;
    downloaded = 0;
    status = DOWNLOADING;

    // Begin the download.
```

```java
    download();
  }

  // Get this download's URL.
  public String getUrl() {
    return url.toString();
  }

  // Get this download's size.
  public int getSize() {
    return size;
  }

  // Get this download's progress.
  public float getProgress() {
    return ((float) downloaded / size) * 100;
  }

  // Get this download's status.
  public int getStatus() {
    return status;
  }

  // Pause this download.
  public void pause() {
    status = PAUSED;
    stateChanged();
  }

  // Resume this download.
  public void resume() {
    status = DOWNLOADING;
    stateChanged();
    download();
  }

  // Cancel this download.
  public void cancel() {
    status = CANCELLED;
    stateChanged();
  }

  // Mark this download as having an error.
  private void error() {
    status = ERROR;
```

```
    stateChanged();
  }

  // Start or resume downloading.
  private void download() {
    Thread thread = new Thread(this);
    thread.start();
  }

  // Get file name portion of URL.
  private String getFileName(URL url) {
    String fileName = url.getFile();
    return fileName.substring(fileName.lastIndexOf('/') + 1);
  }

  // Download file.
  public void run() {
    RandomAccessFile file = null;
    InputStream stream = null;

    try {
      // Open connection to URL.
      HttpURLConnection connection =
        (HttpURLConnection) url.openConnection();

      // Specify what portion of file to download.
      connection.setRequestProperty("Range",
        "bytes=" + downloaded + "-");

      // Connect to server.
      connection.connect();

      // Make sure response code is in the 200 range.
      if (connection.getResponseCode() / 100 != 2) {
        error();
      }

      // Check for valid content length.
      int contentLength = connection.getContentLength();
      if (contentLength < 1) {
        error();
      }

      /* Set the size for this download if it
         hasn't been already set. */
```

```java
    if (size == -1) {
      size = contentLength;
      stateChanged();
    }

    // Open file and seek to the end of it.
    file = new RandomAccessFile(getFileName(url), "rw");
    file.seek(downloaded);

    stream = connection.getInputStream();
    while (status == DOWNLOADING) {
      /* Size buffer according to how much of the
         file is left to download. */
      byte buffer[];
      if (size - downloaded > MAX_BUFFER_SIZE) {
        buffer = new byte[MAX_BUFFER_SIZE];
      } else {
        buffer = new byte[size - downloaded];
      }

      // Read from server into buffer.
      int read = stream.read(buffer);
      if (read == -1)
        break;

      // Write buffer to file.
      file.write(buffer, 0, read);
      downloaded += read;
      stateChanged();
    }

    /* Change status to complete if this point was
       reached because downloading has finished. */
    if (status == DOWNLOADING) {
      status = COMPLETE;
      stateChanged();
    }
  } catch (Exception e) {
    error();
  } finally {
    // Close file.
    if (file != null) {
      try {
        file.close();
      } catch (Exception e) {}
```

```
      }

      // Close connection to server.
      if (stream != null) {
        try {
          stream.close();
        } catch (Exception e) {}
      }
    }
  }

  // Notify observers that this download's status has changed.
  private void stateChanged() {
    setChanged();
    notifyObservers();
  }
}
```

The Download Variables

Download begins by declaring several **static final** variables that specify the various constants used by the class. Next, four instance variables are declared. The **url** variable holds the Internet URL for the file being downloaded; the **size** variable holds the size of the download file in bytes; the **downloaded** variable holds the number of bytes that have been downloaded thus far; and the **status** variable indicates the download's current status.

The Download Constructor

Download's constructor is passed a reference to the URL to download in the form of a **URL** object, which is assigned to the **url** instance variable. It then sets the remaining instance variables to their initial states and calls the **download( )** method. Notice that **size** is set to −1 to indicate there is no size yet.

The download( ) Method

The **download( )** method creates a new **Thread** object, passing it a reference to the invoking **Download** instance. As mentioned before, it's necessary for each download to run independently. In order for the **Download** class to act alone, it must execute in its own thread. Java has excellent built-in support for threads and makes using them a snap. To use threads, the **Download** class simply implements the **Runnable** interface by overriding the **run( )** method. After the **download( )** method has instantiated a new **Thread** instance, passing its constructor the **Runnable Download** class, it calls the thread's **start( )** method. Invoking the **start( )** method causes the **Runnable** instance's (the **Download** class') **run( )** method to be executed.

The run( ) Method

When the **run( )** method executes, the actual downloading gets under way. Because of its size and importance, we will examine it closely, line by line. The **run( )** method begins with these lines:

```
RandomAccessFile file = null;
InputStream stream = null;

try {
  // Open connection to URL.
  HttpURLConnection connection =
    (HttpURLConnection) url.openConnection();
```

First, **run( )** sets up variables for the network stream that the download's contents will be read from and sets up the file that the download's contents will be written to. Next, a connection to the download's URL is opened by calling **url.openConnection( )**. Since we know that the Download Manager supports only HTTP downloads, the connection is cast to the **HttpURLConnection** type. Casting the connection as a **HttpURLConnection** allows us to take advantage of HTTP-specific connection features such as the **getResponseCode( )** method. Note that calling **url.openConnection( )** does not actually create a connection to the URL's server, it simply creates a new **URLConnection** instance associated with the URL that later will be used to connect to the server.

After the **HttpURLConnection** has been created, the connection request property is set by calling **connection.setRequestProperty( )**, as shown here:

```
// Specify what portion of file to download.
connection.setRequestProperty("Range",
  "bytes=" + downloaded + "-");
```

Setting request properties allows extra request information to be sent to the server the download will be coming from. In this case, the "Range" property is set. This is critically important, as the "Range" property specifies the range of bytes that are being requested for download from the server. Normally, all of a file's bytes are downloaded at once. However, if a download has been interrupted or paused, only the download's remaining bytes should be retrieved. Setting the "Range" property is the foundation for the Download Manager's operation.

The "Range" property is specified in this form:

start-byte – end-byte

For example, "0 – 12345". However, the end byte of the range is optional. If the end byte is absent, the range ends at the end of the file. The **run( )** method never specifies the end byte because downloads must run until the entire range is downloaded, unless paused or interrupted.

The next few lines are shown here:

```
// Connect to server.
connection.connect();
```

```
// Make sure response code is in the 200 range.
if (connection.getResponseCode() / 100 != 2) {
  error();
}

// Check for valid content length.
int contentLength = connection.getContentLength();
if (contentLength < 1) {
  error();
}
```

The **connection.connect( )** method is called to make the actual connection to the download's server. Next, the response code returned by the server is checked. The HTTP protocol has a list of response codes that indicate a server's response to a request. HTTP response codes are organized into numeric ranges of 100, and the 200 range indicates success. The server's response code is validated for being in the 200 range by calling **connection.getResponseCode( )** and dividing by 100. If the value of this division is 2, then the connection was successful.

Next, **run( )** gets the content length by calling **connection.getContentLength( )**. The content length represents the number of bytes in the requested file. If the content length is less than 1, the **error( )** method is called. The **error( )** method updates the download's status to **ERROR**, and then calls **stateChanged( )**. The **stateChanged( )** method will be described in detail later.

After getting the content length, the following code checks to see if it has already been assigned to the **size** variable:

```
/* Set the size for this download if it
   hasn't been already set. */
if (size == -1) {
  size = contentLength;
  stateChanged();
}
```

As you can see, instead of assigning the content length to the **size** variable unconditionally, it only gets assigned if it hasn't already been given a value. The reason for this is because the content length reflects how many bytes the server will be sending. If anything other than a 0-based start range is specified, the content length will only represent a portion of the file's size. The **size** variable has to be set to the complete size of the download's file.

The next few lines of code shown here create a new **RandomAccessFile** using the filename portion of the download's URL that is retrieved with a call to the **getFileName( )** method:

```
// Open file and seek to the end of it.
file = new RandomAccessFile(getFileName(url), "rw");
file.seek(downloaded);
```

The **RandomAccessFile** is opened in "rw" mode, which specifies that the file can be written to and read from. Once the file is open, **run( )** seeks to the end of the file by calling the **file.seek( )** method, passing in the **downloaded** variable. This tells the file to position itself at the number of bytes that have been downloaded—in other words, at the end. It's necessary to position the file at the end in case a download has been resumed. If a download is resumed, the newly downloaded bytes are appended to the file and they don't overwrite any previously downloaded bytes. After preparing the output file, a network stream handle to the open server connection is obtained by calling **connection.getInputStream()**, as shown here:

```
stream = connection.getInputStream();
```

The heart of all the action begins next with a **while** loop:

```
while (status == DOWNLOADING) {
  /* Size buffer according to how much of the
     file is left to download. */
  byte buffer[];
  if (size - downloaded > MAX_BUFFER_SIZE) {
    buffer = new byte[MAX_BUFFER_SIZE];
  } else {
    buffer = new byte[size - downloaded];
  }

  // Read from server into buffer.
  int read = stream.read(buffer);
  if (read == -1)
    break;

  // Write buffer to file.
  file.write(buffer, 0, read);
  downloaded += read;
  stateChanged();
}
```

This loop is set up to run until the download's **status** variable changes from **DOWNLOADING**. Inside the loop, a **byte** buffer array is created to hold the bytes that will be downloaded. The buffer is sized according to how much of the download is left to complete. If there is more left to download than the **MAX_BUFFER_SIZE**, the **MAX_BUFFER_SIZE** is used to size the buffer. Otherwise, the buffer is sized exactly at the number of bytes left to download. Once the buffer is sized appropriately, the downloading takes place with a **stream.read( )** call. This call reads bytes from the server and places them into the buffer, returning the count of how many bytes were actually read. If the number of bytes read equals −1, then downloading has completed and the loop is exited. Otherwise, downloading is not finished and the bytes that have been read are written to disk with a call to **file.write( )**. Then the **downloaded** variable is updated, reflecting the number of bytes downloaded thus far. Finally, inside the loop, the **stateChanged( )** method is invoked. More on this later.

After the loop has exited, the following code checks to see why the loop was exited:

```
/* Change status to complete if this point was
   reached because downloading has finished. */
if (status == DOWNLOADING) {
  status = COMPLETE;
  stateChanged();
}
```

If the download's status is still **DOWNLOADING**, this means that the loop exited because downloading has been completed. Otherwise, the loop was exited because the download's status changed to something other than **DOWNLOADING**.

The **run( )** method wraps up with the **catch** and **finally** blocks shown here:

```
} catch (Exception e) {
  error();
} finally {
  // Close file.
  if (file != null) {
    try {
      file.close();
    } catch (Exception e) {}
  }

  // Close connection to server.
  if (stream != null) {
    try {
      stream.close();
    } catch (Exception e) {}
  }
}
```

If an exception is thrown during the download process, the **catch** block captures the exception and calls the **error( )** method. The **finally** block ensures that if the **file** and **stream** connections have been opened, they get closed whether an exception has been thrown or not.

The stateChanged( ) Method

In order for the Download Manager to display up-to-date information on each of the downloads it's managing, it has to know each time a download's information changes. To handle this, the Observer software design pattern is used. The Observer pattern is analogous to an announcement's mailing list where several people register to receive announcements. Each time there's a new announcement, each person on the list receives a message with the announcement. In the Observer pattern's case, there's an observed class with which observer classes can register themselves to receive change notifications.

The **Download** class employs the Observer pattern by extending Java's built-in **Observable** utility class. Extending the **Observable** class allows classes that implement Java's **Observer** interface to register themselves with the **Download** class to receive change notifications. Each time the **Download** class needs to notify its registered **Observer**s of a change, the **stateChanged( )** method is invoked. The **stateChanged( )** method first calls the **Observable** class' **setChanged( )** method to flag the class as having been changed. Next, the **stateChanged( )** method calls **Observable**'s **notifyObservers( )** method, which broadcasts the change notification to the registered **Observer**s.

Action and Accessor Methods

The **Download** class has numerous action and accessor methods for controlling a download and getting data from it. Each of the **pause( )**, **resume( )**, and **cancel( )** action methods simply does as its name implies: pauses, resumes, or cancels the download, respectively. Similarly, the **error( )** method marks the download as having an error. The **getUrl( )**, **getSize( )**, **getProgress( )**, and **getStatus( )** accessor methods each return their current respective values.

The ProgressRenderer Class

The **ProgressRenderer** class is a small utility class that is used to render the current progress of a download listed in the GUI's "Downloads" **JTable** instance. Normally, a **JTable** instance renders each of its table cell's data as text. However, often it's particularly useful to render a cell's data as something other than text. In the Download Manager's case, we want to render each of the table's Progress column cells as progress bars. The **ProgressRenderer** class shown here makes that possible. Notice that it extends **JProgressBar** and implements **TableCellRenderer**:

```java
import java.awt.*;
import javax.swing.*;
import javax.swing.table.*;

// This class renders a JProgressBar in a table cell.
class ProgressRenderer extends JProgressBar
  implements TableCellRenderer
{
  // Constructor for ProgressRenderer.
  public ProgressRenderer(int min, int max) {
    super(min, max);
  }

  /* Returns this JProgressBar as the renderer
     for the given table cell. */
  public Component getTableCellRendererComponent(
    JTable table, Object value, boolean isSelected,
```

```
     boolean hasFocus, int row, int column)
  {
     // Set JProgressBar's percent complete value.
     setValue((int) ((Float) value).floatValue());
     return this;
  }
}
```

The **ProgressRenderer** class takes advantage of the fact that Swing's **JTable** class has a rendering system that can accept "plug-ins" for rendering table cells. To plug into this rendering system, first, the **ProgressRenderer** class has to implement Swing's **TableCellRenderer** interface. Second, a **ProgressRenderer** instance has to be registered with a **JTable** instance; doing so instructs the **JTable** instance as to which cells should be rendered with the "plug-in."

Implementing the **TableCellRenderer** interface requires the class to override the **getTableCellRendererComponent( )** method. The **getTableCellRendererComponent( )** method is invoked each time a **JTable** instance goes to render a cell for which this class has been registered. This method is passed several variables, but in this case only the **value** variable is used. The **value** variable holds the data for the cell being rendered and is passed to **JProgressBar**'s **setValue( )** method. The **getTableCellRendererComponent( )** method wraps up by returning a reference to its class. This works because the **ProgressRenderer** class is a subclass of **JProgessbar**, which is a descendent of the AWT **Component** class.

The DownloadsTableModel Class

The **DownloadsTableModel** class houses the Download Manager's list of downloads and is the backing data source for the GUI's "Downloads" **JTable** instance.

The **DownloadsTableModel** class is shown here. Notice that it extends **AbstractTableModel** and implements the **Observer** interface:

```
import java.util.*;
import javax.swing.*;
import javax.swing.table.*;

// This class manages the download table's data.
class DownloadsTableModel extends AbstractTableModel
  implements Observer
{
  // These are the names for the table's columns.
  private static final String[] columnNames = {"URL", "Size",
    "Progress", "Status"};

  // These are the classes for each column's values.
  private static final Class[] columnClasses = {String.class,
    String.class, JProgressBar.class, String.class};
```

```java
// The table's list of downloads.
private ArrayList downloadList = new ArrayList();

// Add a new download to the table.
public void addDownload(Download download) {
  // Register to be notified when the download changes.
  download.addObserver(this);

  downloadList.add(download);

  // Fire table row insertion notification to table.
  fireTableRowsInserted(getRowCount() - 1, getRowCount() - 1);
}

// Get a download for the specified row.
public Download getDownload(int row) {
  return (Download) downloadList.get(row);
}

// Remove a download from the list.
public void clearDownload(int row) {
  downloadList.remove(row);

  // Fire table row deletion notification to table.
  fireTableRowsDeleted(row, row);
}

// Get table's column count.
public int getColumnCount() {
  return columnNames.length;
}

// Get a column's name.
public String getColumnName(int col) {
    return columnNames[col];
}

// Get a column's class.
public Class getColumnClass(int col) {
  return columnClasses[col];
}

// Get table's row count.
public int getRowCount() {
  return downloadList.size();
```

```
    }

    // Get value for a specific row and column combination.
    public Object getValueAt(int row, int col) {
      Download download = (Download) downloadList.get(row);
      switch (col) {
        case 0: // URL
          return download.getUrl();
        case 1: // Size
          int size = download.getSize();
          return (size == -1) ? "" : Integer.toString(size);
        case 2: // Progress
          return new Float(download.getProgress());
        case 3: // Status
          return Download.STATUSES[download.getStatus()];
      }
      return "";
    }

    /* Update is called when a Download notifies its
       observers of any changes */
    public void update(Observable o, Object arg) {
      int index = downloadList.indexOf(o);

      // Fire table row update notification to table.
      fireTableRowsUpdated(index, index);
    }
  }
```

The **DownloadsTableModel** class essentially is a utility class utilized by the "Downloads" **JTable** instance for managing data in the table. When the **JTable** instance is initialized, it is passed a **DownloadsTableModel** instance. The **JTable** then proceeds to call several methods on the **DownloadsTableModel** instance to populate itself. The **getColumnCount( )** method is called to retrieve the number of columns in the table. Similarly, **getRowCount( )** is used to retrieve the number of rows in the table. The **getColumnName( )** method returns a column's name given its ID. The **getDownload( )** method takes a row ID and returns the associated **Download** object from the list. The rest of the **DownloadsTableModel** class' methods, which are more involved, are detailed in the following sections.

The addDownload( ) Method

The **addDownload( )** method, shown here, adds a new **Download** object to the list of managed downloads and consequently a row to the table:

```
// Add a new download to the table.
public void addDownload(Download download) {
  // Register to be notified when the download changes.
  download.addObserver(this);

  downloadList.add(download);

  // Fire table row insertion notification to table.
  fireTableRowsInserted(getRowCount() - 1, getRowCount() - 1);
}
```

This method first registers itself with the new **Download** as an **Observer** interested in receiving change notifications. Next, the **Download** is added to the internal list of downloads being managed. Finally, a table row insertion event notification is fired to alert the table that a new row has been added.

The clearDownload( ) Method

The **clearDownload( )** method, shown next, removes a **Download** from the list of managed downloads:

```
// Remove a download from the list.
public void clearDownload(int row) {
  downloadList.remove(row);
  fireTableRowsDeleted(row, row);
}
```

After removing the **Download** from the internal list, a table row deleted event notification is fired to alert the table that a row has been deleted.

The getColumnClass( ) Method

The **getColumnClass( )** method, shown here, returns the class type for the data displayed in the specified column.

```
// Get a column's class.
public Class getColumnClass(int col) {
  return columnClasses[col];
}
```

All columns are displayed as text (i.e., **String** objects) except for the Progress column, which is displayed as a progress bar (which is an object of type **JProgressBar**).

The getValueAt( ) Method

The **getValueAt( )** method, shown next, is called to get the current value that should be displayed for each of the table's cells:

```
// Get value for a specific row and column combination.
public Object getValueAt(int row, int col) {
  Download download = (Download) downloadList.get(row);
  switch (col) {
    case 0: // URL
      return download.getUrl();
    case 1: // Size
      int size = download.getSize();
      return (size == -1) ? "" : Integer.toString(size);
    case 2: // Progress
      return new Float(download.getProgress());
    case 3: // Status
      return Download.STATUSES[download.getStatus()];
  }
  return "";
}
```

This method first looks up the **Download** corresponding to the row specified. Next, the column specified is used to determine which one of the **Download**'s property values to return.

The update( ) Method

The **update( )** method is shown here. It fulfills the **Observer** interface contract allowing the **DowloadsTableModel** class to receive notifications from **Download** objects when they change.

```
/* Update is called when a Download notifies its
   observers of any changes. */
public void update(Observable o, Object arg) {
  int index = downloadList.indexOf(o);

  // Fire table row update notification to table.
  fireTableRowsUpdated(index, index);
}
```

This method is passed a reference to the **Download** that has changed, in the form of an **Observable** object. Next, an index to that download is looked up in the list of downloads, and that index is then used to fire a table row update event notification, which alerts the table that the given row has been updated. The table will then rerender the row with the given index, reflecting its new values.

The DownloadManager Class

Now that the foundation has been laid by explaining each of the Download Manager's helper classes, we can look closely at the **DownloadManager** class. The **DownloadManager** class is responsible for creating and running the Download Manager's GUI. This class has a **main( )** method declared, so on execution it will be invoked first. The **main( )** method instantiates a new **DownloadManager** class instance and then calls its **show( )** method, which causes it to be displayed.

The **DownloadManager** class is shown here. Notice that it extends **JFrame** and implements **Observer**. The following sections examine it in detail.

```java
import java.awt.*;
import java.awt.event.*;
import java.net.*;
import java.util.*;
import javax.swing.*;
import javax.swing.event.*;

// The Download Manager.
public class DownloadManager extends JFrame
  implements Observer
{
  // Add download text field.
  private JTextField addTextField;

  // Download table's data model.
  private DownloadsTableModel tableModel;

  // Table listing downloads.
  private JTable table;

  // These are the buttons for managing the selected download.
  private JButton pauseButton, resumeButton;
  private JButton cancelButton, clearButton;

  // Currently selected download.
  private Download selectedDownload;

  // Flag for whether or not table selection is being cleared.
  private boolean clearing;

  // Constructor for Download Manager.
  public DownloadManager()
  {
    // Set application title.
```

```java
    setTitle("Download Manager");

    // Set window size.
    setSize(640, 480);

    // Handle window closing events.
    addWindowListener(new WindowAdapter() {
      public void windowClosing(WindowEvent e) {
        actionExit();
      }
    });

    // Set up file menu.
    JMenuBar menuBar = new JMenuBar();
    JMenu fileMenu = new JMenu("File");
    fileMenu.setMnemonic(KeyEvent.VK_F);
    JMenuItem fileExitMenuItem = new JMenuItem("Exit",
      KeyEvent.VK_X);
    fileExitMenuItem.addActionListener(new ActionListener() {
      public void actionPerformed(ActionEvent e) {
        actionExit();
      }
    });
    fileMenu.add(fileExitMenuItem);
    menuBar.add(fileMenu);
    setJMenuBar(menuBar);

    // Set up add panel.
    JPanel addPanel = new JPanel();
    addTextField = new JTextField(30);
    addPanel.add(addTextField);
    JButton addButton = new JButton("Add Download");
    addButton.addActionListener(new ActionListener() {
      public void actionPerformed(ActionEvent e) {
        actionAdd();
      }
    });
    addPanel.add(addButton);

    // Set up Downloads table.
    tableModel = new DownloadsTableModel();
    table = new JTable(tableModel);
    table.getSelectionModel().addListSelectionListener(new
      ListSelectionListener() {
      public void valueChanged(ListSelectionEvent e) {
```

```java
        tableSelectionChanged();
      }
  });
  // Allow only one row at a time to be selected.
  table.setSelectionMode(ListSelectionModel.SINGLE_SELECTION);

  // Set up ProgressBar as renderer for progress column.
  ProgressRenderer renderer = new ProgressRenderer(0, 100);
  renderer.setStringPainted(true); // show progress text
  table.setDefaultRenderer(JProgressBar.class, renderer);

  // Set table's row height large enough to fit JProgressBar.
  table.setRowHeight(
    (int) renderer.getPreferredSize().getHeight());

  // Set up downloads panel.
  JPanel downloadsPanel = new JPanel();
  downloadsPanel.setBorder(
    BorderFactory.createTitledBorder("Downloads"));
  downloadsPanel.setLayout(new BorderLayout());
  downloadsPanel.add(new JScrollPane(table),
    BorderLayout.CENTER);

  // Set up buttons panel.
  JPanel buttonsPanel = new JPanel();
  pauseButton = new JButton("Pause");
  pauseButton.addActionListener(new ActionListener() {
    public void actionPerformed(ActionEvent e) {
      actionPause();
    }
  });
  pauseButton.setEnabled(false);
  buttonsPanel.add(pauseButton);
  resumeButton = new JButton("Resume");
  resumeButton.addActionListener(new ActionListener() {
    public void actionPerformed(ActionEvent e) {
      actionResume();
    }
  });
  resumeButton.setEnabled(false);
  buttonsPanel.add(resumeButton);
  cancelButton = new JButton("Cancel");
  cancelButton.addActionListener(new ActionListener() {
    public void actionPerformed(ActionEvent e) {
      actionCancel();
```

```
      }
    });
    cancelButton.setEnabled(false);
    buttonsPanel.add(cancelButton);
    clearButton = new JButton("Clear");
    clearButton.addActionListener(new ActionListener() {
      public void actionPerformed(ActionEvent e) {
        actionClear();
      }
    });
    clearButton.setEnabled(false);
    buttonsPanel.add(clearButton);

    // Add panels to display.
    getContentPane().setLayout(new BorderLayout());
    getContentPane().add(addPanel, BorderLayout.NORTH);
    getContentPane().add(downloadsPanel, BorderLayout.CENTER);
    getContentPane().add(buttonsPanel, BorderLayout.SOUTH);
  }

  // Exit this program.
  private void actionExit() {
    System.exit(0);
  }

  // Add a new download.
  private void actionAdd() {
    URL verifiedUrl = verifyUrl(addTextField.getText());
    if (verifiedUrl != null) {
      tableModel.addDownload(new Download(verifiedUrl));
      addTextField.setText(""); // reset add text field
    } else {
      JOptionPane.showMessageDialog(this,
        "Invalid Download URL", "Error",
        JOptionPane.ERROR_MESSAGE);
    }
  }

  // Verify download URL.
  private URL verifyUrl(String url) {
    // Only allow HTTP URLs.
    if (!url.toLowerCase().startsWith("http://"))
      return null;

    // Verify format of URL.
```

```java
  URL verifiedUrl = null;
  try {
    verifiedUrl = new URL(url);
  } catch (Exception e) {
    return null;
  }

  // Make sure URL specifies a file.
  if (verifiedUrl.getFile().length() < 2)
    return null;

  return verifiedUrl;
}


// Called when table row selection changes.
private void tableSelectionChanged() {
  /* Unregister from receiving notifications
     from the last selected download. */
  if (selectedDownload != null)
    selectedDownload.deleteObserver(DownloadManager.this);

  /* If not in the middle of clearing a download,
     set the selected download and register to
     receive notifications from it. */
  if (!clearing) {
    selectedDownload =
      tableModel.getDownload(table.getSelectedRow());
    selectedDownload.addObserver(DownloadManager.this);
    updateButtons();
  }
}


// Pause the selected download.
private void actionPause() {
  selectedDownload.pause();
  updateButtons();
}


// Resume the selected download.
private void actionResume() {
  selectedDownload.resume();
  updateButtons();
}


// Cancel the selected download.
```

```java
private void actionCancel() {
  selectedDownload.cancel();
  updateButtons();
}

// Clear the selected download.
private void actionClear() {
  clearing = true;
  tableModel.clearDownload(table.getSelectedRow());
  clearing = false;
  selectedDownload = null;
  updateButtons();
}

/* Update each button's state based off of the
   currently selected download's status. */
private void updateButtons() {
  if (selectedDownload != null) {
    int status = selectedDownload.getStatus();
    switch (status) {
      case Download.DOWNLOADING:
        pauseButton.setEnabled(true);
        resumeButton.setEnabled(false);
        cancelButton.setEnabled(true);
        clearButton.setEnabled(false);
        break;
      case Download.PAUSED:
        pauseButton.setEnabled(false);
        resumeButton.setEnabled(true);
        cancelButton.setEnabled(true);
        clearButton.setEnabled(false);
        break;
      case Download.ERROR:
        pauseButton.setEnabled(false);
        resumeButton.setEnabled(true);
        cancelButton.setEnabled(false);
        clearButton.setEnabled(true);
        break;
      default: // COMPLETE or CANCELLED
        pauseButton.setEnabled(false);
        resumeButton.setEnabled(false);
        cancelButton.setEnabled(false);
        clearButton.setEnabled(true);
    }
  } else {
```

```
      // No download is selected in table.
      pauseButton.setEnabled(false);
      resumeButton.setEnabled(false);
      cancelButton.setEnabled(false);
      clearButton.setEnabled(false);
    }
  }


  /* Update is called when a Download notifies its
     observers of any changes. */
  public void update(Observable o, Object arg) {
    // Update buttons if the selected download has changed.
    if (selectedDownload != null && selectedDownload.equals(o))
      updateButtons();
  }


  // Run the Download Manager.
  public static void main(String[] args) {
    DownloadManager manager = new DownloadManager();
    manager.show();
  }
}
```

The DownloadManager Variables

DownloadManager starts off by declaring several instance variables, most of which hold references to the GUI controls. The **selectedDownload** variable holds a reference to the **Download** object represented by the selected row in the table. Finally, the **clearing** instance variable is a **boolean** flag that tracks whether or not a download is currently being cleared from the Downloads table.

The DownloadManager Constructor

When the **DownloadManager** is instantiated, all of the GUI's controls are initialized inside its constructor. The constructor contains a lot of code, but most of it is straightforward. The following discussion gives an overview.

First, the window's title is set with a call to **setTitle( )**. Next, the **setSize( )** call establishes the window's width and height in pixels. After that, a window listener is added by calling **addWindowListener( )**, passing a **WindowAdapter** object that overrides the **windowClosing( )** event handler. This handler calls the **actionExit( )** method when the application's window is closed. Next, a menu bar with a "File" menu is added to the application's window. Then the "Add" panel, which has the Add Text field and button, is set up. An **ActionListener** is added to the "Add Download" button so that the **actionAdd( )** method is called each time the button is clicked.

The downloads table is constructed next. A **ListSelectionListener** is added to the table so that each time a row is selected in the table the **tableSelectionChanged( )** method is invoked. The table's selection mode is also updated to **ListSelectionModel.SINGLE_SELECTION** so that only one row at a time can be selected in the table. Limiting row selection to only one row at a time simplifies the logic for determining which buttons should be enabled in the GUI when a row in the download table is selected. Next, a **ProgressRenderer** class is instantiated and registered with the table to handle the "Progress" column. The table's row height is updated to the **ProgressRenderer**'s height by calling **table.setRowHeight( )**. After the table has been assembled and tweaked, it is wrapped in a **JScrollPane** to make it scrollable and then added to a panel.

Finally, the buttons panel is created. The buttons panel has Pause, Resume, Cancel, and Clear buttons. Each of the buttons adds an **ActionListener** that invokes its respective action method when it is clicked. After creating the buttons panel, all of the panels that have been created are added to the window.

The verifyUrl( ) Method

The **verifyUrl( )** method is called by the **actionAdd( )** method each time a download is added to the Download Manager. The **verifyUrl( )** method is shown here:

```
// Verify download URL.
private URL verifyUrl(String url) {
  // Only allow HTTP URLs.
  if (!url.toLowerCase().startsWith("http://"))
    return null;

  // Verify format of URL.
  URL verifiedUrl = null;
  try {
    verifiedUrl = new URL(url);
  } catch (Exception e) {
    return null;
  }

  // Make sure URL specifies a file.
  if (verifiedUrl.getFile().length() < 2)
    return null;

  return verifiedUrl;
}
```

This method first verifies that the URL entered is an HTTP URL since only HTTP is supported. Next, the URL being verified is used to construct a new **URL** class instance.

If the URL is malformed, the **URL** class constructor will throw an exception. Finally, this method verifies that a file is actually specified in the URL.

The tableSelectionChanged( ) Method

The **tableSelectionChanged( )** method, shown here, is called each time a row is selected in the downloads table:

```
// Called when table row selection changes.
private void tableSelectionChanged() {
  /* Unregister from receiving notifications
     from the last selected download. */
  if (selectedDownload != null)
    selectedDownload.deleteObserver(DownloadManager.this);

  /* If not in the middle of clearing a download,
     set the selected download and register to
     receive notifications from it. */
  if (!clearing) {
    selectedDownload =
      tableModel.getDownload(table.getSelectedRow());
    selectedDownload.addObserver(DownloadManager.this);
    updateButtons();
  }
}
```

This method starts by seeing if there is already a row currently selected by checking if the **selectedDownload** variable is **null**. If the **selectedDownload** variable is not null, **DownloadManager** removes itself as an observer of the download so that it no longer receives change notifications. Next the **clearing** flag is checked. If the **clearing** flag is not true, then first the **selectedDownload** variable is updated with the **Download** corresponding to the row selected. Second, the **DownloadManager** is registered as an **Observer** with the newly selected **Download**. Finally, **updateButtons( )** is called to update the button states based on the selected **Download**'s state.

The updateButtons( ) Method

The **updateButtons( )** method updates the state of all the buttons on the button panel based on the state of the selected download. The **updateButtons( )** method is shown here:

```
/* Update each button's state based on the
   currently selected download's status. */
private void updateButtons() {
```

```
    if (selectedDownload != null) {
      int status = selectedDownload.getStatus();
      switch (status) {
        case Download.DOWNLOADING:
          pauseButton.setEnabled(true);
          resumeButton.setEnabled(false);
          cancelButton.setEnabled(true);
          clearButton.setEnabled(false);
          break;
        case Download.PAUSED:
          pauseButton.setEnabled(false);
          resumeButton.setEnabled(true);
          cancelButton.setEnabled(true);
          clearButton.setEnabled(false);
          break;
        case Download.ERROR:
          pauseButton.setEnabled(false);
          resumeButton.setEnabled(true);
          cancelButton.setEnabled(false);
          clearButton.setEnabled(true);
          break;
        default: // COMPLETE or CANCELLED
          pauseButton.setEnabled(false);
          resumeButton.setEnabled(false);
          cancelButton.setEnabled(false);
          clearButton.setEnabled(true);
      }
    } else {
      // No download is selected in table.
      pauseButton.setEnabled(false);
      resumeButton.setEnabled(false);
      cancelButton.setEnabled(false);
      clearButton.setEnabled(false);
    }
  }
```

If no download is selected in the downloads table, all of the buttons are disabled, giving them a grayed-out appearance. However, if there is a selected download, each button's state will be set based on whether the **Download** object has a status of **DOWNLOADING**, **PAUSED**, **ERROR**, **COMPLETE**, or **CANCELLED**.

Handling Action Events

Each of **DownloadManager**'s GUI controls registers an **ActionListener** that invokes its respective action method. **ActionListener**s are triggered each time an action event takes place on a GUI control. For example, when a button is clicked, an **ActionEvent** is generated and each of the button's registered **ActionListener**s are notified. You may have noticed a similarity between the way **ActionListener**s work and the Observer pattern discussed earlier. That is because they are the same pattern with two different naming schemes.

Compiling and Running the Download Manager

Compile **DownloadManager** like this:

```
javac DownloadManager.java DownloadsTableModel.java
ProgressRenderer.java Download.java
```

Run **DownloadManager** like this:

```
javaw DownloadManager
```

The Download Manager is easy to use. First, enter the URL of a file that you want to download in the text field at the top of the screen. For example, to download a file called 0072224207_code.zip from **www.osborne.com**, enter

http://www.osborne.com/products/0072224207/0072224207_code.zip

This is the file that contains the code for Herb's book *Java 2: The Complete Reference.*

After adding a download to the Download Manager, you can manage it by selecting it in the table. Once selected, you can pause, cancel, resume, and clear a download. Figure 4-2 shows the Download Manager in action.

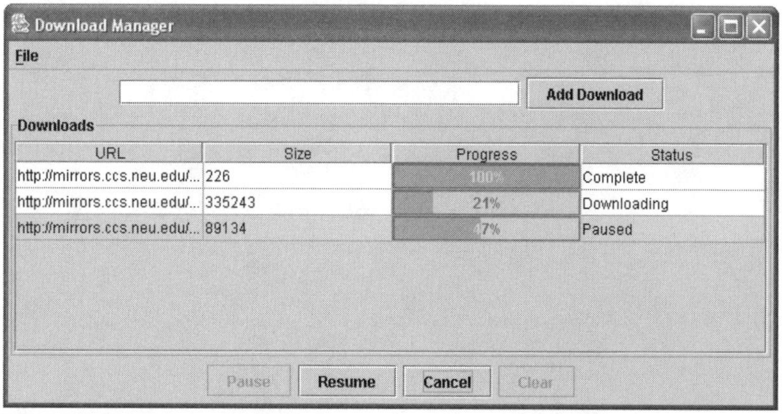

Figure 4-2   *The Download Manager in action*

Enhancing the Download Manager

The Download Manager as it stands is fully functional, with the ability to pause and resume downloads as well as download multiple files at once; however, there are several enhancements that you may want to try on your own. Here are some ideas: proxy server support, FTP and HTTPS support, and drag-and-drop support. A particularly appealing enhancement is a scheduling feature that lets you schedule a download at a specific time, perhaps in the middle of the night when system resources are plentiful.

Note that the techniques illustrated in this chapter are not limited to downloading files in the typical sense. There are many other practical uses for the code. For example, many software programs distributed over the Internet come in two pieces. The first piece is a small, compact application that can be downloaded quickly. This small application contains a mini download manager for downloading the second piece, which is generally much larger. This concept is quite useful, especially as the size of applications increases, which typically leads to an increase in the potential for download interruptions. You might want to try adapting the Download Manager for this purpose.

CHAPTER 5

Implementing an E-mail Client in Java

By James Holmes

As all readers know, there are two primary uses of the Internet: web browsing and e-mail. Although browsing the Web is certainly the more glamorous of the two, it is e-mail that many users have come to rely on. Because e-mail offers a low-cost, high-speed alternative to regular mail and flexibility that is not available with telephone calls, it has become the communication means of choice for many today.

Despite the pervasiveness of e-mail and its importance to the Internet, few programmers know much about how it actually works or how to write applications that use it. Frankly, the ability to send and receive e-mail messages under your direct program control is potentially very valuable. For example, consider an application that monitors the temperature of a commercial freezer. You might want this application to send an e-mail to the plant manager automatically if the temperature rises above zero. Furthermore, you might want to create a specialized e-mail client for the plant manager that monitors all e-mail and sounds an alarm if an e-mail from the freezer is seen.

In addition to dedicated uses of e-mail, such as that just described, there is another reason why you might want the ability to take direct control of e-mail: security. E-mail has evolved significantly from its beginnings where it consisted solely of plaintext messages. Today, e-mail supports much richer formats such as HTML laden with graphics and sounds. It also supports file attachments for transporting data with messages. The trouble is that these extra features and formats have been exploited by malicious programmers who see e-mail as a convenient means of delivering computer viruses, Trojan horses, and the like.

Although today's commercial e-mail programs offer up solutions to combat viruses, with each countermeasure comes a new threat. An alternative approach to the problem is to use an e-mail application that simply receives e-mail but does not take any further action involving its contents. A simple e-mail client that does not render HTML, does not display a graphic, does not preview a photo, and does not play a sound file removes much of the potential for exploitation or threat. Of course, such a solution is not acceptable for the world at large, but such an e-mail client might be quite useful in certain cases—especially in situations in which a cyberattack is ongoing.

Whatever the purpose, the ability to take full control over e-mail is a valuable skill that will find its way into a wide array of applications. Although programming an e-mail application can be difficult, Java—and the JavaMail API—make it easier. In this chapter a simple, text-only e-mail client is developed. The e-mail client serves two purposes. First, it is a fully functional e-mail application that can send and receive text-based messages. It takes no action with other types of content. Thus, it is usable "as is" when such a minimalist e-mail program is required. Second, it demonstrates the techniques needed to send and receive e-mail. You can adapt these techniques for use in your own code.

E-mail Behind the Scenes

Behind the scenes, e-mail is little more than standard client/server networking; there are e-mail clients that communicate with e-mail servers for sending and receiving e-mail messages. E-mail clients come in several varieties, from stand-alone computer applications like the one in this chapter to cell phones that have the ability to receive e-mail messages. Regardless what client is used, it will connect to an e-mail server to transfer e-mail messages, be it to or from the server. Communications between e-mail clients and servers follow defined protocols so that virtually all clients and servers are compatible with one another. There are two protocols for receiving e-mail messages: POP3 and IMAP. SMTP is the dominant protocol for sending e-mail. Each of these protocols is explained in the following sections.

POP3

Post Office Protocol version 3 (POP3) is the dominant protocol for retrieving e-mail from e-mail servers on the Internet. POP3 is very basic, allowing e-mail clients to access only mail in a default "Inbox" folder.

IMAP

Internet Message Access Protocol (IMAP) is another protocol for retrieving e-mail from e-mail servers on the Internet. IMAP has more features than POP and supports retrieving messages from multiple accounts and folders. IMAP also supports the use of public folders where messages are shared.

SMTP

Simple Mail Transfer Protocol (SMTP) is a protocol for sending e-mail on the Internet. When you send a message with SMTP, a server receives the message and then routes it to the recipient's mail server. The message is then available for reading with POP3 or IMAP.

The General Procedure for Sending and Receiving E-mail

As mentioned earlier, both sending and receiving e-mail on the Internet follow defined protocols. Following are samplings of typical client/server communications when sending and receiving e-mail using those protocols.

Sending e-mail with SMTP follows this sequence of events:

1. The client connects to an e-mail server.
2. The client sends an e-mail message to the server.
3. The client closes the connection to the server.

Sending e-mail with SMTP is very simple. Client software establishes a connection with an SMTP server and transmits the message to the server and then closes the connection. The SMTP server then takes the message and routes it to the appropriate recipient e-mail server.

Receiving e-mail with POP3 and IMAP typically follows this process:

1. The client connects to an e-mail server.
2. The client authenticates itself with the server.

3. The client downloads a list of messages from the server.

4. The client closes the connection to the server.

Receiving e-mail is more involved than sending e-mail, but it's still relatively straightforward. First, client software connects to an e-mail server, and then it authenticates itself. Authentication is required to tell the server which account to receive e-mail for and to ensure that only the intended receiver is receiving the messages. After authentication has successfully completed, the client software downloads a list of new messages from the server and, finally, closes the connection to the server.

The JavaMail API

Developing code from scratch to communicate directly with e-mail servers is a considerable undertaking and one that few programmers would want to attempt. Fortunately, Sun Microsystems' JavaSoft division recognized the need for a standard e-mail processing library in Java and created JavaMail. The JavaMail library provides a complete foundation for developing Java-based e-mail applications, including full support for the POP3, IMAP, and SMTP protocols. The e-mail client in this chapter makes heavy use of the JavaMail API, showcasing its robust feature set and ease of use for creating e-mail applications.

In order to compile and run the e-mail client, you will need to have the JavaMail library installed on your computer. JavaMail comes packaged with the Java 2 Software Development Kit, Enterprise Edition (J2SDKEE). If you don't already have the J2SDKEE installed on your computer, you will need to download and install it. Alternatively, you can download just the JavaMail library and its dependent library, the JavaBeans Activation Framework (JAF). Later, in the "Compiling and Running the E-mail Client" section, instructions for using the JavaMail library are detailed. Following are the JavaSoft Web site addresses for downloading JavaMail:

▶   **Java 2 Enterprise Edition**   http://java.sun.com/j2ee/

▶   **JavaMail**   http://java.sun.com/products/javamail/

▶   **JavaBeans Activation Framework (JAF)**
      http://java.sun.com/products/javabeans/glasgow/jaf.html

An Overview of Using JavaMail

JavaMail provides a protocol-independent API for sending and receiving e-mail messages. The API is broken up into several classes that model an e-mail system and abstract the details of the low-level networking protocols such as SMTP and POP. Following is an introduction to the core JavaMail classes you will see used later in this chapter.

javax.mail.Session

The **javax.mail.Session** class defines a basic e-mail session and manages the configuration options and authentication information used to interact with an e-mail server. This class is the entry point for the JavaMail API and is used internally by several of the other classes.

javax.mail.Store

The **javax.mail.Store** class is used to represent a message store, which is analogous to an e-mail account. It also provides the access protocol that is used to store and retrieve messages. **Store** is abstract, and it is essentially an interface used to access an e-mail account with a given protocol such as POP3 or IMAP.

javax.mail.Folder

The **javax.mail.Folder** class represents a mailbox folder for e-mail messages. **Folder** objects are used to provide a tree-like hierarchy for messages and can contain messages, other folders, or both. **Folder** objects are also used for deleting messages. **Folder** is abstract.

javax.mail.Message

The **javax.mail.Message** class encapsulates an e-mail message and houses each of a message's fields such as its sender, recipient, date sent, subject, and the content of the message. **Message** is abstract.

javax.mail.Transport

The **javax.mail.Transport** class encapsulates the code for sending e-mail messages. This class' static **send( )** method is used to send the messages. **Transport** is abstract.

A Simple E-mail Client

The remainder of this chapter develops a simple e-mail client that is capable of sending and receiving text-based messages. This application is useful "as is" when a minimal e-mail client is needed, but its main purpose is to illustrate the techniques needed to access e-mail through the JavaMail API. It also serves as a starting point for your own e-mail application development. Figure 5-1 shows E-mail Client's window.

At the top of the window there is a New Message button for creating new e-mail messages. The center of the window is divided between the table of messages and the message display area. Each message in the table lists its sender, its subject, and the date. When a message in the table is selected, it is loaded into the message display area in the bottom half of the center of the window. The bottom of the window holds the Reply, Forward, and Delete buttons for working with the currently selected message.

E-mail Client's application code is divided among the following classes:

Class	Purpose
EmailClient	Houses the bulk of the application, including code for setting up the GUI and for interfacing with e-mail servers
ConnectDialog	Displays a dialog box into which the user enters the connection settings
DownloadingDialog	Displays a dialog box with a "Downloading" message while e-mail is being downloaded from a server
MessageDialog	Displays a dialog box used for creating messages
MessagesTableModel	Holds the list of messages displayed in the e-mail client's window

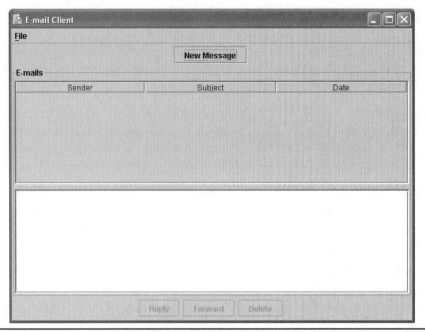

Figure 5-1 *E-mail Client's GUI interface*

The main class of the application is **EmailClient**. It contains the code that actually deals with the sending and receiving of e-mail. The remaining four classes support **EmailClient**. The following sections examine each class in detail, beginning with the support classes.

The ConnectDialog Class

The Connect dialog box, illustrated in Figure 5-2, is displayed when the E-mail Client starts up. This dialog box prompts the user for the settings required to establish a connection to an e-mail server.

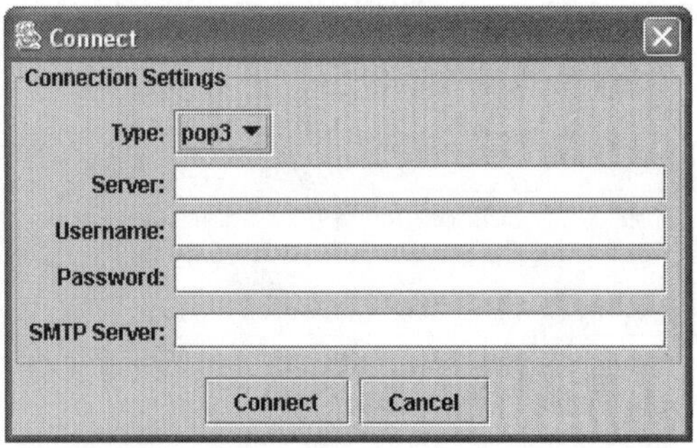

Figure 5-2 *The Connect dialog box window*

The **ConnectDialog** class is shown here. Notice that it extends **JDialog**:

```java
import java.awt.*;
import java.awt.event.*;
import javax.swing.*;

/* This class displays a dialog box for entering e-mail
   server connection settings. */
public class ConnectDialog extends JDialog
{
  // These are the e-mail server types.
  private static final String[] TYPES = {"pop3", "imap"};

  // Combo box for e-mail server types.
  private JComboBox typeComboBox;

  // Server, username, and SMTP server text fields.
  private JTextField serverTextField, usernameTextField;
  private JTextField smtpServerTextField;

  // Password text field.
  private JPasswordField passwordField;

  // Constructor for dialog box.
  public ConnectDialog(Frame parent)
  {
    // Call super constructor, specifying that dialog box is modal.
    super(parent, true);

    // Set dialog box title.
    setTitle("Connect");

    // Handle closing events.
    addWindowListener(new WindowAdapter() {
      public void windowClosing(WindowEvent e) {
        actionCancel();
      }
    });

    // Set up settings panel.
    JPanel settingsPanel = new JPanel();
    settingsPanel.setBorder(
      BorderFactory.createTitledBorder("Connection Settings"));
    GridBagConstraints constraints;
    GridBagLayout layout = new GridBagLayout();
```

```
settingsPanel.setLayout(layout);
JLabel typeLabel = new JLabel("Type:");
constraints = new GridBagConstraints();
constraints.anchor = GridBagConstraints.EAST;
constraints.insets = new Insets(5, 5, 0, 0);
layout.setConstraints(typeLabel, constraints);
settingsPanel.add(typeLabel);
typeComboBox = new JComboBox(TYPES);
constraints = new GridBagConstraints();
constraints.anchor = GridBagConstraints.WEST;
constraints.gridwidth = GridBagConstraints.REMAINDER;
constraints.insets = new Insets(5, 5, 0, 5);
constraints.weightx = 1.0D;
layout.setConstraints(typeComboBox, constraints);
settingsPanel.add(typeComboBox);
JLabel serverLabel = new JLabel("Server:");
constraints = new GridBagConstraints();
constraints.anchor = GridBagConstraints.EAST;
constraints.insets = new Insets(5, 5, 0, 0);
layout.setConstraints(serverLabel, constraints);
settingsPanel.add(serverLabel);
serverTextField = new JTextField(25);
constraints = new GridBagConstraints();
constraints.gridwidth = GridBagConstraints.REMAINDER;
constraints.insets = new Insets(5, 5, 0, 5);
constraints.weightx = 1.0D;
layout.setConstraints(serverTextField, constraints);
settingsPanel.add(serverTextField);
JLabel usernameLabel = new JLabel("Username:");
constraints = new GridBagConstraints();
constraints.anchor = GridBagConstraints.EAST;
constraints.insets = new Insets(5, 5, 0, 0);
layout.setConstraints(usernameLabel, constraints);
settingsPanel.add(usernameLabel);
usernameTextField = new JTextField();
constraints = new GridBagConstraints();
constraints.anchor = GridBagConstraints.WEST;
constraints.fill = GridBagConstraints.HORIZONTAL;
constraints.gridwidth = GridBagConstraints.REMAINDER;
constraints.insets = new Insets(5, 5, 0, 5);
constraints.weightx = 1.0D;
layout.setConstraints(usernameTextField, constraints);
settingsPanel.add(usernameTextField);
JLabel passwordLabel = new JLabel("Password:");
constraints = new GridBagConstraints();
```

```java
constraints.anchor = GridBagConstraints.EAST;
constraints.insets = new Insets(5, 5, 5, 0);
layout.setConstraints(passwordLabel, constraints);
settingsPanel.add(passwordLabel);
passwordField = new JPasswordField();
constraints = new GridBagConstraints();
constraints.anchor = GridBagConstraints.WEST;
constraints.fill = GridBagConstraints.HORIZONTAL;
constraints.gridwidth = GridBagConstraints.REMAINDER;
constraints.insets = new Insets(5, 5, 5, 5);
constraints.weightx = 1.0D;
layout.setConstraints(passwordField, constraints);
settingsPanel.add(passwordField);
JLabel smtpServerLabel = new JLabel("SMTP Server:");
constraints = new GridBagConstraints();
constraints.anchor = GridBagConstraints.EAST;
constraints.insets = new Insets(5, 5, 5, 0);
layout.setConstraints(smtpServerLabel, constraints);
settingsPanel.add(smtpServerLabel);
smtpServerTextField = new JTextField(25);
constraints = new GridBagConstraints();
constraints.gridwidth = GridBagConstraints.REMAINDER;
constraints.insets = new Insets(5, 5, 5, 5);
constraints.weightx = 1.0D;
layout.setConstraints(smtpServerTextField, constraints);
settingsPanel.add(smtpServerTextField);

// Set up buttons panel.
JPanel buttonsPanel = new JPanel();
JButton connectButton = new JButton("Connect");
connectButton.addActionListener(new ActionListener() {
  public void actionPerformed(ActionEvent e) {
    actionConnect();
  }
});
buttonsPanel.add(connectButton);
JButton cancelButton = new JButton("Cancel");
cancelButton.addActionListener(new ActionListener() {
  public void actionPerformed(ActionEvent e) {
    actionCancel();
  }
});
buttonsPanel.add(cancelButton);

// Add panels to display.
```

```java
    getContentPane().setLayout(new BorderLayout());
    getContentPane().add(settingsPanel, BorderLayout.CENTER);
    getContentPane().add(buttonsPanel, BorderLayout.SOUTH);

    // Size dialog box to components.
    pack();

    // Center dialog box over application.
    setLocationRelativeTo(parent);
  }

  // Validate connection settings and close dialog box.
  private void actionConnect() {
    if (serverTextField.getText().trim().length() < 1
        || usernameTextField.getText().trim().length() < 1
        || passwordField.getPassword().length < 1
        || smtpServerTextField.getText().trim().length() < 1) {
      JOptionPane.showMessageDialog(this,
        "One or more settings is missing.",
        "Missing Setting(s)", JOptionPane.ERROR_MESSAGE);
      return;
    }

    // Close dialog box.
    dispose();
  }

  // Cancel connecting and exit program.
  private void actionCancel() {
    System.exit(0);
  }

  // Get e-mail server type.
  public String getType() {
    return (String) typeComboBox.getSelectedItem();
  }

  // Get e-mail server.
  public String getServer() {
    return serverTextField.getText();
  }

  // Get e-mail username.
  public String getUsername() {
    return usernameTextField.getText();
```

```
  }

  // Get e-mail password.
  public String getPassword() {
    return new String(passwordField.getPassword());
  }

  // Get e-mail SMTP server.
  public String getSmtpServer() {
    return smtpServerTextField.getText();
  }
}
```

ConnectDialog begins by declaring a **static final** variable, **TYPES**, to hold the list of e-mail server types. Next, several GUI control variables are declared. The rest of the class is examined in detail in the sections that follow.

The ConnectDialog Constructor

ConnectDialog's constructor is passed a reference to a parent **Frame** with which the dialog box will be associated. The constructor then begins by passing the **Frame** reference to **JDialog**'s constructor with a call to **super( )**. Invoking **JDialog**'s constructor is necessary to specify that the dialog box will be modal. A modal dialog box blocks user input to all other windows in the program. This feature is especially useful in GUI programming to prevent the user from interacting with the rest of the interface elements.

Next, a panel that will hold the connection settings is created. Then each of the controls are initialized and added to the panel. Notice that a grid bag layout is used to position the controls in a well-defined fashion. After the Connection Settings panel has been created, the Connect and Cancel buttons are initialized and added to a buttons panel. Both the settings panel and the buttons panel are then added to the display. Next, **pack( )** is called to size the dialog box window to the minimum size required by its controls. Finally, a call to **setLocationRelativeTo( )** centers the dialog box over the parent window.

The actionConnect( ) Method

The **actionConnect( )** method, shown here, is used to validate that all of the connection settings have been entered and to dispose the dialog box when the Connect button is clicked, removing it from the screen:

```
// Validate connection settings and close dialog box.
private void actionConnect() {
  if (serverTextField.getText().trim().length() < 1
      || usernameTextField.getText().trim().length() < 1
      || passwordField.getPassword().length < 1
      || smtpServerTextField.getText().trim().length() < 1) {
    JOptionPane.showMessageDialog(this,
      "One or more settings is missing.",
```

```
      "Missing Setting(s)", JOptionPane.ERROR_MESSAGE);
    return;
  }

  // Close dialog box.
  dispose();
}
```

Since each of the Connect dialog box's settings are required, **actionConnect( )** begins by validating that they have all been entered. If one or more settings are missing, an error dialog box is displayed to notify the user. Once all the settings have been correctly entered, the **dispose( )** method is called to close the dialog box.

The actionCancel( ) Method

The **actionCancel( )** method, shown here, is called when the Cancel button in the dialog box is clicked or when the dialog box is closed:

```
// Cancel connecting and exit program.
private void actionCancel() {
  System.exit(0);
}
```

Canceling the Connect dialog box results in E-mail Client being shut down with a call to **System.exit( )**. E-mail Client is terminated in this scenario because it cannot function without an e-mail server connection.

Accessor Methods

The **ConnectDialog** class has a number of accessor methods for retrieving the connection settings entered in the dialog box. Each of the **getType( )**, **getServer( )**, **getUsername( )**, **getPassword( )**, and **getSmtpServer( )** methods simply returns the value entered into its corresponding control.

The DownloadingDialog Class

Immediately after the Connect dialog box has been disposed, the Downloading dialog box illustrated in Figure 5-3 is launched. This dialog box tells the user that e-mail messages are being downloaded. Additionally, because the Downloading dialog box is modal, it prevents the user from using any other part of E-mail Client while downloading is under way.

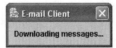

Figure 5-3 *The Downloading dialog box*

The **DownloadingDialog** class is shown here. Notice that it extends **JDialog**:

```java
import java.awt.*;
import javax.swing.*;

/* This class displays a simple dialog box instructing the user
   that messages are being downloaded. */
public class DownloadingDialog extends JDialog
{
  // Constructor for dialog box.
  public DownloadingDialog(Frame parent)
  {
    // Call super constructor, specifying that dialog box is modal.
    super(parent, true);

    // Set dialog box title.
    setTitle("E-mail Client");

    // Instruct window not to close when the "X" is clicked.
    setDefaultCloseOperation(DO_NOTHING_ON_CLOSE);

    // Put a message with a nice border in this dialog box.
    JPanel contentPane = new JPanel();
    contentPane.setBorder(
      BorderFactory.createEmptyBorder(5, 5, 5, 5));
    contentPane.add(new JLabel("Downloading messages..."));
    setContentPane(contentPane);

    // Size dialog box to components.
    pack();

    // Center dialog box over application.
    setLocationRelativeTo(parent);
  }
}
```

The **DownloadingDialog** class is clear cut in that it contains only a constructor method. The constructor begins by mirroring the **ConnectDialog** constructor with **super( )** and **setTitle( )** method calls. Next, the **setDefaultCloseOperation( )** method is called to change the dialog box's behavior so that it doesn't close when the close box is clicked. This prevents the user from being able to close the window prematurely. After that, the message label is added to the display with an empty (invisible) border of 5 pixels for spacing. Next, **pack( )** is invoked to size the dialog box to the minimum size required by its controls. Finally, a call to **setLocationRelativeTo( )** centers the dialog box over the parent window.

The MessageDialog Class

The Message dialog box, shown in Figure 5-4, is used to enter messages that will be sent by the **EmailClient** class. It is created by the **MessageDialog** class. This class is used for new messages, as shown in Figure 5-4, as well as reply to and forward messages.

The **MessageDialog** class is shown here. Notice that it extends **JDialog**:

```java
import java.awt.*;
import java.awt.event.*;
import javax.mail.*;
import javax.swing.*;


// This class displays the dialog box used for creating messages.
public class MessageDialog extends JDialog
{
  // Dialog box message identifiers.
  public static final int NEW = 0;
  public static final int REPLY = 1;
  public static final int FORWARD = 2;

  // Message From, To, and Subject text fields.
  private JTextField fromTextField, toTextField;
  private JTextField subjectTextField;

  // Message content text area.
  private JTextArea contentTextArea;

  // Flag specifying whether or not dialog box was cancelled.
  private boolean cancelled;

  // Constructor for dialog box.
  public MessageDialog(Frame parent, int type, Message message)
    throws Exception
  {
    // Call super constructor, specifying that dialog box is modal.
    super(parent, true);

    /* Set dialog box title and get message's "To", "Subject",
       and "content" values based on message type. */
    String to = "", subject = "", content = "";
    switch (type) {
      // Reply message.
      case REPLY:
        setTitle("Reply To Message");
```

```java
      // Get message "To" value.
      Address[] senders = message.getFrom();
      if (senders != null || senders.length > 0) {
        to = senders[0].toString();
      }
      to = message.getFrom()[0].toString();

      // Get message subject.
      subject = message.getSubject();
      if (subject != null && subject.length() > 0) {
        subject = "RE: " + subject;
      } else {
        subject = "RE:";
      }

      // Get message content and add "REPLIED TO" notation.
      content = "\n---------------- " +
                "REPLIED TO MESSAGE" +
                " ----------------\n" +
                EmailClient.getMessageContent(message);
      break;

  // Forward message.
  case FORWARD:
      setTitle("Forward Message");

      // Get message subject.
      subject = message.getSubject();
      if (subject != null && subject.length() > 0) {
        subject = "FWD: " + subject;
      } else {
        subject = "FWD:";
      }

      // Get message content and add "FORWARDED" notation.
      content = "\n---------------- " +
                "FORWARDED MESSAGE" +
                " ----------------\n" +
                EmailClient.getMessageContent(message);
      break;

  // New message.
  default:
      setTitle("New Message");
}
```

```
// Handle closing events.
addWindowListener(new WindowAdapter() {
  public void windowClosing(WindowEvent e) {
    actionCancel();
  }
});

// Set up fields panel.
JPanel fieldsPanel = new JPanel();
GridBagConstraints constraints;
GridBagLayout layout = new GridBagLayout();
fieldsPanel.setLayout(layout);
JLabel fromLabel = new JLabel("From:");
constraints = new GridBagConstraints();
constraints.anchor = GridBagConstraints.EAST;
constraints.insets = new Insets(5, 5, 0, 0);
layout.setConstraints(fromLabel, constraints);
fieldsPanel.add(fromLabel);
fromTextField = new JTextField();
constraints = new GridBagConstraints();
constraints.fill = GridBagConstraints.HORIZONTAL;
constraints.gridwidth = GridBagConstraints.REMAINDER;
constraints.insets = new Insets(5, 5, 0, 0);
layout.setConstraints(fromTextField, constraints);
fieldsPanel.add(fromTextField);
JLabel toLabel = new JLabel("To:");
constraints = new GridBagConstraints();
constraints.anchor = GridBagConstraints.EAST;
constraints.insets = new Insets(5, 5, 0, 0);
layout.setConstraints(toLabel, constraints);
fieldsPanel.add(toLabel);
toTextField = new JTextField(to);
constraints = new GridBagConstraints();
constraints.fill = GridBagConstraints.HORIZONTAL;
constraints.gridwidth = GridBagConstraints.REMAINDER;
constraints.insets = new Insets(5, 5, 0, 0);
constraints.weightx = 1.0D;
layout.setConstraints(toTextField, constraints);
fieldsPanel.add(toTextField);
JLabel subjectLabel = new JLabel("Subject:");
constraints = new GridBagConstraints();
constraints.insets = new Insets(5, 5, 5, 0);
layout.setConstraints(subjectLabel, constraints);
fieldsPanel.add(subjectLabel);
subjectTextField = new JTextField(subject);
constraints = new GridBagConstraints();
constraints.fill = GridBagConstraints.HORIZONTAL;
```

```java
      constraints.gridwidth = GridBagConstraints.REMAINDER;
      constraints.insets = new Insets(5, 5, 5, 0);
      layout.setConstraints(subjectTextField, constraints);
      fieldsPanel.add(subjectTextField);

      // Set up content panel.
      JScrollPane contentPanel = new JScrollPane();
      contentTextArea = new JTextArea(content, 10, 50);
      contentPanel.setViewportView(contentTextArea);

      // Set up buttons panel.
      JPanel buttonsPanel = new JPanel();
      JButton sendButton = new JButton("Send");
      sendButton.addActionListener(new ActionListener() {
        public void actionPerformed(ActionEvent e) {
          actionSend();
        }
      });
      buttonsPanel.add(sendButton);
      JButton cancelButton = new JButton("Cancel");
      cancelButton.addActionListener(new ActionListener() {
        public void actionPerformed(ActionEvent e) {
          actionCancel();
        }
      });
      buttonsPanel.add(cancelButton);

      // Add panels to display.
      getContentPane().setLayout(new BorderLayout());
      getContentPane().add(fieldsPanel, BorderLayout.NORTH);
      getContentPane().add(contentPanel, BorderLayout.CENTER);
      getContentPane().add(buttonsPanel, BorderLayout.SOUTH);

      // Size dialog box to components.
      pack();

      // Center dialog box over application.
      setLocationRelativeTo(parent);
    }

    // Validate message fields and close dialog box.
    private void actionSend() {
      if (fromTextField.getText().trim().length() < 1
          || toTextField.getText().trim().length() < 1
          || subjectTextField.getText().trim().length() < 1
          || contentTextArea.getText().trim().length() < 1) {
```

```java
      JOptionPane.showMessageDialog(this,
        "One or more fields is missing.",
        "Missing Field(s)", JOptionPane.ERROR_MESSAGE);
      return;
    }

    // Close dialog box.
    dispose();
  }

  // Cancel creation of this message and close dialog box.
  private void actionCancel() {
    cancelled = true;

    // Close dialog box.
    dispose();
  }

  // Show dialog box.
  public boolean display() {
    show();

    // Return whether or not display was successful.
    return !cancelled;
  }

  // Get message's "From" field value.
  public String getFrom() {
    return fromTextField.getText();
  }

  // Get message's "To" field value.
  public String getTo() {
    return toTextField.getText();
  }

  // Get message's "Subject" field value.
  public String getSubject() {
    return subjectTextField.getText();
  }

  // Get message's "content" field value.
  public String getContent() {
    return contentTextArea.getText();
  }
}
```

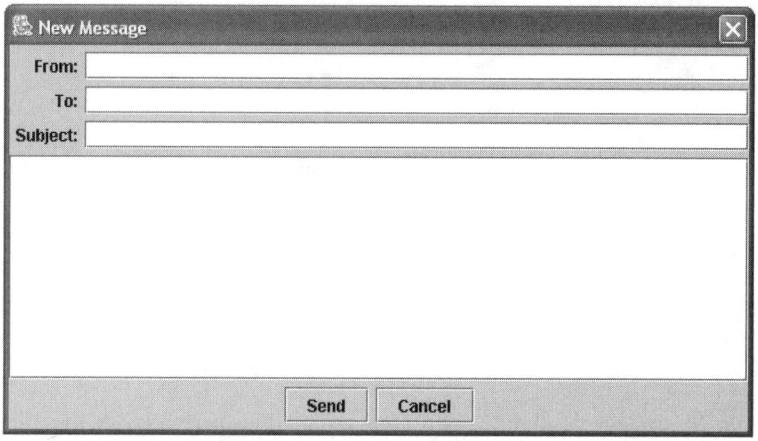

Figure 5-4   *The Message dialog box*

The MessageDialog Variables

MessageDialog begins by declaring three **static final** variables, **NEW**, **REPLY**, and **FORWARD**, that specify the types of messages that the dialog box handles. Next, several GUI control variables are declared. Finally, the **cancelled** flag is declared for tracking whether or not the dialog box was cancelled.

The MessageDialog Constructor

Similar to the previous two dialog classes, the **MessageDialog** constructor begins by calling its parent class constructor to specify that the dialog box is modal. Next, a **switch** statement is used to set the dialog box's title based on the type of message being created. The **switch** statement also serves to retrieve message fields from an original message supplied as an argument to the constructor (**REPLY** and **FORWARD** types). These original message fields are then used to populate **MessageDialog**'s fields later in the constructor. Notice that the **REPLY** and **FORWARD** messages' content is prefixed with text to denote the original message.

After the **switch** statement has concluded, the fields panel is created, and each field's control is initialized and added to the panel. The content and buttons panels are set up next, and then all the panels are added to the display. Next, **pack( )** is called to size the dialog box window to the minimum size required by its GUI controls. Finally, a call to **setLocation-RelativeTo( )** centers the dialog box over the parent window.

The actionSend( ) Method

The **actionSend( )** method, shown here, confirms that all the message fields have been entered and then disposes the dialog box when the Send button is clicked:

```
// Validate message fields and close dialog box.
private void actionSend() {
  if (fromTextField.getText().trim().length() < 1
```

```
        || toTextField.getText().trim().length() < 1
        || subjectTextField.getText().trim().length() < 1
        || contentTextArea.getText().trim().length() < 1) {
    JOptionPane.showMessageDialog(this,
      "One or more fields is missing.",
      "Missing Field(s)", JOptionPane.ERROR_MESSAGE);
    return;
  }


  // Close dialog box.
  dispose();
}
```

Each of the Message dialog box's fields are required, thus **actionSend( )** verifies that all the fields have been entered before completing successfully. If one or more fields have not been entered, an error dialog box is displayed to notify the user. Once all the field validations are successful, the **dispose( )** method is called to close the dialog box window.

The actionCancel( ) Method

The **actionCancel( )** method, shown here, is called when the Cancel button in the dialog box is clicked or when the dialog box is closed:

```
// Cancel creation of this message and close dialog box.
private void actionCancel() {
  cancelled = true;

  // Close dialog box.
  dispose();
}
```

Before closing the dialog box with a call to **dispose( )**, the **actionCancel( )** method sets the **cancelled** flag to **true**. The **cancelled** flag is used by the **display( )** method to determine if the dialog box has been cancelled.

The display( ) Method

Normally, a dialog box is displayed on the screen by calling its **show( )** method. However, in the case of the Message dialog box, it is essential to know whether or not the dialog box was cancelled when it was disposed. The **display( )** method, shown here, does just that, acting as a proxy for the **show( )** method:

```
// Show dialog box.
public boolean display() {
  show();

  // Return whether or not display was successful.
```

```
    return !cancelled;
}
```

Notice that the inverse of the cancelled flag is returned to indicate whether the **display( )** method was successful or not.

Accessor Methods

The **MessageDialog** class has a number of accessor methods for retrieving the message properties entered in the dialog box. Each of the **getFrom( )**, **getTo( )**, **getSubject( )**, and **getContent( )** methods simply returns the value entered into its corresponding control.

The MessagesTableModel Class

The **MessagesTableModel** class houses E-mail Client's list of messages and is the backing data source for the "Messages" **JTable** instance.

The **MessagesTableModel** class is shown here. Notice that it extends **AbstractTableModel**:

```
import java.util.*;
import javax.mail.*;
import javax.swing.*;
import javax.swing.table.*;

// This class manages the e-mail table's data.
public class MessagesTableModel extends AbstractTableModel
{
  // These are the names for the table's columns.
  private static final String[] columnNames = {"Sender",
    "Subject", "Date"};

  // The table's list of messages.
  private ArrayList messageList = new ArrayList();

  // Sets the table's list of messages.
  public void setMessages(Message[] messages) {
    for (int i = messages.length - 1; i >= 0; i--) {
      messageList.add(messages[i]);
    }

    // Fire table data change notification to table.
    fireTableDataChanged();
  }

  // Get a message for the specified row.
  public Message getMessage(int row) {
    return (Message) messageList.get(row);
```

```java
  }

  // Remove a message from the list.
  public void deleteMessage(int row) {
    messageList.remove(row);

    // Fire table row deletion notification to table.
    fireTableRowsDeleted(row, row);
  }

  // Get table's column count.
  public int getColumnCount() {
    return columnNames.length;
  }

  // Get a column's name.
  public String getColumnName(int col) {
      return columnNames[col];
  }

  // Get table's row count.
  public int getRowCount() {
    return messageList.size();
  }

  // Get value for a specific row and column combination.
  public Object getValueAt(int row, int col) {
    try {
      Message message = (Message) messageList.get(row);
      switch (col) {
        case 0: // Sender
          Address[] senders = message.getFrom();
          if (senders != null || senders.length > 0) {
            return senders[0].toString();
          } else {
            return "[none]";
          }
        case 1: // Subject
          String subject = message.getSubject();
          if (subject != null && subject.length() > 0) {
            return subject;
          } else {
            return "[none]";
          }
        case 2: // Date
```

```
          Date date = message.getSentDate();
          if (date != null) {
            return date.toString();
          } else {
            return "[none]";
          }
      }
    } catch (Exception e) {
      // Fail silently.
      return "";
    }

    return "";
  }
}
```

The **MessagesTableModel** class is a utility class used by the "Messages" **JTable** instance for managing data in the table. When the **JTable** instance is initialized, it is passed a **MessagesTableModel** instance. The **JTable** then proceeds to call several methods on the **MessagesTableModel** instance to populate itself. The **getColumnCount( )** method is called to retrieve the number of columns in the table. Similarly, **getRowCount( )** is used to retrieve the number of rows in the table. The **getColumnName( )** method returns a column's name given its ID. The **getMessage( )** method takes a row ID and returns the associated **Message** object from the list. The rest of the **MessagesTableModel** methods, which are more involved, are detailed in the following sections.

The setMessages( ) Method

The **setMessages( )** method, shown here, sets the list of **Message**s that will be displayed in the table:

```
// Sets the table's list of messages.
public void setMessages(Message[] messages) {
  for (int i = messages.length - 1; i >= 0; i--) {
    messageList.add(messages[i]);
  }

  // Fire table data change notification to table.
  fireTableDataChanged();
}
```

This method first iterates through the array of **Message** objects passed to the **messages** parameter, adding each individual **Message** to the message list. Normally in this scenario, the **messages** array itself would be used as the backing data source for the table model. However, since messages can be deleted from the **MessagesTableModel**, using an **ArrayList** to hold the messages is more convenient. After adding the messages to the message list, a table row data change event notification is fired to alert the table that its data has been changed.

The deleteMessage( ) Method

The **deleteMessage( )** method, shown next, removes a **Message** from the list of managed messages:

```
// Remove a message from the list.
public void deleteMessage(int row) {
  messageList.remove(row);

  // Fire table row deletion notification to table.
  fireTableRowsDeleted(row, row);
}
```

After removing the **Message** from the internal list, a table row deleted event notification is fired to alert the table that a row has been deleted.

The getValueAt( ) Method

The **getValueAt( )** method, shown next, is called to get the current value to display for each of the table's cells:

```
// Get value for a specific row and column combination.
public Object getValueAt(int row, int col) {
  try {
    Message message = (Message) messageList.get(row);
    switch (col) {
      case 0: // Sender
        Address[] senders = message.getFrom();
        if (senders != null || senders.length > 0) {
          return senders[0].toString();
        } else {
          return "[none]";
        }
      case 1: // Subject
        String subject = message.getSubject();
        if (subject != null && subject.length() > 0) {
          return subject;
        } else {
          return "[none]";
        }
      case 2: // Date
        Date date = message.getSentDate();
        if (date != null) {
          return date.toString();
        } else {
          return "[none]";
        }
```

```
      }
    } catch (Exception e) {
      // Fail silently.
      return "";
    }


    return "";
  }
```

This method first looks up the **Message** object corresponding to the selected row. Next, the selected column is used to determine which of the **Message**'s property values to return. Notice that each property retrieved from the **Message** is checked to see if it is **null**. If the property is **null**, then "[none]" is returned in lieu of the property's value. This is necessary because some **Message** properties may be absent. For example, an e-mail message can be sent without a subject or return address. Observe, also, that this method's body is wrapped in a **try-catch** block. If one of the **Message** object's methods throws an exception, it is caught with the **catch** block and an empty value is returned.

The EmailClient Class

Now that the foundation has been laid by explaining each of E-mail Client's helper classes, we can look closely at the **EmailClient** class. The **EmailClient** class is responsible for creating and running E-mail Client's GUI as well as performing the communications with an e-mail server.

EmailClient has a **main( )** method, so on execution it will be invoked first. The **main( )** method instantiates a new **EmailClient** object and then calls its **show( )** method, which causes it to be displayed. After E-mail Client has been displayed on the screen, the **connect( )** method is called to prompt the user for connection settings.

The **EmailClient** class is shown here and examined in detail in the following sections. Notice that it extends **JFrame**.

```
import java.awt.*;
import java.awt.event.*;
import java.net.*;
import java.util.*;
import javax.mail.*;
import javax.mail.internet.*;
import javax.swing.*;
import javax.swing.event.*;

// The E-mail Client.
public class EmailClient extends JFrame
{
  // Message table's data model.
  private MessagesTableModel tableModel;
```

```java
    // Table listing messages.
    private JTable table;

    // This is the text area for displaying messages.
    private JTextArea messageTextArea;

    /* This is the split panel that holds the messages
       table and the message view panel. */
    private JSplitPane splitPane;

    // These are the buttons for managing the selected message.
    private JButton replyButton, forwardButton, deleteButton;

    // Currently selected message in table.
    private Message selectedMessage;

    // Flag for whether or not a message is being deleted.
    private boolean deleting;

    // This is the JavaMail session.
    private Session session;

    // Constructor for E-mail Client.
    public EmailClient()
    {
      // Set application title.
      setTitle("E-mail Client");

      // Set window size.
      setSize(640, 480);

      // Handle window closing events.
      addWindowListener(new WindowAdapter() {
        public void windowClosing(WindowEvent e) {
          actionExit();
        }
      });

      // Set up File menu.
      JMenuBar menuBar = new JMenuBar();
      JMenu fileMenu = new JMenu("File");
      fileMenu.setMnemonic(KeyEvent.VK_F);
      JMenuItem fileExitMenuItem = new JMenuItem("Exit",
        KeyEvent.VK_X);
      fileExitMenuItem.addActionListener(new ActionListener() {
```

```java
      public void actionPerformed(ActionEvent e) {
        actionExit();
      }
   });
   fileMenu.add(fileExitMenuItem);
   menuBar.add(fileMenu);
   setJMenuBar(menuBar);

   // Set up buttons panel.
   JPanel buttonPanel = new JPanel();
   JButton newButton = new JButton("New Message");
   newButton.addActionListener(new ActionListener() {
      public void actionPerformed(ActionEvent e) {
        actionNew ();
      }
   });
   buttonPanel.add(newButton);

   // Set up messages table.
   tableModel = new MessagesTableModel();
   table = new JTable(tableModel);
   table.getSelectionModel().addListSelectionListener(new
      ListSelectionListener() {
      public void valueChanged(ListSelectionEvent e) {
        tableSelectionChanged();
      }
   });
   // Allow only one row at a time to be selected.
   table.setSelectionMode(ListSelectionModel.SINGLE_SELECTION);

   // Set up E-mails panel.
   JPanel emailsPanel = new JPanel();
   emailsPanel.setBorder(
      BorderFactory.createTitledBorder("E-mails"));
   messageTextArea = new JTextArea();
   messageTextArea.setEditable(false);
   splitPane = new JSplitPane(JSplitPane.VERTICAL_SPLIT,
      new JScrollPane(table), new JScrollPane(messageTextArea));
   emailsPanel.setLayout(new BorderLayout());
   emailsPanel.add(splitPane, BorderLayout.CENTER);

   // Set up buttons panel 2.
   JPanel buttonPanel2 = new JPanel();
   replyButton = new JButton("Reply");
   replyButton.addActionListener(new ActionListener() {
```

```java
      public void actionPerformed(ActionEvent e) {
        actionReply();
      }
    });
    replyButton.setEnabled(false);
    buttonPanel2.add(replyButton);
    forwardButton = new JButton("Forward");
    forwardButton.addActionListener(new ActionListener() {
      public void actionPerformed(ActionEvent e) {
        actionForward();
      }
    });
    forwardButton.setEnabled(false);
    buttonPanel2.add(forwardButton);
    deleteButton = new JButton("Delete");
    deleteButton.addActionListener(new ActionListener() {
      public void actionPerformed(ActionEvent e) {
        actionDelete();
      }
    });
    deleteButton.setEnabled(false);
    buttonPanel2.add(deleteButton);

    // Add panels to display.
    getContentPane().setLayout(new BorderLayout());
    getContentPane().add(buttonPanel, BorderLayout.NORTH);
    getContentPane().add(emailsPanel, BorderLayout.CENTER);
    getContentPane().add(buttonPanel2, BorderLayout.SOUTH);
  }

  // Exit this program.
  private void actionExit() {
    System.exit(0);
  }

  // Create a new message.
  private void actionNew () {
    sendMessage(MessageDialog.NEW, null);
  }

  // Called when table row selection changes.
  private void tableSelectionChanged() {
    /* If not in the middle of deleting a message, set
       the selected message and display it. */
    if (!deleting) {
```

```java
      selectedMessage =
        tableModel.getMessage(table.getSelectedRow());
      showSelectedMessage();
      updateButtons();
    }
  }

  // Reply to a message.
  private void actionReply() {
    sendMessage(MessageDialog.REPLY, selectedMessage);
  }

  // Forward a message.
  private void actionForward() {
    sendMessage(MessageDialog.FORWARD, selectedMessage);
  }

  // Delete the selected message.
  private void actionDelete() {
    deleting = true;

    try {
      // Delete message from server.
      selectedMessage.setFlag(Flags.Flag.DELETED, true);
      Folder folder = selectedMessage.getFolder();
      folder.close(true);
      folder.open(Folder.READ_WRITE);
    } catch (Exception e) {
      showError("Unable to delete message.", false);
    }

    // Delete message from table.
    tableModel.deleteMessage(table.getSelectedRow());

    // Update GUI.
    messageTextArea.setText("");
    deleting = false;
    selectedMessage = null;
    updateButtons();
  }

  // Send the specified message.
  private void sendMessage(int type, Message message) {
    // Display message dialog box to get message values.
    MessageDialog dialog;
```

```
  try {
    dialog = new MessageDialog(this, type, message);
    if (!dialog.display()) {
      // Return if dialog box was cancelled.
      return;
    }
  } catch (Exception e) {
    showError("Unable to send message.", false);
    return;
  }

  try {
    // Create a new message with values from dialog box.
    Message newMessage = new MimeMessage(session);
    newMessage.setFrom(new InternetAddress(dialog.getFrom()));
    newMessage.setRecipient(Message.RecipientType.TO,
      new InternetAddress(dialog.getTo()));
    newMessage.setSubject(dialog.getSubject());
    newMessage.setSentDate(new Date());
    newMessage.setText(dialog.getContent());

    // Send new message.
    Transport.send(newMessage);
  } catch (Exception e) {
    showError("Unable to send message.", false);
  }
}

// Show the selected message in the content panel.
private void showSelectedMessage() {
  // Show hour glass cursor while message is loaded.
  setCursor(Cursor.getPredefinedCursor(Cursor.WAIT_CURSOR));
  try {
    messageTextArea.setText(
      getMessageContent(selectedMessage));
    messageTextArea.setCaretPosition(0);
  } catch (Exception e) {
    showError("Unabled to load message.", false);
  } finally {
    // Return to default cursor.
    setCursor(Cursor.getDefaultCursor());
  }
}

/* Update each button's state based on whether or not
```

```
      there is a message currently selected in the table. */
private void updateButtons() {
  if (selectedMessage != null) {
    replyButton.setEnabled(true);
    forwardButton.setEnabled(true);
    deleteButton.setEnabled(true);
  } else {
    replyButton.setEnabled(false);
    forwardButton.setEnabled(false);
    deleteButton.setEnabled(false);
  }
}

// Show the application window on the screen.
public void show() {
  super.show();

  // Update the split panel to be divided 50/50.
  splitPane.setDividerLocation(.5);
}

// Connect to e-mail server.
public void connect() {
  // Display Connect dialog box.
  ConnectDialog dialog = new ConnectDialog(this);
  dialog.show();

  // Build connection URL from Connect dialog box settings.
  StringBuffer connectionUrl = new StringBuffer();
  connectionUrl.append(dialog.getType() + "://");
  connectionUrl.append(dialog.getUsername() + ":");
  connectionUrl.append(dialog.getPassword() + "@");
  connectionUrl.append(dialog.getServer() + "/");

  /* Display dialog box stating that messages are
     currently being downloaded from server. */
  final DownloadingDialog downloadingDialog =
    new DownloadingDialog(this);
  SwingUtilities.invokeLater(new Runnable() {
    public void run() {
      downloadingDialog.show();
    }
  });

  // Establish JavaMail session and connect to server.
```

```java
Store store = null;
try {
  // Initialize JavaMail session with SMTP server.
  Properties props = new Properties();
  props.put("mail.smtp.host", dialog.getSmtpServer());
  session = Session.getDefaultInstance(props, null);

  // Connect to e-mail server.
  URLName urln = new URLName(connectionUrl.toString());
  store = session.getStore(urln);
  store.connect();
} catch (Exception e) {
  // Close the Downloading dialog box.
  downloadingDialog.dispose();

  // Show error dialog box.
  showError("Unable to connect.", true);
}

// Download message headers from server.
try {
  // Open main "INBOX" folder.
  Folder folder = store.getFolder("INBOX");
  folder.open(Folder.READ_WRITE);

  // Get folder's list of messages.
  Message[] messages = folder.getMessages();

  // Retrieve message headers for each message in folder.
  FetchProfile profile = new FetchProfile();
  profile.add(FetchProfile.Item.ENVELOPE);
  folder.fetch(messages, profile);

  // Put messages in table.
  tableModel.setMessages(messages);
} catch (Exception e) {
  // Close the Downloading dialog box.
  downloadingDialog.dispose();

  // Show error dialog box.
  showError("Unable to download messages.", true);
}

// Close the Downloading dialog box.
downloadingDialog.dispose();
```

```
  }

  // Show error dialog box and exit afterward if necessary.
  private void showError(String message, boolean exit) {
    JOptionPane.showMessageDialog(this, message, "Error",
      JOptionPane.ERROR_MESSAGE);
    if (exit)
      System.exit(0);
  }

  // Get a message's content.
  public static String getMessageContent(Message message)
    throws Exception {
    Object content = message.getContent();
    if (content instanceof Multipart) {
      StringBuffer messageContent = new StringBuffer();
      Multipart multipart = (Multipart) content;
      for (int i = 0; i < multipart.getCount(); i++) {
        Part part = (Part) multipart.getBodyPart(i);
          if (part.isMimeType("text/plain")) {
            messageContent.append(part.getContent().toString());
          }
        }
      }
      return messageContent.toString();
    } else {
      return content.toString();
    }
  }

  // Run E-mail Client.
  public static void main(String[] args) {
    EmailClient client = new EmailClient();
    client.show();

    // Display Connect dialog box.
    client.connect();
  }
}
```

The EmailClient Variables

EmailClient begins by declaring several instance variables, most of which hold references
to the controls. The **selectedMessage** variable holds a reference to the **Message** object
represented by the selected row in the message table. The **deleting** instance variable is
a **boolean** flag that tracks whether or not a message is currently being deleted from the

messages table. Finally, the **session** variable contains a reference to the JavaMail session established in the **connect( )** method.

The EmailClient Constructor

When the **EmailClient** is instantiated, all the controls are initialized inside its constructor. The constructor contains a lot of code, but most of it is straightforward. The following discussion gives an overview.

First, the window's title is set with a call to **setTitle( )**. Next, the **setSize( )** call establishes the window's width and height in pixels. After that, a window listener is added by calling **addWindowListener( )**, passing a **WindowAdapter** object that overrides the **windowClosing( )** event handler. This handler calls the **actionExit( )** method when the application's window is closed. Next, a menu bar with a File menu is added to the application's window. Then the first buttons panel, which has the New Message button, is set up. An **ActionListener** is added to the New Message button so that the **actionNew( )** method is called each time the button is clicked.

The messages table is constructed next. A **ListSelectionListener** is added to the table so that each time a row is selected in the table the **tableSelectionChanged( )** method is invoked. The table's selection mode is also updated to **ListSelectionModel.SINGLE_SELECTION** so that only one row at a time can be selected in the table. Limiting row selection to only one row simplifies the logic for determining which buttons should be enabled in the GUI when a row (or message) is selected.

Next, the E-mails panel is created to house the messages table and the **JTextArea** in which messages will be displayed when they are selected. After that, a titled border is added to the panel. The message text area is set up next. Take note that the **messageTextArea** **.setEditable( )** method is called with a parameter of **false**. This disables the text in the text area from being modified. Next, a **JSplitPane** is created to divide the E-mails panel between the messages table and the message text area. The **JSplitPane** creates a divider between the two components so that each section of the panel can be sized as desired. Initially, each section of the **JSplitPane** is set to 50% in the **show( )** method, effectively dividing the panel in half.

Finally, the second buttons panel is created. This buttons panel has a Reply, a Forward, and a Delete button. Each of the buttons adds an **ActionListener** that invokes the corresponding action method when a button is clicked. After creating the second button panel, all of the panels that have been created are added to the window.

The tableSelectionChanged( ) Method

The **tableSelectionChanged( )** method, shown here, is called each time a row is selected in the messages table:

```
// Called when table row selection changes.
private void tableSelectionChanged() {
  /* If not in the middle of deleting a message, set
     the selected message and display it. */
  if (!deleting) {
    selectedMessage =
```

```
      tableModel.getMessage(table.getSelectedRow());
    showSelectedMessage();
    updateButtons();
  }
}
```

This method starts by checking the **deleting** flag. If the **deleting** flag is not true, then, first, the **selectedMessage** variable is updated with the **Message** corresponding to the row selected. Second, the **showSeletedMessage( )** method is called to display the message that has just been selected. Finally, **updateButtons( )** is called to update the state of the buttons.

The actionNew( ), actionForward( ), and actionReply( ) Methods

Each of the **actionNew( )**, **actionForward( )**, and **actionReply( )** methods serves to invoke the **sendMessage( )** method when its respective button is clicked. The **sendMessage( )** method is passed an identifier specifying the type of message being sent and the **selectedMessage** if applicable.

The actionDelete( ) Method

As E-mail Client is currently written, it does not automatically remove messages from the server. Instead, you must explicitly request that they be deleted. This is a safety feature built into the program that allows you to experiment freely without worrying about losing an important message. If you don't explicitly delete a message, it will remain on the server where it can be retrieved by another e-mail application.

The **actionDelete( )** method shown in this section deletes an e-mail message from the server. It works by flagging the selected message as being deleted and then instructing the selected message's folder to expunge any deleted messages it contains.

In general, messages can be removed from JavaMail folders by calling the **expunge( )** method of the **Folder** object or by closing the folder with the expunge flag set to **true**. JavaMail defines several message flags which are supported by the **javax.mail.Flags** class and specified by its inner class, **javax.mail.Flags.Flag**. Of these flags, **DELETED** is the one that marks a message as deleted.

Because JavaMail's built-in POP3 code does not support the **Folder** object's **expunge( )** method, the **actionDelete( )** method removes the deleted message by closing the folder with the expunge flag set to **true**.

```
// Delete the selected message.
private void actionDelete() {
  deleting = true;

  try {
    // Delete message from server.
    selectedMessage.setFlag(Flags.Flag.DELETED, true);
    Folder folder = selectedMessage.getFolder();
    folder.close(true);
    folder.open(Folder.READ_WRITE);
```

```
    } catch (Exception e) {
      showError("Unable to delete message.", false);
    }

    // Delete message from table.
    tableModel.deleteMessage(table.getSelectedRow());

    // Update GUI.
    messageTextArea.setText("");
    deleting = false;
    selectedMessage = null;
    updateButtons();
  }
```

The **actionDelete( )** method begins by setting the **deleting** flag to **true**. Setting the **deleting** flag alerts the **tableSelectionChanged( )** method to ignore table changes while a message is being deleted. Next, the actual message deleting takes place in a few steps. First, the **selectedMessage** is marked as having been deleted by a call to **setFlag( )** with the **Flags.Flag.DELETED** flag. Second, the **selectedMessage**'s folder is closed. When folders are closed in JavaMail, any messages in the folder that have a **DELETED** flag are deleted. Third, the closed folder is reopened so that any other messages it contains can be accessed again.

After the message is deleted from the server, it is removed from the messages table with a call to **tableModel.deleteMessage( )**. Finally, **actionDelete( )** updates the GUI by clearing the message text area and updating the button states.

The sendMessage( ) Method

The **sendMessage( )** method, shown here, performs the actual sending of a message. In general, it works by displaying a Message dialog box and then using the data entered in the Message dialog box to create a new **Message** object. The new **Message** object is then sent with JavaMail's **Transport** class.

```
// Send the specified message.
private void sendMessage(int type, Message message) {
  // Display message dialog box to get message values.
  MessageDialog dialog;
  try {
    dialog = new MessageDialog(this, type, message);
    if (!dialog.display()) {
      // Return if dialog box was cancelled.
      return;
    }
  } catch (Exception e) {
    showError("Unable to send message.", false);
    return;
  }
```

```
try {
  // Create a new message with values from dialog box.
  Message newMessage = new MimeMessage(session);
  newMessage.setFrom(new InternetAddress(dialog.getFrom()));
  newMessage.setRecipient(Message.RecipientType.TO,
    new InternetAddress(dialog.getTo()));
  newMessage.setSubject(dialog.getSubject());
  newMessage.setSentDate(new Date());
  newMessage.setText(dialog.getContent());

  // Send new message.
  Transport.send(newMessage);
} catch (Exception e) {
  showError("Unable to send message.", false);
}
}
```

First, **sendMessage( )** creates a **MessageDialog** forwarding it the message type and message passed in as arguments. The **MessageDialog** then collects the message properties such as the To address, the From address, and the Subject. After the message properties have been collected, a new **Message** object is created and populated with the properties. The new message's From address is set with the **Message** object's **setFrom( )** method. Similarly, the **Message** object's **setRecipient( )** method sets the new message's To address. Take note that the **setRecipient( )** method also serves to set a message's CC and BCC addresses by specifying the recipient type as **Message.RecipientType.CC** or **Message.RecipientType** **.BCC**, respectively. The **Messsage** object's **setSubject( )** method does just that—it sets the message's subject. The **setSentDate( )** method specifies the timestamp placed on the message. The **setText( )** method specifies the message's text content.

Finally, the message is sent with a call to **Transport.send( )**. JavaMail's **Transport** class encapsulates the protocol-specific code for sending the message, which typically is SMTP.

The showSelectedMessage( ) Method

The **showSelectedMessage( )** method, shown here, loads and then displays the **selectedMessage** in the message text area:

```
// Show the selected message in the content panel.
private void showSelectedMessage() {
  // Show hour glass cursor while message is being loaded.
  setCursor(Cursor.getPredefinedCursor(Cursor.WAIT_CURSOR));
  try {
    messageTextArea.setText(
      getMessageContent(selectedMessage));
    messageTextArea.setCaretPosition(0);
  } catch (Exception e) {
    showError("Unable to load message.", false);
```

```
    } finally {
      // Return to default cursor.
      setCursor(Cursor.getDefaultCursor());
    }
}
```

Before the **selectedMessage** is loaded, the application's cursor is set to the **WAIT_CURSOR** to signify that the application is busy. On most operating systems, the **WAIT_CURSOR** is an hour glass. After the cursor has been set, the selected message's content is loaded with a call to **getMessageContent( )**. Next, the content is displayed in the text area and the **setCaretPosition( )** method is called to reset the text area's caret position to the beginning. Setting the caret position at the beginning ensures that the text area is scrolled to the top. Finally, the application cursor is set back to the default cursor.

The udpateButtons( ) Method

The **updateButtons( )** method updates the state of all the buttons on the button panel based on whether or not there is a message currently selected. The **updateButtons( )** method is shown here:

```
/* Update each button's state based on whether or not
   there is a message currently selected in the table. */
private void updateButtons() {
  if (selectedMessage != null) {
    replyButton.setEnabled(true);
    forwardButton.setEnabled(true);
    deleteButton.setEnabled(true);
  } else {
    replyButton.setEnabled(false);
    forwardButton.setEnabled(false);
    deleteButton.setEnabled(false);
  }
}
```

If no message is selected in the messages table, all of the buttons are disabled, giving them a grayed-out appearance. However, if there is a selected message, each button is enabled for use.

The show( ) Method

The **show( )** method overrides its parent method in the **JFrame** class so that the E-mails panel's split pane divider location can be updated. By default, **JSplitPane** uses the preferred sizes of its components to determine where the divider should be located. Since the message table doesn't have any messages in it to start with, the message table's preferred size is set just high enough to show the column headers. To properly position the divider in the middle of the panel, the **show( )** method, shown here, makes a call to **setDividerLocation( )**:

```
// Show the application window on the screen.
public void show() {
```

```
super.show();

// Update the split panel to be divided 50/50.
splitPane.setDividerLocation(.5);
}
```

The connect( ) Method

Because of the **connect( )** method's size and importance, we will examine it closely, line by line. The **connect( )** method begins with these lines:

```
// Display Connect dialog box.
ConnectDialog dialog = new ConnectDialog(this);
dialog.show();
```

Before a connection can be made to an e-mail server, the connection settings have to be entered into the application. A **ConnectDialog** is instantiated and displayed to capture the connection settings.

Once the connection settings have been captured by the **ConnectDialog**, they are used to create a JavaMail connection URL.

```
// Build connection URL from Connect dialog box settings.
StringBuffer connectionUrl = new StringBuffer();
connectionUrl.append(dialog.getType() + "://");
connectionUrl.append(dialog.getUsername() + ":");
connectionUrl.append(dialog.getPassword() + "@");
connectionUrl.append(dialog.getServer() + "/");
```

JavaMail connection URLs have the following scheme:

protocol://*username*:*password*@*hostname*

For example, to connect to a server named **mailserver.com** with a username of **johndoe** and a password of **pass1234** using the POP3 protocol, the URL would be:

pop3://johndoe:pass1234@mailserver.com

Next, a **DownloadingDialog** is instantiated and then run to display an informational message on the screen while e-mail is being downloaded.

```
/* Display dialog box stating that messages are
   currently being downloaded from server. */
final DownloadingDialog downloadingDialog =
  new DownloadingDialog(this);
SwingUtilities.invokeLater(new Runnable() {
  public void run() {
    downloadingDialog.show();
```

```
    }
});
```

When a modal dialog box, like **DownloadingDialog**, is displayed on the screen, the current thread of execution is halted until the dialog box is terminated. This behavior is normally the desired effect; however, it is not desirable for E-mail Client. In the case of E-mail Client, the **DownloadingDialog** needs to be displayed while downloading is taking place, not prior to downloading. To achieve this, the Downloading dialog box is run in a separate thread from Swing's main event execution thread with a call to **SwingUtilities.invokeLater( )**.

After launching the Downloading dialog box, the actual work of connecting to the e-mail server takes place. First, a JavaMail session is initialized by the following sequence:

```
// Establish JavaMail session and connect to server.
Store store = null;
try {
  // Initialize JavaMail session with SMTP server.
  Properties props = new Properties();
  props.put("mail.smtp.host", dialog.getSmtpServer());
  session = Session.getDefaultInstance(props, null);
```

Notice that the JavaMail session is passed a set of properties that contains the SMTP server address. JavaMail sessions store the configuration options and authentication information used to interact with an e-mail server. Storing this information in the **Session** object allows it to be reused throughout the application by JavaMail's classes. In E-mail Client's case, the session data is used by the **Transport** class to send messages in the **sendMessage( )** method.

After initializing the JavaMail session, the connection to the e-mail server is made in the following code:

```
  // Connect to mail server.
  URLName urln = new URLName(connectionUrl.toString());
  store = session.getStore(urln);
  store.connect();
} catch (Exception e) {
  // Close the Downloading dialog box.
  downloadingDialog.dispose();

  // Show error dialog box.
  showError("Unable to connect.", true);
}
```

JavaMail uses **Store** objects to represent a message store and its access protocol for storing and retrieving messages. A message store is analogous to an e-mail account; thus **Store** objects essentially are an interface to accessing an e-mail account with a given protocol such as POP3 or IMAP. In the preceding code, the actual network connection to the e-mail server is established by retrieving a **Store** based on the protocol entered in the Connect dialog box and then calling its **connect( )** method.

First, a **URLName** object is instantiated with the connection URL constructed earlier using data entered in the Connect dialog box. The **URLName** object is then passed to the session's **getStore( )** method. The **getStore( )** method returns a **Store** object based on the **URLName** object's protocol. After the **store** has been retrieved, its **connect( )** method is invoked.

Remember that POP3 servers only support the notion of one folder, whereas IMAP servers can have multiple folders. Thus, once the connection has been successfully established with the e-mail server, the default "INBOX" folder is opened and its messages are retrieved as shown in the following code:

```
// Download message headers from server.
try {
  // Open main "INBOX" folder.
  Folder folder = store.getFolder("INBOX");
  folder.open(Folder.READ_WRITE);

  // Get folder's list of messages.
  Message[] messages = folder.getMessages();
```

When a list of messages is retrieved from a folder, as shown in the preceding listing, each **Message** object is empty. The **Folder** object's **getMessages( )** method simply returns an array of empty **Message** objects, each one representing a message in the folder. JavaMail uses this technique to allow messages to be downloaded on demand, thus minimizing the amount of data being downloaded from an e-mail server.

Since E-mail Client needs to have each message's data available when displaying the list of messages in the table, the following code retrieves the message headers ahead of time instead of having them loaded on demand:

```
  // Retrieve message headers for each message in folder.
  FetchProfile profile = new FetchProfile();
  profile.add(FetchProfile.Item.ENVELOPE);
  folder.fetch(messages, profile);

  // Put messages in table.
  tableModel.setMessages(messages);
} catch (Exception e) {
  // Close the Downloading dialog box.
  downloadingDialog.dispose();

  // Show error dialog box.
```

```
  showError("Unable to download messages.", true);
}
```

In order to load the messages ahead of time, a **FetchProfile** object is created. Fetch profiles are used to specify the portions of a message that should be loaded or "fetched" ahead of time. The **FetchProfile** created in the preceding code fetches the "envelope" portion of messages. Message envelopes are an aggregation of the most common message headers, such as the sender, recipient, and subject.

After retrieving the message fields ahead of time with a **FetchProfile**, the messages are added to the messages table with a call to **tableModel.setMessages( )**. The messages table is then updated, listing each of the messages downloaded from the server.

The **connect( )** method wraps up by closing the modal **DownloadingDialog**, as shown here. The user is now free to interact with the application again.

```
// Close the Downloading dialog box.
downloadingDialog.dispose();
```

The showError( ) Method

The **showError( )** method, shown here, displays an error dialog box on the screen with the given message. Observe also that the **showError( )** method takes an **exit** flag to specify whether or not the application should exit after displaying the error message.

```
// Show error dialog box and exit afterward if necessary.
private void showError(String message, boolean exit) {
  JOptionPane.showMessageDialog(this, message, "Error",
    JOptionPane.ERROR_MESSAGE);
  if (exit)
    System.exit(0);
}
```

The getMessageContent( ) Method

The **getMessageContent( )** method, shown here, retrieves a message's content. Notice that this method is declared **public** and **static** so that it can be accessed from other classes without requiring a reference to the **EmailClient** class:

```
// Get a message's content.
public static String getMessageContent(Message message)
  throws Exception {
  Object content = message.getContent();
  if (content instanceof Multipart) {
    StringBuffer messageContent = new StringBuffer();
    Multipart multipart = (Multipart) content;
    for (int i = 0; i < multipart.getCount(); i++) {
      Part part = (Part) multipart.getBodyPart(i);
```

```
        if (part.isMimeType("text/plain")) {
          messageContent.append(part.getContent().toString());
        }
      }
    return messageContent.toString();
  } else {
    return content.toString();
  }
}
```

Most e-mail messages contain only plaintext, but there are many messages that contain other information. For instance, some messages contain HTML or file attachments. When a message contains HTML, typically it also contains a plaintext version of the HTML. In this case, both the HTML and plaintext pieces of the message are distinguished as separate "parts." Messages with more than one piece, or "part," are called *multipart* messages. Messages with file attachments work much the same way as messages containing HTML; the file attachment is contained in its own part.

Because E-mail Client handles only text-based messages, the **getMessageContent( )** method begins by checking the given message's content to see whether or not it is multipart. If the content is multipart, then **message.getContent( )** will return a **Multipart** object. JavaMail's **Multipart** object is similar to a standard Java collection; it encapsulates a list of parts for a multipart message.

If **message.getContent( )** returns a **Multipart** object, each of its parts are iterated over in an effort to find and extract the plaintext parts of the message content. Conversely, if the content object returned from **message.getContent( )** is not **Multipart**, then the returned object's **toString( )** method is called to simply return its text.

Compiling and Running the E-mail Client

As mentioned earlier, you will need to have the JavaMail and the JavaBeans Activation Framework libraries installed on your computer before you can compile or run the E-mail Client code. Once the libraries have been installed, they must be added to your Java classpath. You could do this by updating your CLASSPATH environmental variable. Alternatively, you can just specify the path when you compile and run E-mail Client. For example, if the top-level directory for JavaMail is **javamail-1.3** and the top-level directory for JavaBeans Activation Framework is **jaf-1.0.2**, then the following command line will compile E-mail Client:

```
javac -classpath .;c:\javamail-1.3\mail.jar;c:\jaf-1.0.2\activation.jar
      EmailClient.java MessagesTableModel.java ConnectDialog.java
      DownloadingDialog.java MessageDialog.java
```

The **mail.jar** and the **activation.jar** files contain the classes used by JavaMail and JavaBeans Activation Framework.

To run **EmailClient**, use the following command line:

```
javaw -cp .;c:\javamail-1.3\mail.jar;c:\jaf-1.0.2\activation.jar EmailClient
```

Notice that you must specify the paths to the **mail.jar** and **activation.jar** files explicitly. Of course, if you update CLASSPATH, this explicit specification is not needed.

Once E-mail Client has been started, its use is straightforward. First, the Connect dialog box will appear on the screen prompting for connection settings. Enter the settings and then click the Connect button. After the connection with the server is established, the e-mail messages will be downloaded and displayed in the table. To view a message, simply select it from the table, and it will be displayed in the area below the table. Once a message is selected, it can be replied to, forwarded, or deleted by clicking the buttons at the bottom of the application. Remember two points: First, only text messages are fully supported. Second, no message is deleted on the server unless you explicitly request it. Figure 5-5 shows E-mail Client in action.

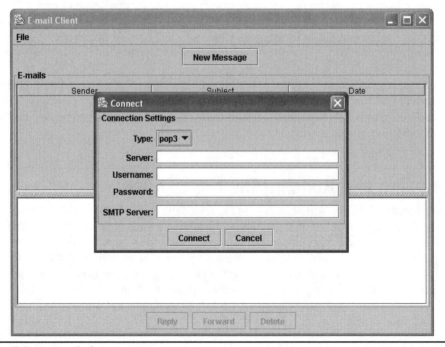

Figure 5-5   *E-mail Client in action*

Expanding Beyond the Basic E-mail Client

The code in this chapter provides an excellent experimental platform for e-mail application development. It is also a good starting point for creating your own custom e-mail application. Here are some enhancements that you might want to try adding to E-mail Client:

▶   Add support for saving connection settings so that they don't have to be entered each time.

▶   Add the ability to check for and download new e-mail from the server.

▶   Add the ability to save e-mail attachments.

▶   Add the ability to render HTML messages.

▶   Add an address book.

Conversely, you might want to try removing functionality, too. For example, you might want to try integrating into another application only that part of the code that sends a message. Doing so would allow that application to send an e-mail message automatically when some event has occurred. The ability to take complete programmatic control over e-mail opens the door to many exciting possibilities.

CHAPTER 6

Crawling the Web with Java

By James Holmes

Have you ever wondered how Internet search engines like Google and Yahoo! can search the Internet on virtually any topic and return a list of results so quickly? Obviously it would be impossible to scour the Internet each time a search request was initiated. Instead search engines query highly optimized databases of Web pages that have been aggregated and indexed ahead of time. Compiling these databases ahead of time allows search engines to scan billions of Web pages for something as esoteric as "astrophysics" or as common as "weather" and return the results almost instantly.

The real mystery of search engines does not lie in their databases of Web pages, but rather in how the databases are created. Search engines use software known as *Web crawlers* to traverse the Internet and to save each of the individual pages passed by along the way. Search engines then use additional software to index each of the saved pages, creating a database containing all the words in the pages.

Web crawlers are an essential component to search engines; however, their use is not limited to just creating databases of Web pages. In fact, Web crawlers have many practical uses. For example, you might use a crawler to look for broken links in a commercial Web site. You might also use a crawler to find changes to a Web site. To do so, first, crawl the site, creating a record of the links contained in the site. At a later date, crawl the site again and then compare the two sets of links, looking for changes. A crawler could also be used to archive the contents of a site. Frankly, crawler technology is useful in many types of Web-related applications.

Although Web crawlers are conceptually easy in that you just follow the links from one site to another, they are a bit challenging to create. One complication is that a list of links to be crawled must be maintained, and this list grows and shrinks as sites are searched. Another complication is the complexity of handling absolute versus relative links. Fortunately, Java contains features that help make it easier to implement a Web crawler. First, Java's support for networking makes downloading Web pages simple. Second, Java's support for regular expression processing simplifies the finding of links. Third, Java's Collection Framework supplies the mechanisms needed to store a list of links.

The Web crawler developed in this chapter is called Search Crawler. It crawls the Web, looking for sites that contain strings matching those specified by the user. It displays the URLs of the sites in which matches are found. Although Search Crawler is a useful utility as is, its greatest benefit is found when it is used as a starting point for your own crawler-based applications.

Fundamentals of a Web Crawler

Despite the numerous applications for Web crawlers, at the core they are all fundamentally the same. Following is the process by which Web crawlers work:

1. Download the Web page.
2. Parse through the downloaded page and retrieve all the links.
3. For each link retrieved, repeat the process.

Now let's look at each step of the process in more detail.

In the first step, a Web crawler takes a URL and downloads the page from the Internet at the given URL. Oftentimes the downloaded page is saved to a file on disk or put in a database. Saving the page allows the crawler or other software to go back later and manipulate the page, be it for indexing words (as in the case with a search engine) or for archiving the page for use by an automated archiver.

In the second step, a Web crawler parses through the downloaded page and retrieves the links to other pages. Each link in the page is defined with an HTML anchor tag similar to the one shown here:

<A HREF="http://www.host.com/directory/file.html">Link</A>

After the crawler has retrieved the links from the page, each link is added to a list of links to be crawled.

The third step of Web crawling repeats the process. All crawlers work in a recursive or loop fashion, but there are two different ways to handle it. Links can be crawled in a depth-first or breadth-first manner. *Depth-first crawling* follows each possible path to its conclusion before another path is tried. It works by finding the first link on the first page. It then crawls the page associated with that link, finding the first link on the new page, and so on, until the end of the path has been reached. The process continues until all the branches of all the links have been exhausted.

Breadth-first crawling checks each link on a page before proceeding to the next page. Thus, it crawls each link on the first page and then crawls each link on the first page's first link, and so on, until each level of links has been exhausted. Choosing whether to use depth- or breadth-first crawling often depends on the crawling application and its needs. Search Crawler uses breadth-first crawling, but you can change this behavior if you like.

Although Web crawling seems quite simple at first glance, there's actually a lot that goes into creating a full-fledged Web crawling application. For example, Web crawlers need to adhere to the "Robot protocol," as explained in the following section. Web crawlers also have to handle many "exception" scenarios such as Web server errors, redirects, and so on.

Adhering to the Robot Protocol

As you can imagine, crawling a Web site can put an enormous strain on a Web server's resources as a myriad of requests are made back to back. Typically, a few pages are downloaded at a time from a Web site, not hundreds or thousands in succession. Web sites also often have restricted areas that crawlers should not crawl. To address these concerns, many Web sites adopted the *Robot protocol,* which establishes guidelines that crawlers should follow. Over time, the protocol has become the unwritten law of the Internet for Web crawlers.

The Robot protocol specifies that Web sites wishing to restrict certain areas or pages from crawling have a file called **robots.txt** placed at the root of the Web site. Ethical crawlers will reference the robot file and determine which parts of the site are disallowed for crawling. The disallowed areas will then be skipped by the ethical crawlers. Following is an example **robots.txt** file and an explanation of its format:

```
# robots.txt for http://somehost.com/

User-agent: *
Disallow: /cgi-bin/
Disallow: /registration  # Disallow robots on registration page
Disallow: /login
```

The first line of the sample file has a comment on it, as denoted by the use of a hash (#) character. Comments can be on lines unto themselves or on statement lines, as shown on the fifth line of the preceding sample file. Crawlers reading **robots.txt** files should ignore any comments.

The third line of the sample file specifies the *User-agent* to which the *Disallow* rules following it apply. User-agent is a term used for the programs that access a Web site. For example, when accessing a Web site with Microsoft's Internet Explorer, the User-agent is "Mozilla/4.0 (compatible; MSIE 6.0; Windows NT 5.0)" or something similar to it. Each browser has a unique User-agent value that it sends along with each request to a Web server. Web crawlers also typically send a User-agent value along with each request to a Web server. The use of User-agents in the **robots.txt** file allows Web sites to set rules on a User-agent–by–User-agent basis. However, typically Web sites want to disallow all robots (or User-agents) access to certain areas, so they use a value of asterisk (*) for the User-agent. This specifies that all User-agents are disallowed for the rules that follow it. You might be thinking that the use of an asterisk to disallow all User-agents from accessing a site would prevent standard browser software from working with certain sections of Web sites. This is not a problem, though, because browsers do not observe the Robot protocol and are not expected to.

The lines following the User-agent line are called *disallow statements*. The disallow statements define the Web site paths that crawlers are not allowed to access. For example, the first disallow statement in the sample file tells crawlers not to crawl any links that begin with "/cgi-bin/". Thus, the URLs

> http://somehost.com/cgi-bin/
> http://somehost.com/cgi-bin/register

are both off limits to crawlers according to that line. Disallow statements are for paths and not specific files; thus any link being requested that contains a path on the disallow list is off limits.

An Overview of the Search Crawler

Search Crawler is a basic Web crawler for searching the Web, and it illustrates the fundamental structure of crawler-based applications. With Search Crawler, you can enter search criteria and then search the Web in real time, URL by URL, looking for matches to the criteria.

Search Crawler's interface, as shown in Figure 6-1, has three prominent sections, which we will refer to as *Search, Stats,* and *Matches.* The Search section at the top of the window has controls for entering search criteria, including the start URL for the search, the maximum number of URLs to crawl, and the search string. The search criteria can be additionally tweaked by choosing to limit the search to the site of the beginning URL and by selecting the Case Sensitive check box for the search string.

The Stats section, located in the middle of the window, has controls showing the current status of crawling when searching is underway. This section also has a progress bar to indicate the progress toward completing the search.

The Matches section at the bottom of the window has a table listing all the matches found by a search. These are the URLs of the Web pages that contain the search string.

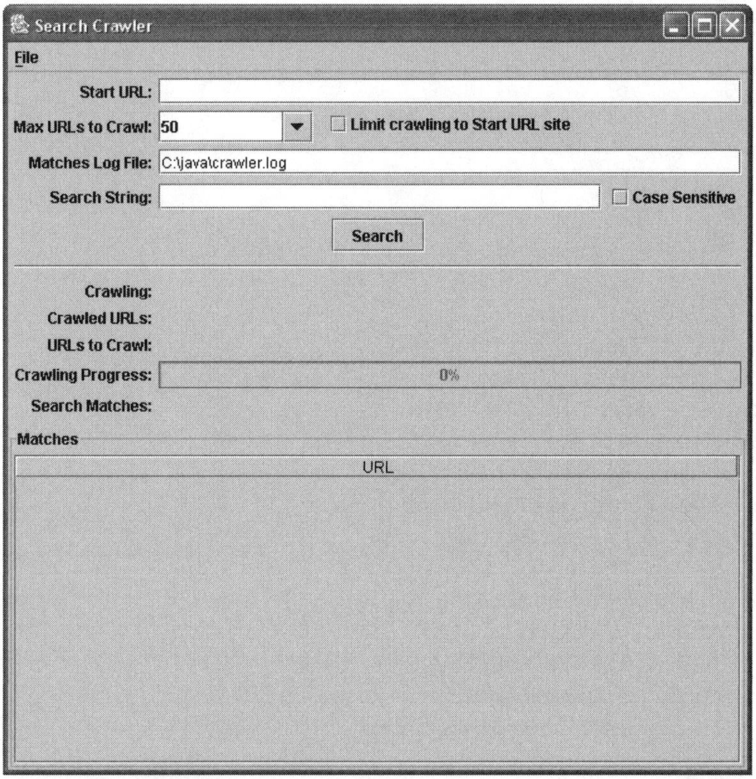

Figure 6-1   *The Search Crawler GUI interface*

The SearchCrawler Class

SearchCrawler has a **main( )** method, so on execution it will be invoked first. The **main( )** method instantiates a new **SearchCrawler** object and then calls its **show( )** method, which causes it to be displayed.

The **SearchCrawler** class is shown here and is examined in detail in the following sections. Notice that it extends **JFrame**:

```java
import java.awt.*;
import java.awt.event.*;
import java.io.*;
import java.net.*;
import java.util.*;
import java.util.regex.*;
import javax.swing.*;
import javax.swing.table.*;

// The Search Web Crawler
public class SearchCrawler extends JFrame
{
  // Max URLs drop-down values.
  private static final String[] MAX_URLS =
    {"50", "100", "500", "1000"};

  // Cache of robot disallow lists.
  private HashMap disallowListCache = new HashMap();

  // Search GUI controls.
  private JTextField startTextField;
  private JComboBox maxComboBox;
  private JCheckBox limitCheckBox;
  private JTextField logTextField;
  private JTextField searchTextField;
  private JCheckBox caseCheckBox;
  private JButton searchButton;

  // Search stats GUI controls.
  private JLabel crawlingLabel2;
  private JLabel crawledLabel2;
  private JLabel toCrawlLabel2;
  private JProgressBar progressBar;
  private JLabel matchesLabel2;

  // Table listing search matches.
  private JTable table;
```

```java
// Flag for whether or not crawling is underway.
private boolean crawling;

// Matches log file print writer.
private PrintWriter logFileWriter;

// Constructor for Search Web Crawler.
public SearchCrawler()
{
  // Set application title.
  setTitle("Search Crawler");

  // Set window size.
  setSize(600, 600);

   // Handle window closing events.
  addWindowListener(new WindowAdapter() {
    public void windowClosing(WindowEvent e) {
      actionExit();
    }
  });

  // Set up File menu.
  JMenuBar menuBar = new JMenuBar();
  JMenu fileMenu = new JMenu("File");
  fileMenu.setMnemonic(KeyEvent.VK_F);
  JMenuItem fileExitMenuItem = new JMenuItem("Exit",
    KeyEvent.VK_X);
  fileExitMenuItem.addActionListener(new ActionListener() {
    public void actionPerformed(ActionEvent e) {
      actionExit();
    }
  });
  fileMenu.add(fileExitMenuItem);
  menuBar.add(fileMenu);
  setJMenuBar(menuBar);

  // Set up search panel.
  JPanel searchPanel = new JPanel();
  GridBagConstraints constraints;
  GridBagLayout layout = new GridBagLayout();
  searchPanel.setLayout(layout);

  JLabel startLabel = new JLabel("Start URL:");
  constraints = new GridBagConstraints();
```

```java
constraints.anchor = GridBagConstraints.EAST;
constraints.insets = new Insets(5, 5, 0, 0);
layout.setConstraints(startLabel, constraints);
searchPanel.add(startLabel);

startTextField = new JTextField();
constraints = new GridBagConstraints();
constraints.fill = GridBagConstraints.HORIZONTAL;
constraints.gridwidth = GridBagConstraints.REMAINDER;
constraints.insets = new Insets(5, 5, 0, 5);
layout.setConstraints(startTextField, constraints);
searchPanel.add(startTextField);

JLabel maxLabel = new JLabel("Max URLs to Crawl:");
constraints = new GridBagConstraints();
constraints.anchor = GridBagConstraints.EAST;
constraints.insets = new Insets(5, 5, 0, 0);
layout.setConstraints(maxLabel, constraints);
searchPanel.add(maxLabel);

maxComboBox = new JComboBox(MAX_URLS);
maxComboBox.setEditable(true);
constraints = new GridBagConstraints();
constraints.insets = new Insets(5, 5, 0, 0);
layout.setConstraints(maxComboBox, constraints);
searchPanel.add(maxComboBox);

limitCheckBox =
  new JCheckBox("Limit crawling to Start URL site");
constraints = new GridBagConstraints();
constraints.anchor = GridBagConstraints.WEST;
constraints.insets = new Insets(0, 10, 0, 0);
layout.setConstraints(limitCheckBox, constraints);
searchPanel.add(limitCheckBox);

JLabel blankLabel = new JLabel();
constraints = new GridBagConstraints();
constraints.gridwidth = GridBagConstraints.REMAINDER;
layout.setConstraints(blankLabel, constraints);
searchPanel.add(blankLabel);

JLabel logLabel = new JLabel("Matches Log File:");
constraints = new GridBagConstraints();
constraints.anchor = GridBagConstraints.EAST;
constraints.insets = new Insets(5, 5, 0, 0);
```

```
layout.setConstraints(logLabel, constraints);
searchPanel.add(logLabel);

String file =
  System.getProperty("user.dir") +
  System.getProperty("file.separator") +
  "crawler.log";
logTextField = new JTextField(file);
constraints = new GridBagConstraints();
constraints.fill = GridBagConstraints.HORIZONTAL;
constraints.gridwidth = GridBagConstraints.REMAINDER;
constraints.insets = new Insets(5, 5, 0, 5);
layout.setConstraints(logTextField, constraints);
searchPanel.add(logTextField);

JLabel searchLabel = new JLabel("Search String:");
constraints = new GridBagConstraints();
constraints.anchor = GridBagConstraints.EAST;
constraints.insets = new Insets(5, 5, 0, 0);
layout.setConstraints(searchLabel, constraints);
searchPanel.add(searchLabel);

searchTextField = new JTextField();
constraints = new GridBagConstraints();
constraints.fill = GridBagConstraints.HORIZONTAL;
constraints.insets = new Insets(5, 5, 0, 0);
constraints.gridwidth= 2;
constraints.weightx = 1.0d;
layout.setConstraints(searchTextField, constraints);
searchPanel.add(searchTextField);

caseCheckBox = new JCheckBox("Case Sensitive");
constraints = new GridBagConstraints();
constraints.insets = new Insets(5, 5, 0, 5);
constraints.gridwidth = GridBagConstraints.REMAINDER;
layout.setConstraints(caseCheckBox, constraints);
searchPanel.add(caseCheckBox);

searchButton = new JButton("Search");
searchButton.addActionListener(new ActionListener() {
  public void actionPerformed(ActionEvent e) {
    actionSearch();
  }
});
constraints = new GridBagConstraints();
```

```
constraints.gridwidth = GridBagConstraints.REMAINDER;
constraints.insets = new Insets(5, 5, 5, 5);
layout.setConstraints(searchButton, constraints);
searchPanel.add(searchButton);

JSeparator separator = new JSeparator();
constraints = new GridBagConstraints();
constraints.fill = GridBagConstraints.HORIZONTAL;
constraints.gridwidth = GridBagConstraints.REMAINDER;
constraints.insets = new Insets(5, 5, 5, 5);
layout.setConstraints(separator, constraints);
searchPanel.add(separator);

JLabel crawlingLabel1 = new JLabel("Crawling:");
constraints = new GridBagConstraints();
constraints.anchor = GridBagConstraints.EAST;
constraints.insets = new Insets(5, 5, 0, 0);
layout.setConstraints(crawlingLabel1, constraints);
searchPanel.add(crawlingLabel1);

crawlingLabel2 = new JLabel();
crawlingLabel2.setFont(
  crawlingLabel2.getFont().deriveFont(Font.PLAIN));
constraints = new GridBagConstraints();
constraints.fill = GridBagConstraints.HORIZONTAL;
constraints.gridwidth = GridBagConstraints.REMAINDER;
constraints.insets = new Insets(5, 5, 0, 5);
layout.setConstraints(crawlingLabel2, constraints);
searchPanel.add(crawlingLabel2);

JLabel crawledLabel1 = new JLabel("Crawled URLs:");
constraints = new GridBagConstraints();
constraints.anchor = GridBagConstraints.EAST;
constraints.insets = new Insets(5, 5, 0, 0);
layout.setConstraints(crawledLabel1, constraints);
searchPanel.add(crawledLabel1);

crawledLabel2 = new JLabel();
crawledLabel2.setFont(
  crawledLabel2.getFont().deriveFont(Font.PLAIN));
constraints = new GridBagConstraints();
constraints.fill = GridBagConstraints.HORIZONTAL;
constraints.gridwidth = GridBagConstraints.REMAINDER;
constraints.insets = new Insets(5, 5, 0, 5);
```

```
layout.setConstraints(crawledLabel2, constraints);
searchPanel.add(crawledLabel2);

JLabel toCrawlLabel1 = new JLabel("URLs to Crawl:");
constraints = new GridBagConstraints();
constraints.anchor = GridBagConstraints.EAST;
constraints.insets = new Insets(5, 5, 0, 0);
layout.setConstraints(toCrawlLabel1, constraints);
searchPanel.add(toCrawlLabel1);

toCrawlLabel2 = new JLabel();
toCrawlLabel2.setFont(
  toCrawlLabel2.getFont().deriveFont(Font.PLAIN));
constraints = new GridBagConstraints();
constraints.fill = GridBagConstraints.HORIZONTAL;
constraints.gridwidth = GridBagConstraints.REMAINDER;
constraints.insets = new Insets(5, 5, 0, 5);
layout.setConstraints(toCrawlLabel2, constraints);
searchPanel.add(toCrawlLabel2);

JLabel progressLabel = new JLabel("Crawling Progress:");
constraints = new GridBagConstraints();
constraints.anchor = GridBagConstraints.EAST;
constraints.insets = new Insets(5, 5, 0, 0);
layout.setConstraints(progressLabel, constraints);
searchPanel.add(progressLabel);

progressBar = new JProgressBar();
progressBar.setMinimum(0);
progressBar.setStringPainted(true);
constraints = new GridBagConstraints();
constraints.fill = GridBagConstraints.HORIZONTAL;
constraints.gridwidth = GridBagConstraints.REMAINDER;
constraints.insets = new Insets(5, 5, 0, 5);
layout.setConstraints(progressBar, constraints);
searchPanel.add(progressBar);

JLabel matchesLabel1 = new JLabel("Search Matches:");
constraints = new GridBagConstraints();
constraints.anchor = GridBagConstraints.EAST;
constraints.insets = new Insets(5, 5, 10, 0);
layout.setConstraints(matchesLabel1, constraints);
searchPanel.add(matchesLabel1);
```

```
matchesLabel2 = new JLabel();
matchesLabel2.setFont(
  matchesLabel2.getFont().deriveFont(Font.PLAIN));
constraints = new GridBagConstraints();
constraints.fill = GridBagConstraints.HORIZONTAL;
constraints.gridwidth = GridBagConstraints.REMAINDER;
constraints.insets = new Insets(5, 5, 10, 5);
layout.setConstraints(matchesLabel2, constraints);
searchPanel.add(matchesLabel2);

// Set up matches table.
table =
  new JTable(new DefaultTableModel(new Object[][]{},
    new String[]{"URL"}) {
  public boolean isCellEditable(int row, int column)
  {
    return false;
  }
});

// Set up Matches panel.
JPanel matchesPanel = new JPanel();
matchesPanel.setBorder(
  BorderFactory.createTitledBorder("Matches"));
matchesPanel.setLayout(new BorderLayout());
matchesPanel.add(new JScrollPane(table),
  BorderLayout.CENTER);

// Add panels to display.
getContentPane().setLayout(new BorderLayout());
getContentPane().add(searchPanel, BorderLayout.NORTH);
getContentPane().add(matchesPanel, BorderLayout.CENTER);
}

// Exit this program.
private void actionExit() {
  System.exit(0);
}

// Handle Search/Stop button being clicked.
private void actionSearch() {
  // If stop button clicked, turn crawling flag off.
  if (crawling) {
    crawling = false;
    return;
```

```java
}

ArrayList errorList = new ArrayList();

// Validate that start URL has been entered.
String startUrl = startTextField.getText().trim();
if (startUrl.length() < 1) {
  errorList.add("Missing Start URL.");
}
// Verify start URL.
else if (verifyUrl(startUrl) == null) {
  errorList.add("Invalid Start URL.");
}

// Validate that Max URLs is either empty or is a number.
int maxUrls = 0;
String max = ((String) maxComboBox.getSelectedItem()).trim();
if (max.length() > 0) {
  try {
    maxUrls = Integer.parseInt(max);
  } catch (NumberFormatException e) {
  }
  if (maxUrls < 1) {
    errorList.add("Invalid Max URLs value.");
  }
}

// Validate that matches log file has been entered.
String logFile = logTextField.getText().trim();
if (logFile.length() < 1) {
  errorList.add("Missing Matches Log File.");
}

// Validate that search string has been entered.
String searchString = searchTextField.getText().trim();
if (searchString.length() < 1) {
  errorList.add("Missing Search String.");
}

// Show errors, if any, and return.
if (errorList.size() > 0) {
  StringBuffer message = new StringBuffer();

  // Concatenate errors into single message.
  for (int i = 0; i < errorList.size(); i++) {
```

```
        message.append(errorList.get(i));
        if (i + 1 < errorList.size()) {
          message.append("\n");
        }
      }
    }

    showError(message.toString());
    return;
  }

  // Remove "www" from start URL if present.
  startUrl = removeWwwFromUrl(startUrl);

  // Start the Search Crawler.
  search(logFile, startUrl, maxUrls, searchString);
}

private void search(final String logFile, final String startUrl,
  final int maxUrls, final String searchString)
{
  // Start the search in a new thread.
  Thread thread = new Thread(new Runnable() {
    public void run() {
      // Show hour glass cursor while crawling is under way.
      setCursor(Cursor.getPredefinedCursor(Cursor.WAIT_CURSOR));

      // Disable search controls.
      startTextField.setEnabled(false);
      maxComboBox.setEnabled(false);
      limitCheckBox.setEnabled(false);
      logTextField.setEnabled(false);
      searchTextField.setEnabled(false);
      caseCheckBox.setEnabled(false);

      // Switch Search button to "Stop."
      searchButton.setText("Stop");

      // Reset stats.
      table.setModel(new DefaultTableModel(new Object[][]{},
        new String[]{"URL"}) {
        public boolean isCellEditable(int row, int column)
        {
          return false;
        }
      });
```

```java
    updateStats(startUrl, 0, 0, maxUrls);

    // Open matches log file.
    try {
      logFileWriter = new PrintWriter(new FileWriter(logFile));
    } catch (Exception e) {
      showError("Unable to open matches log file.");
      return;
    }

    // Turn crawling flag on.
    crawling = true;

    // Perform the actual crawling.
    crawl(startUrl, maxUrls, limitCheckBox.isSelected(),
      searchString, caseCheckBox.isSelected());

    // Turn crawling flag off.
    crawling = false;

    // Close matches log file.
    try {
      logFileWriter.close();
    } catch (Exception e) {
      showError("Unable to close matches log file.");
    }

    // Mark search as done.
    crawlingLabel2.setText("Done");

    // Enable search controls.
    startTextField.setEnabled(true);
    maxComboBox.setEnabled(true);
    limitCheckBox.setEnabled(true);
    logTextField.setEnabled(true);
    searchTextField.setEnabled(true);
    caseCheckBox.setEnabled(true);

    // Switch search button back to "Search."
    searchButton.setText("Search");

    // Return to default cursor.
    setCursor(Cursor.getDefaultCursor());

    // Show message if search string not found.
```

```
        if (table.getRowCount() == 0) {
          JOptionPane.showMessageDialog(SearchCrawler.this,
            "Your Search String was not found. Please try another.",
            "Search String Not Found",
            JOptionPane.WARNING_MESSAGE);
        }
      }
    });
    thread.start();
  }

  // Show dialog box with error message.
  private void showError(String message) {
    JOptionPane.showMessageDialog(this, message, "Error",
      JOptionPane.ERROR_MESSAGE);
  }

  // Update crawling stats.
  private void updateStats(
    String crawling, int crawled, int toCrawl, int maxUrls)
  {
    crawlingLabel2.setText(crawling);
    crawledLabel2.setText("" + crawled);
    toCrawlLabel2.setText("" + toCrawl);

    // Update progress bar.
    if (maxUrls == -1) {
      progressBar.setMaximum(crawled + toCrawl);
    } else {
      progressBar.setMaximum(maxUrls);
    }
    progressBar.setValue(crawled);

    matchesLabel2.setText("" + table.getRowCount());
  }

  // Add match to matches table and log file.
  private void addMatch(String url) {
    // Add URL to matches table.
    DefaultTableModel model =
      (DefaultTableModel) table.getModel();
    model.addRow(new Object[]{url});

    // Add URL to matches log file.
    try {
```

```
      logFileWriter.println(url);
    } catch (Exception e) {
      showError("Unable to log match.");
    }
  }

  // Verify URL format.
  private URL verifyUrl(String url) {
    // Only allow HTTP URLs.
    if (!url.toLowerCase().startsWith("http://"))
      return null;

    // Verify format of URL.
    URL verifiedUrl = null;
    try {
      verifiedUrl = new URL(url);
    } catch (Exception e) {
      return null;
    }

    return verifiedUrl;
  }

  // Check if robot is allowed to access the given URL.
  private boolean isRobotAllowed(URL urlToCheck) {
    String host = urlToCheck.getHost().toLowerCase();

    // Retrieve host's disallow list from cache.
    ArrayList disallowList =
      (ArrayList) disallowListCache.get(host);

    // If list is not in the cache, download and cache it.
    if (disallowList == null) {
      disallowList = new ArrayList();

      try {
        URL robotsFileUrl =
          new URL("http://" + host + "/robots.txt");

        // Open connection to robot file URL for reading.
        BufferedReader reader =
          new BufferedReader(new InputStreamReader(
            robotsFileUrl.openStream()));

        // Read robot file, creating list of disallowed paths.
```

```java
      String line;
      while ((line = reader.readLine()) != null) {
        if (line.indexOf("Disallow:") == 0) {
          String disallowPath =
            line.substring("Disallow:".length());

          // Check disallow path for comments and remove if present.
          int commentIndex = disallowPath.indexOf("#");
          if (commentIndex != - 1) {
            disallowPath =
              disallowPath.substring(0, commentIndex);
          }

          // Remove leading or trailing spaces from disallow path.
          disallowPath = disallowPath.trim();

          // Add disallow path to list.
          disallowList.add(disallowPath);
        }
      }

      // Add new disallow list to cache.
      disallowListCache.put(host, disallowList);
    }
    catch (Exception e) {
      /* Assume robot is allowed since an exception
         is thrown if the robot file doesn't exist. */
      return true;
    }
  }

  /* Loop through disallow list to see if
     crawling is allowed for the given URL. */
  String file = urlToCheck.getFile();
  for (int i = 0; i < disallowList.size(); i++) {
    String disallow = (String) disallowList.get(i);
    if (file.startsWith(disallow)) {
      return false;
    }
  }

  return true;
}

// Download page at given URL.
```

```java
private String downloadPage(URL pageUrl) {
    try {
        // Open connection to URL for reading.
        BufferedReader reader =
            new BufferedReader(new InputStreamReader(
                pageUrl.openStream()));

        // Read page into buffer.
        String line;
        StringBuffer pageBuffer = new StringBuffer();
        while ((line = reader.readLine()) != null) {
            pageBuffer.append(line);
        }

        return pageBuffer.toString();
    } catch (Exception e) {
    }

    return null;
}


// Remove leading "www" from a URL's host if present.
private String removeWwwFromUrl(String url) {
    int index = url.indexOf("://www.");
    if (index != -1) {
        return url.substring(0, index + 3) +
            url.substring(index + 7);
    }

    return (url);
}


// Parse through page contents and retrieve links.
private ArrayList retrieveLinks(
    URL pageUrl, String pageContents, HashSet crawledList,
    boolean limitHost)
{
    // Compile link matching pattern.
    Pattern p =
        Pattern.compile("<a\\s+href\\s*=\\s*\"?(.*?)[\"|>]",
            Pattern.CASE_INSENSITIVE);
    Matcher m = p.matcher(pageContents);

    // Create list of link matches.
    ArrayList linkList = new ArrayList();
```

```
while (m.find()) {
  String link = m.group(1).trim();

  // Skip empty links.
  if (link.length() < 1) {
    continue;
  }

  // Skip links that are just page anchors.
  if (link.charAt(0) == '#') {
    continue;
  }

  // Skip mailto links.
  if (link.indexOf("mailto:") != -1) {
    continue;
  }

  // Skip JavaScript links.
  if (link.toLowerCase().indexOf("javascript") != -1) {
    continue;
  }

  // Prefix absolute and relative URLs if necessary.
  if (link.indexOf("://") == -1) {
    // Handle absolute URLs.
    if (link.charAt(0) == '/') {
      link = "http://" + pageUrl.getHost() + link;
    // Handle relative URLs.
    } else {
      String file = pageUrl.getFile();
      if (file.indexOf('/') == -1) {
        link = "http://" + pageUrl.getHost() + "/" + link;
      } else {
        String path =
          file.substring(0, file.lastIndexOf('/') + 1);
        link = "http://" + pageUrl.getHost() + path + link;
      }
    }
  }

  // Remove anchors from link.
  int index = link.indexOf('#');
  if (index != -1) {
    link = link.substring(0, index);
```

```
    }

    // Remove leading "www" from URL's host if present.
    link = removeWwwFromUrl(link);

    // Verify link and skip if invalid.
    URL verifiedLink = verifyUrl(link);
    if (verifiedLink == null) {
      continue;
    }

    /* If specified, limit links to those
       having the same host as the start URL. */
    if (limitHost &&
        !pageUrl.getHost().toLowerCase().equals(
          verifiedLink.getHost().toLowerCase()))
    {
      continue;
    }

    // Skip link if it has already been crawled.
    if (crawledList.contains(link)) {
      continue;
    }

    // Add link to list.
    linkList.add(link);
  }

  return (linkList);
}

/* Determine whether or not search string is
   matched in the given page contents. */
private boolean searchStringMatches(
  String pageContents, String searchString,
  boolean caseSensitive)
{
  String searchContents = pageContents;

  /* If case-sensitive search, lowercase
     page contents for comparison. */
  if (!caseSensitive) {
    searchContents = pageContents.toLowerCase();
  }
```

```java
    // Split search string into individual terms.
    Pattern p = Pattern.compile("[\\s]+");
    String[] terms = p.split(searchString);

    // Check to see if each term matches.
    for (int i = 0; i < terms.length; i++) {
      if (caseSensitive) {
        if (searchContents.indexOf(terms[i]) == -1) {
          return false;
        }
      } else {
        if (searchContents.indexOf(terms[i].toLowerCase()) == -1) {
          return false;
        }
      }
    }

    return true;
  }

  // Perform the actual crawling, searching for the search string.
  public void crawl(
    String startUrl, int maxUrls, boolean limitHost,
    String searchString, boolean caseSensitive)
  {
    // Set up crawl lists.
    HashSet crawledList = new HashSet();
    LinkedHashSet toCrawlList = new LinkedHashSet();

    // Add start URL to the to crawl list.
    toCrawlList.add(startUrl);

    /* Perform actual crawling by looping
       through the To Crawl list. */
    while (crawling && toCrawlList.size() > 0)
    {
      /* Check to see if the max URL count has
         been reached, if it was specified.*/
      if (maxUrls != -1) {
        if (crawledList.size() == maxUrls) {
          break;
        }
      }

      // Get URL at bottom of the list.
```

```java
String url = (String) toCrawlList.iterator().next();

// Remove URL from the To Crawl list.
toCrawlList.remove(url);

// Convert string url to URL object.
URL verifiedUrl = verifyUrl(url);

// Skip URL if robots are not allowed to access it.
if (!isRobotAllowed(verifiedUrl)) {
  continue;
}

// Update crawling stats.
updateStats(url, crawledList.size(), toCrawlList.size(),
  maxUrls);

// Add page to the crawled list.
crawledList.add(url);

// Download the page at the given URL.
String pageContents = downloadPage(verifiedUrl);

/* If the page was downloaded successfully, retrieve all its
   links and then see if it contains the search string. */
if (pageContents != null && pageContents.length() > 0)
{
  // Retrieve list of valid links from page.
  ArrayList links =
    retrieveLinks(verifiedUrl, pageContents, crawledList,
      limitHost);

  // Add links to the To Crawl list.
  toCrawlList.addAll(links);

  /* Check if search string is present in
     page, and if so, record a match. */
  if (searchStringMatches(pageContents, searchString,
      caseSensitive))
  {
    addMatch(url);
  }
}

// Update crawling stats.
```

```
        updateStats(url, crawledList.size(), toCrawlList.size(),
          maxUrls);
      }
    }

    // Run the Search Crawler.
    public static void main(String[] args) {
      SearchCrawler crawler = new SearchCrawler();
      crawler.show();
    }
  }
```

The SearchCrawler Variables

SearchCrawler starts off by declaring several instance variables, most of which hold references to the interface controls. First, the **MAX_URLS String** array declares the list of values to be displayed in the Max URLs to Crawl combo box. Second, **disallowListCache** is defined for caching robot disallow lists so that they don't have to be retrieved for each URL being crawled. Next, each of the interface controls is declared for the Search, Stats, and Matches sections of the interface. After the interface controls have been declared, the **crawling** flag is defined for tracking whether or not crawling is underway. Finally, the **logFileWriter** instance variable, which is used for printing search matches to a log file, is declared.

The SearchCrawler Constructor

When the **SearchCrawler** is instantiated, all the interface controls are initialized inside its constructor. The constructor contains a lot of code, but most of it is straightforward. The following discussion gives an overview.

First, the application's window title is set with a call to **setTitle( )**. Next, the **setSize( )** call establishes the window's width and height in pixels. After that, a window listener is added by calling **addWindowListener( )**, which passes a **WindowAdapter** object that overrides the **windowClosing( )** event handler. This handler calls the **actionExit( )** method when the application's window is closed. Next, a menu bar with a File menu is added to the application's window.

The next several lines of the constructor initiate and lay out the interface controls. Similar to other applications in this book, the layout is arranged using the **GridBagLayout** class and its associated **GridBagConstraints** class. First, the Search section of the interface is laid out, followed by the Stats section. The Search section includes all the controls for entering the search criteria and constraints. The Stats section holds all the controls for displaying the current crawling status, such as how many URLs have been crawled and how many URLs are left to crawl.

It's important to point out three things in the Search and Stats sections. First, the Matches Log File text field control is initialized with a string containing a filename. This string is set to a file called **crawler.log** in the directory the application is run from, as specified by the Java environment variable **user.dir**. Second, an **ActionListener** is added to the Search button so that the **actionSearch( )** method is called each time the button is clicked. Third, the font for each label that is used to display results is updated with a call to **setFont( )**. The **setFont( )** call is used to turn off the bolding of the label fonts so that they are distinguished in the interface.

Following the Search and Stats sections of the interface is the Matches section that consists of the matches table, which contains the URLs containing the search string. The matches table is instantiated with a new **DefaultTableModel** subclass passed to its constructor. Typically a fully qualified subclass of **DefaultTableModel** is used to customize the data model used by a **JTable**; however, in this case only the **isCellEditable( )** method needs to be implemented. The **isCellEditable( )** method instructs the table that no cells should be editable by returning **false**, regardless of the row and column specified.

Once the matches table is initialized, it is added to the Matches panel. Finally, the Search panel and Matches panel are added to the interface.

The actionSearch( ) Method

The **actionSearch( )** method is invoked each time the Search (or Stop) button is clicked. The **actionSearch( )** method starts with these lines of code:

```
// If stop button clicked, turn crawling flag off.
if (crawling) {
  crawling = false;
  return;
}
```

Since the Search button in the interface doubles as both the Search button and the Stop button, it's necessary to know which of the two buttons was clicked. When crawling is underway, the **crawling** flag is set to **true**. Thus if the **crawling** flag is **true** when the **actionsearch( )** method is invoked, the Stop button was clicked. In this scenario, the **crawling** flag is set to **false** and **actionSearch( )** returns so that the rest of the method is not executed.

Next, an **ArrayList** variable, **errorList**, is initialized:

```
ArrayList errorList = new ArrayList();
```

The **errorList** is used to hold any error messages generated by the next several lines of code that validate all required search fields have been entered.

It goes without saying that the Search Crawler will not function without a URL that specifies the location at which to start crawling. The following code verifies that a starting URL has been entered and that the URL is valid:

```
// Validate that the start URL has been entered.
String startUrl = startTextField.getText().trim();
if (startUrl.length() < 1) {
  errorList.add("Missing Start URL.");
```

```
}
// Verify start URL.
else if (verifyUrl(startUrl) == null) {
  errorList.add("Invalid Start URL.");
}
```

If either of these checks fails, an error message is added to the error list.
Next, the Max URLs to Crawl combo box value is validated:

```
// Validate that Max URLs is either empty or is a number.
int maxUrls = -1;
String max = ((String) maxComboBox.getSelectedItem()).trim();
if (max.length() > 0) {
  try {
    maxUrls = Integer.parseInt(max);
  } catch (NumberFormatException e) {
  }
  if (maxUrls < 1) {
    errorList.add("Invalid Max URLs value.");
  }
}
```

Validating the maximum number of URLs to crawl is a bit more involved than the other validations in this method. This is because the Max URLs to Crawl field can either contain a positive number that indicates the maximum number of URLs to crawl or can be left blank to indicate that no maximum should be used. Initially, **maxUrls** is defaulted to −1 to indicate no maximum. If the user enters something into the Max URLs to Crawl field, it is validated as being a valid numeric value with a call to **Integer.parseInt( )**. **Integer.parseInt( )** converts a **String** representation of an integer into an **int** value. If the **String** representation cannot be converted to an integer, a **NumberFormatException** is thrown and the **maxUrls** value is not set. Next, **maxUrls** is checked to see if it is less than 1. If so, an error is added to the error list.

Next, the Matches Log File and Search String fields are validated:

```
// Validate that the matches log file has been entered.
String logFile = logTextField.getText().trim();
if (logFile.length() < 1) {
  errorList.add("Missing Matches Log File.");
}

// Validate that the search string has been entered.
String searchString = searchTextField.getText().trim();
if (searchString.length() < 1) {
  errorList.add("Missing Search String.");
}
```

If either of these fields has not been entered, an error message is added to the error list.

The following code checks to see if any errors have been recorded during validation. If so, all the errors are concatenated into a single message and displayed with a call to **showError( )**.

```
// Show errors, if any, and return.
if (errorList.size() > 0) {
  StringBuffer message = new StringBuffer();

  // Concatenate errors into single message.
  for (int i = 0; i < errorList.size(); i++) {
    message.append(errorList.get(i));
    if (i + 1 < errorList.size()) {
      message.append("\n");
    }
  }

  showError(message.toString());
  return;
}
```

For efficiency's sake, a **StringBuffer** object (referred to by **message**) is used to hold the concatenated message. The error list is iterated over with a **for** loop, adding each message to **message**. Notice that each time a message is added, a check is performed to see if the message is the last in the list or not. If the message is not the last message in the list, a newline (**\n**) character is added so that each message will be displayed on its own line in the error dialog box shown with the **showError( )** method.

Finally, after all the field validations are successful, **actionSearch( )** concludes by removing "www" from the starting URL and then calling the **search( )** method:

```
// Remove "www" from start URL if present.
startUrl = removeWwwFromUrl(startUrl);

// Start the Search Crawler.
search(logFile, startUrl, maxUrls, searchString);
```

The search( ) Method

The **search( )** method is used to begin the Web crawling process. Since this process can take a considerable amount of time to complete, a new thread is created so that the search code can run independently. This frees up Swing's event thread, allowing changes in the interface to take place while crawling is underway.

The **search( )** method starts with these lines of code:

```
// Start the search in a new thread.
Thread thread = new Thread(new Runnable() {
  public void run() {
```

To run the search code in a separate thread, a new **Thread** object is instantiated with a **Runnable** instance passed to its constructor. Instead of creating a separate class that implements the **Runnable** interface, the code is in-lined.

Before the search starts, the interface controls are updated to indicate that crawling is underway, as shown here:

```
// Show hour glass cursor while crawling is under way.
setCursor(Cursor.getPredefinedCursor(Cursor.WAIT_CURSOR));

// Disable search controls.
startTextField.setEnabled(false);
maxComboBox.setEnabled(false);
limitCheckBox.setEnabled(false);
logTextField.setEnabled(false);
searchTextField.setEnabled(false);
caseCheckBox.setEnabled(false);

// Switch search button to "Stop."
searchButton.setText("Stop");
```

First, the application's cursor is set to the **WAIT_CURSOR** to signify that the application is busy. On most operating systems, the **WAIT_CURSOR** is an hourglass. After the cursor has been set, each of the search interface controls is disabled by calling the **setEnabled( )** method with a **false** flag on the control. Next, the Search button is changed to read "Stop." The Search button is changed, because when searching is underway the button doubles as a control for stopping the current search.

After disabling the search controls, the Stats section of the interface is reset, as shown here:

```
// Reset stats.
table.setModel(new DefaultTableModel(new Object[][]{},
  new String[]{"URL"}) {
  public boolean isCellEditable(int row, int column)
  {
    return false;
  }
});
updateStats(startUrl, 0, 0, maxUrls);
```

First, the matches table's data model is reset by passing the **setModel( )** method an all new, empty **DefaultTableModel** instance. Second, the **updateStats( )** method is called to refresh the progress bar and the status labels.

Next, the log file is opened and the **crawling** flag is turned on:

```
// Open matches log file.
try {
  logFileWriter = new PrintWriter(new FileWriter(logFile));
} catch (Exception e) {
```

```
    showError("Unable to open matches log file.");
    return;
}


// Turn crawling flag on.
crawling = true;
```

The log file is opened by way of creating a new **PrintWriter** instance for writing to the file. If the file cannot be opened, an error dialog box is displayed by calling **showError( )**. The **crawling** flag is set to **true** to indicate to the **actionSearch( )** method that crawling is underway.

The following code kicks off the actual search crawling by invoking the **crawl( )** method:

```
// Perform the actual crawling.
crawl(startUrl, maxUrls, limitCheckBox.isSelected(),
  searchString, caseCheckBox.isSelected());
```

After crawling has completed, the **crawling** flag is turned off and the matches log file is closed, as shown here:

```
// Turn crawling flag off.
crawling = false;

// Close matches log file.
try {
  logFileWriter.close();
} catch (Exception e) {
  showError("Unable to close matches log file.");
}
```

The **crawling** flag is set to **false** to indicate that crawling is no longer underway. Next, the matches log file is closed since crawling is finished. Similar to opening the file, if an exception is thrown while trying to close the file, an error dialog box will be shown with a call to **showError( )**.

Because crawling is finished, the search controls are reactivated by the following code:

```
// Mark search as done.
crawlingLabel2.setText("Done");

// Enable search controls.
startTextField.setEnabled(true);
maxComboBox.setEnabled(true);
limitCheckBox.setEnabled(true);
logTextField.setEnabled(true);
searchTextField.setEnabled(true);
caseCheckBox.setEnabled(true);
```

```
// Switch search button back to "Search."
searchButton.setText("Search");

// Return to default cursor.
setCursor(Cursor.getDefaultCursor());
```

First, the Crawling field is updated to display "Done." Second, each of the search controls is reenabled. Third, the Stop button is reverted back to displaying "Search." Finally, the cursor is reverted back to the default application cursor.

If the search did not yield any matches, the following code displays a dialog box to indicate this fact:

```
// Show message if search string not found.
if (table.getRowCount() == 0) {
  JOptionPane.showMessageDialog(SearchCrawler.this,
    "Your Search String was not found. Please try another.",
    "Search String Not Found",
    JOptionPane.WARNING_MESSAGE);
}
```

The **search( )** method wraps up with the following lines of code:

```
  }
});
thread.start();
```

After the **Runnable** implementation's **run( )** method has been defined, the search thread is started with a call to **thread.start( )**. Upon the thread's execution, the **Runnable** instance's **run( )** method will be invoked.

The showError( ) Method

The **showError( )** method, shown here, displays an error dialog box on the screen with the given message. This method is invoked if any required search options are missing or if there are any problems opening, writing to, or closing the log file.

```
// Show dialog box with error message.
private void showError(String message) {
  JOptionPane.showMessageDialog(this, message, "Error",
    JOptionPane.ERROR_MESSAGE);
}
```

The updateStats( ) Method

The **updateStats( )** method, shown here, updates the values displayed in the Stats section of the interface:

```
// Update crawling stats.
private void updateStats(
  String crawling, int crawled, int toCrawl, int maxUrls)
{
  crawlingLabel2.setText(crawling);
  crawledLabel2.setText("" + crawled);
  toCrawlLabel2.setText("" + toCrawl);

  // Update progress bar.
  if (maxUrls == -1) {
    progressBar.setMaximum(crawled + toCrawl);
  } else {
    progressBar.setMaximum(maxUrls);
  }
  progressBar.setValue(crawled);

  matchesLabel2.setText("" + table.getRowCount());
}
```

First, the crawling results are updated to reflect the current URL being crawled, the number of URLs crawled thus far, and the number of URLs that are left to crawl. Take note that the URLs to Crawl field may be misleading. It displays the number of links that have been aggregated and put in the To Crawl queue, not the difference between the specified maximum URLs and the number of URLs that have been crawled thus far. Notice also that when **setText( )** is called with **crawled** and **toCrawl**, it is passed an empty string (" ") plus an **int** value. This is so that Java will convert the **int** values into **String** objects, which the **setText( )** method requires.

Next, the progress bar is updated to reflect the current progress made toward finishing crawling. If the Max URLs to Crawl text field was left blank, which specifies that crawling should not be capped, the **maxUrls** variable will have the value –1. In this case, the progress bar's maximum is set to the number of URLs that have been crawled plus the number of URLs left to crawl. If, on the other hand, a Max URLs to Crawl value was specified, it will be used as the progress bar's maximum. After establishing the progress bar's maximum value, its current value is set. The **JProgressBar** class uses the maximum and current values to calculate the percentage shown in text on the progress bar.

Finally, the Search Matches label is updated to reflect the current number of URLs that contain the specified search string.

The addMatch( ) Method

The **addMatch( )** method is called by the **crawl( )** method each time a match with the search string is found. The **addMatch( )** method, shown here, adds a URL to both the matches table and the log file:

```
// Add match to matches table and log file.
private void addMatch(String url) {
```

```
  // Add URL to matches table.
  DefaultTableModel model =
    (DefaultTableModel) table.getModel();
  model.addRow(new Object[]{url});

  // Add URL to matches log file.
  try {
    logFileWriter.println(url);
  } catch (Exception e) {
    showError("Unable to log match.");
  }
}
```

This method first adds the URL to the matches table by retrieving the table's data model and calling its **addRow( )** method. Notice that the **addRow( )** method takes an **Object** array as input. In order to satisfy that requirement, the **url String** object is wrapped in an **Object** array. After adding the URL to the matches table, the URL is written to the log file with a call to **logFileWriter.println( )**. This call is wrapped in a **try-catch** block; and if an exception is thrown, the **showError( )** method is called to alert the user that an error has occurred while trying to write to the log file.

The verifyUrl( ) Method

The **verifyUrl( )** method, shown here, is used throughout **SearchCrawler** to verify the format of a URL. Additionally, this method serves to convert a string representation of a URL into a **URL** object:

```
// Verify URL format.
private URL verifyUrl(String url) {
  // Only allow HTTP URLs.
  if (!url.toLowerCase().startsWith("http://"))
    return null;

  // Verify format of URL.
  URL verifiedUrl = null;
  try {
    verifiedUrl = new URL(url);
  } catch (Exception e) {
    return null;
  }

  return verifiedUrl;
}
```

This method first verifies that the given URL is an HTTP URL since only HTTP URLs are supported by Search Crawler. Next, the URL being verified is used to construct a new **URL** object. If the URL is malformed, the **URL** class constructor will throw an exception resulting in **null** being returned from this method. A **null** return value is used to denote that the string passed to **url** is not valid or verified.

The isRobotAllowed( ) Method

The **isRobotAllowed( )** method fulfills the robot protocol. In order to fully explain this method, we'll review it line by line.

The **isRobotAllowed( )** method starts with these lines of code:

```
String host = urlToCheck.getHost().toLowerCase();

// Retrieve host's disallow list from cache.
ArrayList disallowList =
  (ArrayList) disallowListCache.get(host);

// If list is not in the cache, download and cache it.
if (disallowList == null) {
  disallowList = new ArrayList();
```

In order to efficiently check whether or not robots are allowed to access a URL, Search Crawler caches each host's disallow list after it has been retrieved. This significantly improves the performance of Search Crawler because it avoids downloading the disallow list for each URL being verified. Instead, it just retrieves the list from cache.

The disallow list cache is keyed on the host portion of a URL, so **isRobotAllowed( )** starts out by retrieving the **urlToCheck**'s host by calling its **getHost( )** method. Notice that **toLowerCase( )** is tacked on to the end of the **getHost( )** call. Lowercasing the host ensures that duplicate host entries are not placed in the cache. Take note that the host portion of URLs is case insensitive on the Internet; however, the cache keys are case-sensitive strings. After retrieving the **urlToCheck**'s host, an attempt to retrieve a disallow list from the cache for the host is made. If there is not a list in cache already, **null** is returned, signaling that the disallow list must be downloaded from the host. The process of retrieving the disallow list from a host starts by creating a new **ArrayList** object.

Next, the contents of the disallow list are populated, beginning with the following lines of code:

```
try {
  URL robotsFileUrl =
    new URL("http://" + host + "/robots.txt");

  // Open connection to robot file URL for reading.
  BufferedReader reader =
    new BufferedReader(new InputStreamReader(
      robotsFileUrl.openStream()));
```

As mentioned earlier, Web site owners wishing to prevent Web crawlers from crawling their site, or portions of their site, must have a file called **robots.txt** at the root of their Web site hierarchy. The host portion of the **urlToCheck** is used to construct a URL, **robotsFileUrl**, pointing to the **robots.txt** file. Then a **BufferedReader** object is created for reading the contents of the **robots.txt** file. The **BufferedReader**'s constructor is passed an instance of **InputStreamReader**, whose constructor is passed the **InputStream** object returned from calling **robotsFileUrl.openStream( )**.

The following sequence sets up a **while** loop for reading the contents of the **robots.txt** file:

```
// Read robot file, creating list of disallowed paths.
String line;
while ((line = reader.readLine()) != null) {
  if (line.indexOf("Disallow:") == 0) {
    String disallowPath =
      line.substring("Disallow:".length());
```

The loop reads the contents of the file, line by line, until the **reader.readLine( )** method returns **null**, signaling that all lines have been read. Each line that is read is checked to see if it has a Disallow statement by using the **indexOf( )** method defined by **String**. If the line does in fact have a Disallow statement, the disallow path is culled from the line by taking a substring of the line from the point where the string "Disallow:" ends.

As discussed, comments can be interspersed in the **robots.txt** file by using a hash (#) character followed by a comment. Since comments will interfere with the Disallow statement comparisons, they are removed in the following lines of code:

```
    // Check disallow path for comments and remove if present.
    int commentIndex = disallowPath.indexOf("#");
    if (commentIndex != - 1) {
      disallowPath =
        disallowPath.substring(0, commentIndex);
    }

    // Remove leading or trailing spaces from disallow path.
    disallowPath = disallowPath.trim();

    // Add disallow path to list.
    disallowList.add(disallowPath);
  }
}
```

First, the disallow path is searched to see if it contains a hash character. If it does, the disallow path is substringed, removing the comment from the end of the string. After checking and potentially removing a comment from the disallow path, **disallowPath.trim( )** is called to remove any leading or trailing space characters. Similar to comments, extraneous space characters will trip up comparisons, so they are removed. Finally, the disallow path is added to the list of disallow paths.

After the disallow path list has been created, it is added to the disallow list cache, as shown here:

```
    // Add new disallow list to cache.
    disallowListCache.put(host, disallowList);
  }
  catch (Exception e) {
    /* Assume robot is allowed since an exception
       is thrown if the robot file doesn't exist. */
    return true;
  }
}
```

The disallow path is added to the disallow list cache so that subsequent requests for the list can be quickly retrieved from cache instead of having to be downloaded again.

If an error occurs while opening the input stream to the robot file URL or while reading the contents of the file, an exception will be thrown. Since an exception will be thrown if the **robots.txt** file does not exist, we'll assume robots are allowed if an exception is thrown. Normally, the error checking in this scenario should be more robust; however, for simplicity and brevity's sake, we'll make the blanket decision that robots are allowed.

Next, the following code iterates over the disallow list to see if the **urlToCheck** is allowed or not:

```
/* Loop through disallow list to see if the
   crawling is allowed for the given URL. */
String file = urlToCheck.getFile();
for (int i = 0; i < disallowList.size(); i++) {
  String disallow = (String) disallowList.get(i);
  if (file.startsWith(disallow)) {
    return false;
  }
}

return true;
```

Each iteration of the **for** loop checks to see if the file portion of the **urlToCheck** is found in the disallow list. If the **urlToCheck**'s file does in fact match one of the statements in the disallow list, then **false** is returned, indicating that crawlers are not allowed to crawl the given URL. However, if the list is iterated over and no match is made, **true** is returned, indicating that crawling is allowed.

The downloadPage( ) Method

The **downloadPage( )** method, shown here, simply does as its name implies: it downloads the Web page at the given URL and returns the contents of the page as a large string:

```
// Download page at given URL.
private String downloadPage(URL pageUrl) {
    try {
        // Open connection to URL for reading.
        BufferedReader reader =
            new BufferedReader(new InputStreamReader(
                pageUrl.openStream()));

        // Read page into buffer.
        String line;
        StringBuffer pageBuffer = new StringBuffer();
        while ((line = reader.readLine()) != null) {
            pageBuffer.append(line);
        }

        return pageBuffer.toString();
    } catch (Exception e) {
    }

    return null;
}
```

Downloading Web pages from the Internet in Java is quite simple, as evidenced by this method. First, a **BufferedReader** object is created for reading the contents of the page at the given URL. The **BufferedReader**'s constructor is passed an instance of **InputStreamReader**, whose constructor is passed the **InputStream** object returned from calling **pageUrl.openStream( )**. Next, a **while** loop is used to read the contents of the page, line by line, until the **reader.readLine( )** method returns **null**, signaling that all lines have been read. Each line that is read with the **while** loop is added to the **pageBuffer StringBuffer** instance. After the page has been downloaded, its contents are returned as a **String** by calling **pageBuffer.toString( )**.

If an error occurs when opening the input stream to the page URL or while reading the contents of the Web page, an exception will be thrown. This exception will be caught by the empty catch block. The **catch** block has purposefully been left blank so that execution will continue to the remaining **return null** line. A return value of **null** from this method indicates to callers that an error occurred.

The removeWwwFromUrl( ) Method

The **removeWwwFromUrl( )** method is a simple utility method used to remove the "www" portion of a URL's host. For example, take the URL:

> http://www.osborne.com

This method removes the "www." piece of the URL, yielding:

> http://osborne.com

Because many Web sites intermingle URLs that do and don't start with "www", the Search Crawler uses this technique to find the "lowest common denominator" URL. Effectively, both URLs are the same on most Web sites, and having the lowest common denominator allows the Search Crawler to skip over duplicate URLs that would otherwise be redundantly crawled.

The **removeWwwFromUrl( )** method is shown here:

```
// Remove leading "www" from a URL's host if present.
private String removeWwwFromUrl(String url) {
  int index = url.indexOf("://www.");
  if (index != -1) {
    return url.substring(0, index + 3) +
      url.substring(index + 7);
  }

  return (url);
}
```

The **removeWwwFromUrl( )** method starts out by finding the index of "://www." inside the string passed to **url**. The "://" at the beginning of the string passed to the **indexOf( )** method indicates that "www" should be found at the beginning of a URL where the protocol is defined (for example, http://www.osborne.com). This way, URLs that simply contain the string "www" are not tampered with. If **url** contains "://www.", the characters before and after "www." are concatenated and returned. Otherwise, the string passed to **url** is returned.

The retrieveLinks( ) Method

The **retrieveLinks( )** method parses through the contents of a Web page and retrieves all the relevant links. The Web page for which links are being retrieved is stored in a large **String** object. To say the least, parsing through this string, looking for specific character sequences, would be quite cumbersome using the methods defined by the **String** class. Fortunately, beginning with Java 2, v1.4, Java comes standard with a regular expression API library that makes easy work of parsing through strings.

The regular expression API is contained in **java.util.regex**. The topic of regular expressions is fairly large, and a complete discussion is beyond the scope of this book. However, because parsing regular expressions is key to Search Crawler, a brief overview is presented here.

An Overview of Regular Expression Processing

As the term is used here, a *regular expression* is a sequence of characters that describes a character sequence. This general description, called a *pattern,* can then be used to find matches in other character sequences. Regular expressions can specify wildcard characters, sets of characters, and various quantifiers. Thus, you can specify a regular expression that represents a general form that can match several different specific character sequences. There are two classes that support regular expression processing: **Pattern** and **Matcher**. You use **Pattern** to define a regular expression. To match the pattern against another sequence, use **Matcher**.

The **Pattern** class defines no constructors. Instead, a pattern is created by calling the **compile( )** factory method. The form used here is

    static Pattern compile(String *pattern,* int *options*)

Here, *pattern* is the regular expression that you want to use, and *options* specifies one or more options that affect matching. The option used by Search Crawler is **Pattern.CASE_INSENSITIVE**, which causes the case of the strings to be ignored. The **compile( )** method transforms the string in *pattern* into a pattern that can be used for pattern matching by the **Matcher** class. It returns a **Pattern** object that contains the pattern.

Once you have created a **Pattern** object, you will use it to create a **Matcher**. This is done by calling the **matcher( )** factory method defined by **Pattern**. It is shown here:

    Matcher matcher(CharSequence *str*)

Here, *str* is the character sequence that the pattern will be matched against. This is called the *input sequence.* **CharSequence** is an interface that was added by Java 2, v1.4 and defines a read-only set of characters. It is implemented by the **String** class, among others. Thus, you can pass a string to **matcher( )**.

You will use methods defined by **Matcher** to perform various pattern-matching operations. The ones used by **retrieveLinks( )** are **find( )** and **group( )**. The **find( )** method determines if a subsequence of the input sequence matches the pattern. The version used by Search Crawler is shown here:

    boolean find( )

It returns **true** if there is a matching subsequence and **false** otherwise. This method can be called repeatedly, allowing it to find all matching subsequences. Each call to **find( )** begins where the previous one left off.

You can obtain a string containing a matching sequence by calling **group( )**. The form used by Search Crawler is shown here:

> String group(int *which*)

Here, *which* specifies the sequence (group of characters), with the first group being 1. The matching string is returned.

Regular Expression Syntax

The syntax and rules that define a regular expression are similar to those used by Perl 5. Although no single rule is complicated, there are a large number of them, and a complete discussion is beyond the scope of this book. However, a few of the more commonly used constructs are described here.

In general, a regular expression is comprised of normal characters, character classes (sets of characters), wildcard characters, and quantifiers. A normal character is matched as is. Thus, if a pattern consists of "xy", the only input sequence that will match it is "xy". Characters such as newlines and tabs are specified using the standard escape sequences, which begin with a backslash (\). For example, a newline is specified by **\n**. In the language of regular expressions, a normal character is also called a *literal*.

A character class is a set of characters. A character class is specified by putting the characters in the class between brackets. For example, the class **[wxyz]** matches w, x, y, or z. To specify an inverted set, precede the characters with a circumflex (^). For example, **[^wxyz]** matches any character except w, x, y, or z. You can specify a range of characters using a hyphen. For example, to specify a character class that will match the digits 1 through 9, use **[1–9]**.

The wildcard character is the dot (**.**), and it matches any character. Thus, a pattern that consists of "." will match these (and other) input sequences: "A", "a", "x", and so on.

A quantifier determines how many times an expression is matched. The quantifiers are shown here:

+	Match one or more.
*	Match zero or more.
?	Match zero or one.

For example, the pattern **"x+"** will match **"x"**, **"xx"**, and **"xxx"**, among others.

A Close Look at retrieveLinks( )

The **retrieveLinks( )** method uses the regular expression API to obtain the links from a page. It begins with these lines of code:

```
// Compile link matching pattern.
Pattern p =
  Pattern.compile("<a\\s+href\\s*=\\s*\"?(.*?)[\"|>]",
    Pattern.CASE_INSENSITIVE);
Matcher m = p.matcher(pageContents);
```

The regular expression used to obtain links can be broken down as a series of steps, as shown in the following table:

Character Sequence	Explanation
<a	Look for the characters "<a".
\\s+	Look for one or more space characters.
href	Look for the characters "href".
\\s*	Look for zero or more space characters.
=	Look for the character "=".
\\s*	Look for zero or more space characters.
\"?	Look for zero or one quote character.
(.*?)	Look for zero or more of any character until the next part of the pattern is matched, and place the results in a group.
[\"|>]	Look for quote character or greater than (">") character.

Notice that **Pattern.CASE_INSENSITIVE** is passed to the pattern compiler. As mentioned, this indicates that the pattern should ignore case when searching for matches.

Next, a list to hold the links is created, and the search for the links begins, as shown here:

```
// Create list of link matches.
ArrayList linkList = new ArrayList();
while (m.find()) {
  String link = m.group(1).trim();
```

Each link is found by cycling through **m** with a **while** loop. The **find( )** method of **Matcher** returns **true** until no more matches are found. Each match (link) found is retrieved by calling the **group( )** method defined by **Matcher**. Notice that **group( )** takes 1 as an argument. This specifies that the first group from the matching sequences be returned. Notice also that **trim( )** is called on the return value from the **group( )** method. This removes any unnecessary leading or trailing space from the value.

Many of the links found in Web pages are not suited for crawling. The following code filters out several links that the Search Crawler is uninterested in:

```
// Skip empty links.
if (link.length() < 1) {
  continue;
}

// Skip links that are just page anchors.
if (link.charAt(0) == '#') {
  continue;
}

// Skip mailto links.
```

```
if (link.indexOf("mailto:") != -1) {
  continue;
}

// Skip JavaScript links.
if (link.toLowerCase().indexOf("javascript") != -1) {
  continue;
}
```

First, empty links are skipped so as not to waste any more time on them. Second, links that are simply anchors into a page are skipped by checking to see if the first character of the link is a hash (#).

Page anchors allow for links to be made to a certain section of a page. Take, for example, this URL:

> http://osborne.com/#contact

This URL has an anchor to the "contact" section of the page located at http://osborne.com. Links inside the page at http://osborne.com can reference the section relatively as just "#contact". Since anchors are not links to "new" pages, they are skipped over.

Next, "mailto" links are skipped. Mailto links are used for specifying an e-mail link in a Web page. For example, the link

> mailto:books@osborne.com

is a mailto link. Since mailto links don't point to Web pages and cannot be crawled, they are skipped over. Finally, JavaScript links are skipped. JavaScript is a scripting language that can be embedded in Web pages for adding interactive functionality to the page. Additionally, JavaScript functionality can be accessed from links. Similar to mailto links, JavaScript links cannot be crawled; thus they are overlooked.

As you've just seen, the links in Web pages can take many formats, such as mailto and JavaScript formats. Additionally, traditional links inside Web pages can take a few different formats as well. Following are the three formats that traditional links can take:

▶   http://osborne.com/books/ArtofJava

▶   /books/ArtofJava

▶   books/ArtofJava

The first of the three links shown here is considered to be a fully qualified URL. The second example is a shortened version of the first URL, omitting the "host" portion of the URL. Notice the slash (/) at the beginning of the URL. The slash indicates that the URL is what's called "absolute." *Absolute URLs* are URLs that start at the root of a Web site. The third example is again a shortened version of the first URL, omitting the "host" portion of the URL. Notice that this third example does not have the leading slash. Since the leading slash is absent, the URL is considered to be "relative." *Relative,* in the realm of URLs, means that the URL address is relative to the URL on which the link is found.

The lines of code in the next section handle converting absolute and relative links into fully qualified URLs:

```
// Prefix absolute and relative URLs if necessary.
if (link.indexOf("://") == -1) {
  // Handle absolute URLs.
  if (link.charAt(0) == '/') {
    link = "http://" + pageUrl.getHost() + link;
  // Handle relative URLs.
  } else {
    String file = pageUrl.getFile();
    if (file.indexOf('/') == -1) {
      link = "http://" + pageUrl.getHost() + "/" + link;
    } else {
      String path =
        file.substring(0, file.lastIndexOf('/') + 1);
      link = "http://" + pageUrl.getHost() + path + link;
    }
  }
}
```

First, the link is checked to see whether or not it is fully qualified by looking for the presence of "://" in the link. If these characters exist, the URL is assumed to be fully qualified. However, if they are not present, the link is converted to a fully qualified URL. As discussed, links beginning with a slash (/) are absolute, so this code adds "http://" and the current page's URL host to the link to fully qualify it. Relative links are converted here in a similar fashion.

For relative links, the current page URL's filename is taken and checked to see if it contains a slash (/). A slash in the filename indicates that the file is in a directory hierarchy. For example, a file may look like this:

   dir1/dir2/file.html

or simply like this:

   file.html

In the latter case, "http://", the current page's URL host, and "/" are added to the link since the current page is at the root of the Web site. In the former case, the "path" (or directory) portion of the filename is retrieved to create the fully qualified URL. This case concatenates "http://", the current page's URL host, the path, and the link together to create a fully qualified URL.

Next, page anchors and "www" are removed from the fully qualified link:

```
// Remove anchors from link.
int index = link.indexOf('#');
if (index != -1) {
  link = link.substring(0, index);
}


// Remove leading "www" from URL's host if present.
link = removeWwwFromUrl(link);
```

For the same reason that anchor-only links are skipped over, links with anchors tacked on to the end are skipped over. The leading "www" is also removed from links so that duplicate links are skipped over later in this method.

Next, the link is verified to make sure it is a valid URL:

```
// Verify link and skip if invalid.
URL verifiedLink = verifyUrl(link);
if (verifiedLink == null) {
  continue;
}
```

After validating that the link is a URL, the following code checks to see if the link's host is the same as the one specified by Start URL and checks to see if the link has already been crawled:

```
/* If specified, limit links to those
   having the same host as the start URL. */
if (limitHost &&
    !pageUrl.getHost().toLowerCase().equals(
      verifiedLink.getHost().toLowerCase()))
{
  continue;
}

// Skip link if it has already been crawled.
if (crawledList.contains(link)) {
  continue;
}
```

Finally, the **retrieveLinks( )** method ends by adding each link that passes all filters to the link list.

```
  // Add link to list.
  linkList.add(link);
```

```
}

return (linkList);
```

After the **while** loop finishes and all links have been added to the link list, the link list is returned.

The searchStringMatches( ) Method

The **searchStringMatches( )** method, shown here, is used to search through the contents of a Web page downloaded during crawling, determining whether or not the specified search string is present in the page:

```
/* Determine whether or not search string is
   present in the given page contents. */
private boolean searchStringMatches(
  String pageContents, String searchString,
  boolean caseSensitive)
{
  String searchContents = pageContents;

  /* If case-sensitive search, lowercase
     page contents before comparison. */
  if (!caseSensitive) {
    searchContents = pageContents.toLowerCase();
  }

  // Split search string into individual terms.
  Pattern p = Pattern.compile("[\\s]+");
  String[] terms = p.split(searchString);

  // Check to see if each term matches.
  for (int i = 0; i < terms.length; i++) {
    if (caseSensitive) {
      if (searchContents.indexOf(terms[i]) == -1) {
        return false;
      }
    } else {
      if (searchContents.indexOf(terms[i].toLowerCase()) == -1) {
        return false;
      }
    }
  }

  return true;
}
```

Because the search string can be either case insensitive (default) or case sensitive, **searchStringMatches( )** starts out by declaring a local variable, **searchContents**, that refers to the string to be searched. By default, the **pageContents** variable is assigned to **searchContents**. If the search is case sensitive, however, the **searchContents** variable is set to a lowercased version of the **pageContents** string.

Next, the search string is split into individual search terms using Java's regular expression library. To split the search string, first, a regular expression pattern is compiled with the **Pattern** object's static **compile( )** method. The pattern used here, "[\\s]+", states that one or more white space characters (that is, spaces, tabs, or newlines) should be matched. Second, the compiled **Pattern**'s **split( )** method is invoked with the search string, which yields a **String** array containing individual search terms.

After breaking the search string up, the individual terms are cycled through, checking to see if each term is found in the page's contents. The **indexOf( )** method defined by **String** is used to search through the **searchContents** variable. A return value of –1 indicates that the search term was not found, and thus **false** is returned since all terms must be found in order to have a match. Notice that if the search is case insensitive, the search term is lowercased in the comparison. This coincides with the value assigned to the **searchContents** variable at the beginning of this method. If the **for** loop executes in its entirety, the **searchStringMatches( )** method concludes by returning **true**, indicating that all terms in the search string matched.

The crawl( ) Method

The **crawl( )** method is the core of the search Web crawler because it performs the actual crawling. It begins with these lines of code:

```
// Set up crawl lists.
HashSet crawledList = new HashSet();
LinkedHashSet toCrawlList = new LinkedHashSet();

// Add start URL to the To Crawl list.
toCrawlList.add(startUrl);
```

There are several techniques that can be employed to crawl Web sites, recursion being a natural choice because crawling itself is recursive. Recursion, however, can be quite resource intensive, so the Search Crawler uses a queue technique. Here, **toCrawlList** is initialized to hold the queue of links to crawl. The start URL is then added to **toCrawlList** to begin the crawling process.

After initializing the To Crawl list and adding the start URL, crawling begins with a **while** loop set up to run until the **crawling** flag is turned off or until the To Crawl list has been exhausted, as shown here:

```
/* Perform actual crawling by looping
   through the To Crawl list. */
while (crawling && toCrawlList.size() > 0)
{
   /* Check to see if the max URL count has
```

```
   been reached, if it was specified.*/
 if (maxUrls != -1) {
   if (crawledList.size() == maxUrls) {
     break;
   }
 }
```

Remember that the **crawling** flag is used to stop crawling prematurely. If the Stop button on the interface is clicked during crawling, **crawling** is set to **false**. The next time the **while** loop's expression is evaluated, the loop will end because the **crawling** flag is **false**. The first section of code inside the **while** loop checks to see if the crawling limit specified by **maxUrls** has been reached. This check is performed only if the **maxUrls** variable has been set, as indicated by a value other than –1.

Upon each iteration of the **while** loop, the following code is executed:

```
// Get URL at bottom of the list.
String url = (String) toCrawlList.iterator().next();

// Remove URL from the To Crawl list.
toCrawlList.remove(url);

// Convert string url to URL object.
URL verifiedUrl = verifyUrl(url);

// Skip URL if robots are not allowed to access it.
if (!isRobotAllowed(verifiedUrl)) {
  continue;
}
```

First, the URL at the bottom of the To Crawl list is "popped" off. Thus, the list works in a first in, first out (FIFO) manner. Since the URLs are stored in a **LinkedHashSet** object, there is not actually a "pop" method. Instead, the functionality of a pop method is simulated by first retrieving the value at the bottom of the list with a call to **toCrawlList.iterator( ).next( )**. Then the URL retrieved from the list is removed from the list by calling **toCrawlList.remove( )**, passing in the URL as an argument.

After retrieving the next URL from the To Crawl list, the string representation of the URL is converted to a **URL** object using the **verifyUrl( )** method. Next, the URL is checked to see whether or not it is allowed to be crawled by calling the **isRobotAllowed( )** method. If the crawler is not allowed to crawl the given URL, then **continue** is executed to skip to the next iteration of the **while** loop.

After retrieving and verifying the next URL on the crawl list, the results are updated in the Stats section, as shown here:

```
// Update crawling stats.
updateStats(url, crawledList.size(), toCrawlList.size(),
```

```
    maxUrls);

// Add page to the crawled list.
crawledList.add(url);

// Download the page at the given URL.
String pageContents = downloadPage(verifiedUrl);
```

The output is updated with a call to **updateStats( )**. The URL is then added to the crawled list, indicating that it has been crawled and that subsequent references to the URL should be skipped. Next, the page at the given URL is downloaded with a call to **downloadPage( )**.

If the **downloadPage( )** method successfully downloads the page at the given URL, the following code is executed:

```
/* If the page was downloaded successfully, retrieve all of its
   links and then see if it contains the search string. */
if (pageContents != null && pageContents.length() > 0)
{
  // Retrieve list of valid links from page.
  ArrayList links =
    retrieveLinks(verifiedUrl, pageContents, crawledList,
      limitHost);

  // Add links to the To Crawl list.
  toCrawlList.addAll(links);

  /* Check if search string is present in
     page, and if so, record a match. */
  if (searchStringMatches(pageContents, searchString,
      caseSensitive))
  {
    addMatch(url);
  }
}
```

First, the page links are retrieved by calling the **retrieveLinks( )** method. Each of the links returned from the **retrieveLinks( )** call is then added to the To Crawl list. Next, the downloaded page is searched to see if the search string is found in the page with a call to **searchStringMatches( )**. If the search string is found in the page, the page is recorded as a match with the **addMatch( )** method.

The **crawl( )** method finishes by calling **updateStats( )** again at the end of the **while** loop:

```
  // Update crawling stats.
  updateStats(url, crawledList.size(), toCrawlList.size(),
    maxUrls);
}
```

The first call to **updateStats( )**, earlier in this method, updates the label that indicates which URL is being crawled. This second call updates all the other values because they will have changed since the first call.

Compiling and Running the Search Web Crawler

As mentioned earlier, **SearchCrawler** takes advantage of Java's new regular expression package: **java.util.regex**. The regular expression package was introduced in JDK 1.4; thus you will need to use JDK 1.4 or later to compile and run **SearchCrawler**.

Compile **SearchCrawler** like this:

```
javac SearchCrawler.java
```

Run **SearchCrawler** like this:

```
javaw SearchCrawler
```

Search Crawler has a simple, yet feature-rich, interface that's easy to use. First, in the Start URL field, enter the URL at which you want your search to begin. Next, choose the maximum number of URLs you want to crawl and whether or not you want to limit crawling to only the Web site specified in the Start URL field. If you want the crawler to continue crawling until it has exhausted all links it finds, you can leave the Max URLs to Crawl field blank. Be forewarned, however, that choosing not to set a maximum value will likely result in a search that will run for a very long time.

Next you'll notice a Matches Log File specified for you. This text field is prepopulated, specifying that the log file be written to a file called **crawler.log** in the directory that you are running the Search Crawler from. If you'd like to have the log file written to a different file, simply enter the new filename. Next, enter the string you want to search for and then select whether or not you want the search to be case sensitive. Note that entering a search string containing multiple words requires matching pages to include all the words specified.

Once you have entered all your search criteria and configured the search constraints, click the Search button. You'll notice that the search controls become disabled and the Search button changes to a Stop button. After searching has completed, the search controls will be reenabled, and the Stop button will revert back to being the Search button. Clicking the Stop button will cause the crawler to stop crawling after it has finished crawling the URL it is currently crawling. Figure 6-2 shows the Search Crawler in action.

A few key points about Search Crawler's functionality:

▶ Only HTTP links are supported, not HTTPS or FTP.

▶ URLs that redirect to another URL are not supported.

▶ Similar links such as "http://osborne.com" and "http://osborne.com/" (notice the trailing slash) are treated as separate unique links. This is because the Search Crawler cannot categorically know that both are the same in all instances.

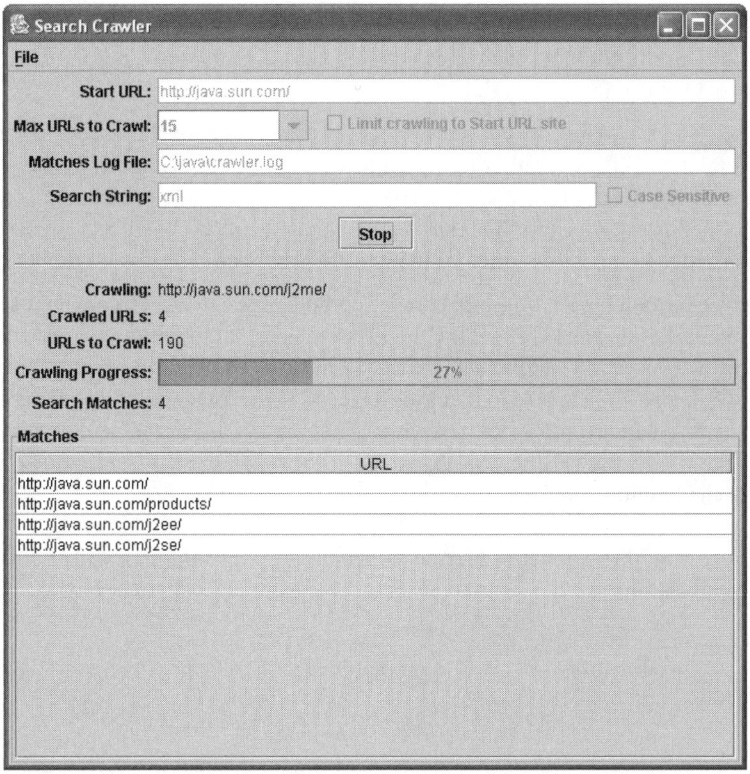

Figure 6-2   *The Search Crawler in action*

Web Crawler Ideas

Search Crawler is an excellent illustration of Java's networking capabilities. It is also an application that demonstrates the core technology associated with Web crawling. As mentioned at the start of this chapter, although Search Crawler is useful as is, its greatest benefit is as a starting point for your own crawler-based projects.

To begin, you might try enhancing Search Crawler. Try changing the way it follows links, perhaps to use depth-first crawling rather than breadth-first. Also try adding support for URLs that redirect to other URLs. Experiment with optimizing the search, perhaps by using additional threads to download multiple pages at the same time.

Next, you will want to try creating your own crawler-based projects. Here are some ideas:

► **Broken Link Crawler**   A broken link crawler could be used to crawl a Web site and find any links that are broken. Each broken link would be recorded. At the end of crawling, a report would be generated listing each page that had broken links along with a breakdown of each broken link on that page. This application would be especially useful for large Web sites where there are hundreds if not thousands of pages to check for broken links.

▶ **Comparison Crawler**   A comparison crawler could be used to crawl several Web sites in an effort to find the lowest price for a list of products. For example, a comparison crawler might visit Amazon.com, Barnes&Noble.com, and a few others to find the lowest prices for books. This technique is often called "screen scraping" and is used to compare the price of many different types of goods on the Internet.

▶ **Archiver Crawler**   An archiver crawler could be used to crawl a site and save or "archive" all of its pages. There are many reasons for archiving a site, including having the ability to view the site offline, creating a backup, or obtaining a snapshot in time of the Web site. In fact, a search engine's use of crawler technology is actually in the capacity of an archiver crawler. Search engines crawl the Internet and save all the pages along the way. Afterward they go back and sift through the data and index it so it can be searched rapidly.

As the preceding ideas show, crawler-based technology is useful in a wide variety of Web-based applications.

Rendering HTML
with Java

By James Holmes

A s all readers know, HTML is at the foundation of the Web. Through the mechanism of hyperlinks, HTML enables text to be organized in nonlinear ways—something that is not possible with the traditional, top-down representation. Because of the power of hyperlinks, HTML is being used in increasing numbers of non-Web-related applications, too. For example, today many Help files use HTML to represent their information. Because of the importance of HTML to the modern computing environment, it is not uncommon to encounter a situation in which the rendering of HTML is either required or desired. In the past, such a task was challenging because of the richness of the HTML command set and the need to process hyperlinks. Fortunately, Java simplifies this task, although not all Java programmers are aware of it.

Support for HTML is included in the Swing framework. This support includes the ability to display (render) HTML and handle hyperlink event notifications. HTML can be rendered by the **JEditorPane** class. Hyperlink events are managed via the **HyperlinkEvent** class and the **HyperlinkListener** interface. Java's built-in support for HTML is a capability that is often overlooked.

This chapter begins by describing how to render HTML by using **JEditorPane** and how to handle hyperlink events. It then demonstrates these capabilities by creating a simple Web browser. Of course, the rendering of HTML is not limited to browsers. You can use the techniques described here whenever you need to display and process HTML.

Rendering HTML with JEditorPane

Swing's **JEditorPane** class makes the rendering of HTML easy. Simply instantiate a **JEditorPane** and then set its content type to "text/html". When displaying HTML, you will also need to disable editing. The following sequence shows the procedure to follow:

```
JEditorPane htmlViewer = new JEditorPane();
htmlViewer.setContentType("text/html");
htmlViewer.setEditable(false);
```

After instantiating a **JEditorPane** instance called **htmlViewer**, **setContentType( )** is called to cause **htmlViewer** to render its content as HTML. Calling **setEditable( )** with a parameter of **false** prevents the contents of the editor pane from being changed. It also allows HTML tags to be rendered rather than displayed as tags. These steps are all that is required to prepare a **JEditorPane** for rendering HTML and are a perfect example of the art of Java!

Once you have prepared a **JEditorPane** for HTML, there are two ways you can load (or display) HTML pages, as shown here:

```
// Method 1.
htmlViewer.setText("<html>Hello World!</html>");

// Method 2.
try {
  htmlViewer.setPage("http://www.dmoz.org/");
```

```
} catch (Exception e) {
  // Handle error here.
}
```

The first method makes a call to **setText( )**, passing in the HTML as a string. The rendered HTML is then displayed. The second method makes a call to **setPage( )**, passing in the URL of a page to display. The browser in this chapter makes exclusive use of the second method.

At the time of this writing, there is one limitation to **JEditorPane**'s capabilities: it supports HTML version 3.2. This means that HTML based on a newer specification will not display correctly. Subsequent releases of Java may change this situation.

CAUTION

*At the time of this writing, **JEditorPane** handles only HTML version 3.2. HTML based on a new version will not be displayed correctly.*

Handling Hyperlink Events

In addition to supporting HTML rendering, Java supports the ability to capture hyperlink events in HTML pages and act on them accordingly. To capture events from HTML being rendered in a **JEditorPane**, a **HyperlinkListener** has to be registered with the **JEditorPane** instance. **HyperlinkListener** defines only one method, **hyperlinkUpdate( )**, which has this general form:

public void hyperlinkUpdate(HyperlinkEvent *event*)

Here, *event* contains the hyperlink event that was generated.

To add a **HyperlinkListener**, use **addHyperlinkListener( )** defined by **JEditorPane**. For example, here is one way to add a **HyperlinkListener** to the **htmlViewer** object created in the previous section:

```
htmlViewer.addHyperlinkListener(new HyperlinkListener() {
  public void hyperlinkUpdate(HyperlinkEvent event) {
    // Handle event here.
  }
});
```

Each time a hyperlink is clicked, a **HyperlinkEvent** is generated and each registered **HyperlinkListener** will be notified by its **hyperlinkUpdate( )** method being called. Typically the **hyperlinkUpdate( )** method implementation consists of code for displaying the clicked link in the **JEditorPane**. This is how the browser in this chapter handles hyperlink updates.

HyperlinkEvent defines four methods that obtain information about the link: **getDescription( )**, **getURL( )**, **getEventType( )**, and **getSourceElement( )**. Each returns the indicated item. The methods used in this chapter are **getURL( )**, which returns a **URL** object corresponding to the link that was clicked, and **getEventType( )**, which returns a

HyperlinkEvent.EventType object that specifies the type of the event. There are three possible event types: **ACTIVATED**, **ENTERED**, and **EXITED**. The only one used here is **ACTIVATED**, which means that a link has been clicked.

Both **HyperlinkEvent** and **HyperlinkListener** are contained in **javax.swing.event**.

Creating a Mini Web Browser

To illustrate the power of Java's built-in HTML-rendering functionality, the remainder of this chapter develops a simple Web browser called Mini Browser. Mini Browser provides basic Web browsing functionality, such as the ability to move forward and back. Because it uses the HTML-rendering capabilities of **JEditorPane**, it supports only HTML 3.2 at the time of this writing; thus there are some pages that it won't display properly if they are built using a newer HTML specification. Although Mini Browser has only minimal browsing functionality, it is easily enhanced. It can also serve as a starting point for your own application development. Figure 7-1 shows Mini Browser's window.

At the top of the window there are buttons for moving back and forward through the list of pages that have been displayed in the browser. There is also a text field for entering the URL of a page to be displayed in the browser. After a URL has been entered in the text field, the Go button is used to load the page in the display part of the window.

Figure 7-1   *The Mini Browser GUI interface*

The MiniBrowser Class

The code for Mini Browser is contained in the **MiniBrowser** class. **MiniBrowser** has a **main( )** method, so on execution it will be invoked first. The **main( )** method instantiates a new **MiniBrowser** object and then calls its **show( )** method, which causes it to be displayed.

The **MiniBrowser** class is shown here and examined in detail in the following sections. Notice that it extends **JFrame** and implements **HyperlinkListener**:

```java
import java.awt.*;
import java.awt.event.*;
import java.net.*;
import java.util.*;
import javax.swing.*;
import javax.swing.event.*;
import javax.swing.text.html.*;

// The Mini Browser.
public class MiniBrowser extends JFrame
  implements HyperlinkListener
{
  // These are the buttons for iterating through the page list.
  private JButton backButton, forwardButton;

  // Page location text field.
  private JTextField locationTextField;

  // Editor pane for displaying pages.
  private JEditorPane displayEditorPane;

  // Browser's list of pages that have been visited.
  private ArrayList pageList = new ArrayList();

  // Constructor for Mini Browser.
  public MiniBrowser()
  {
    // Set application title.
    super("Mini Browser");

    // Set window size.
    setSize(640, 480);

    // Handle closing events.
    addWindowListener(new WindowAdapter() {
```

```
      public void windowClosing(WindowEvent e) {
        actionExit();
      }
    });

    // Set up File menu.
    JMenuBar menuBar = new JMenuBar();
    JMenu fileMenu = new JMenu("File");
    fileMenu.setMnemonic(KeyEvent.VK_F);
    JMenuItem fileExitMenuItem = new JMenuItem("Exit",
      KeyEvent.VK_X);
    fileExitMenuItem.addActionListener(new ActionListener() {
      public void actionPerformed(ActionEvent e) {
        actionExit();
      }
    });
    fileMenu.add(fileExitMenuItem);
    menuBar.add(fileMenu);
    setJMenuBar(menuBar);

    // Set up button panel.
    JPanel buttonPanel = new JPanel();
    backButton = new JButton("< Back");
    backButton.addActionListener(new ActionListener() {
      public void actionPerformed(ActionEvent e) {
        actionBack();
      }
    });
    backButton.setEnabled(false);
    buttonPanel.add(backButton);
    forwardButton = new JButton("Forward >");
    forwardButton.addActionListener(new ActionListener() {
      public void actionPerformed(ActionEvent e) {
        actionForward();
      }
    });
    forwardButton.setEnabled(false);
    buttonPanel.add(forwardButton);
    locationTextField = new JTextField(35);
    locationTextField.addKeyListener(new KeyAdapter() {
      public void keyReleased(KeyEvent e) {
        if (e.getKeyCode() == KeyEvent.VK_ENTER) {
          actionGo();
        }
      }
```

```
    });
    buttonPanel.add(locationTextField);
    JButton goButton = new JButton("GO");
    goButton.addActionListener(new ActionListener() {
      public void actionPerformed(ActionEvent e) {
        actionGo();
      }
    });
    buttonPanel.add(goButton);

    // Set up page display.
    displayEditorPane = new JEditorPane();
    displayEditorPane.setContentType("text/html");
    displayEditorPane.setEditable(false);
    displayEditorPane.addHyperlinkListener(this);

    getContentPane().setLayout(new BorderLayout());
    getContentPane().add(buttonPanel, BorderLayout.NORTH);
    getContentPane().add(new JScrollPane(displayEditorPane),
      BorderLayout.CENTER);
  }

  // Exit this program.
  private void actionExit() {
    System.exit(0);
  }

  // Go back to the page viewed before the current page.
  private void actionBack() {
    URL currentUrl = displayEditorPane.getPage();
    int pageIndex = pageList.indexOf(currentUrl.toString());
    try {
      showPage(
        new URL((String) pageList.get(pageIndex - 1)), false);
    }
    catch (Exception e) {}
  }

  // Go forward to the page viewed after the current page.
  private void actionForward() {
    URL currentUrl = displayEditorPane.getPage();
    int pageIndex = pageList.indexOf(currentUrl.toString());
    try {
      showPage(
        new URL((String) pageList.get(pageIndex + 1)), false);
```

```java
    }
    catch (Exception e) {}
  }

  // Load and show the page specified in the location text field.
  private void actionGo() {
    URL verifiedUrl = verifyUrl(locationTextField.getText());
    if (verifiedUrl != null) {
      showPage(verifiedUrl, true);
    } else {
      showError("Invalid URL");
    }
  }

  // Show dialog box with error message.
  private void showError(String errorMessage) {
    JOptionPane.showMessageDialog(this, errorMessage,
      "Error", JOptionPane.ERROR_MESSAGE);
  }

  // Verify URL format.
  private URL verifyUrl(String url) {
    // Only allow HTTP URLs.
    if (!url.toLowerCase().startsWith("http://"))
      return null;

    // Verify format of URL.
    URL verifiedUrl = null;
    try {
      verifiedUrl = new URL(url);
    } catch (Exception e) {
      return null;
    }

    return verifiedUrl;
  }

  /* Show the specified page and add it to
     the page list if specified. */
  private void showPage(URL pageUrl, boolean addToList)
  {
    // Show hourglass cursor while crawling is under way.
    setCursor(Cursor.getPredefinedCursor(Cursor.WAIT_CURSOR));

    try {
```

```java
      // Get URL of page currently being displayed.
      URL currentUrl = displayEditorPane.getPage();

      // Load and display specified page.
      displayEditorPane.setPage(pageUrl);

      // Get URL of new page being displayed.
      URL newUrl = displayEditorPane.getPage();

      // Add page to list if specified.
      if (addToList) {
        int listSize = pageList.size();
        if (listSize > 0) {
          int pageIndex =
            pageList.indexOf(currentUrl.toString());
          if (pageIndex < listSize - 1) {
            for (int i = listSize - 1; i > pageIndex; i--) {
              pageList.remove(i);
            }
          }
        }
        pageList.add(newUrl.toString());
      }

      // Update location text field with URL of current page.
      locationTextField.setText(newUrl.toString());

      // Update buttons based on the page being displayed.
      updateButtons();
    }
    catch (Exception e)
    {
      // Show error message.
      showError("Unable to load page");
    }
    finally
    {
      // Return to default cursor.
      setCursor(Cursor.getDefaultCursor());
    }
}

/* Update Back and Forward buttons based on
   the page being displayed. */
private void updateButtons() {
```

```
      if (pageList.size() < 2) {
        backButton.setEnabled(false);
        forwardButton.setEnabled(false);
      } else {
        URL currentUrl = displayEditorPane.getPage();
        int pageIndex = pageList.indexOf(currentUrl.toString());
        backButton.setEnabled(pageIndex > 0);
        forwardButton.setEnabled(
          pageIndex < (pageList.size() - 1));
      }
    }


    // Handle hyperlinks being clicked.
    public void hyperlinkUpdate(HyperlinkEvent event) {
      HyperlinkEvent.EventType eventType = event.getEventType();
      if (eventType == HyperlinkEvent.EventType.ACTIVATED) {
        if (event instanceof HTMLFrameHyperlinkEvent) {
          HTMLFrameHyperlinkEvent linkEvent =
            (HTMLFrameHyperlinkEvent) event;
          HTMLDocument document =
            (HTMLDocument) displayEditorPane.getDocument();
          document.processHTMLFrameHyperlinkEvent(linkEvent);
        } else {
            showPage(event.getURL(), true);
        }
      }
    }


    // Run Mini Browser.
    public static void main(String[] args) {
      MiniBrowser browser = new MiniBrowser();
      browser.show();
    }
}
```

The MiniBrowser Variables

MiniBrowser begins by declaring a few instance variables, most of which hold references to the interface controls. First, the **JButton** instances that support the Back and Forward buttons are declared. These buttons are used to navigate through the list of pages visited in the browser. Second, **locationTextField**, which is a reference to a **JTextField**, is declared. Into this text field the user enters the location (or URL) of pages to be displayed in the browser. Next, **displayEditorPane** is declared. This is a reference to the **JEditorPane** instance that will be used to display the Web pages. Finally, **pageList** is declared. It will refer to the list of pages the browser has visited.

The MiniBrowser Constructor

When **MiniBrowser** is instantiated, all the interface controls are initialized inside its constructor. The constructor contains a lot of code, but most of it is straightforward. The following discussion gives an overview.

First, the window title is set. Next, the call to **setSize( )** establishes the window's width and height in pixels. After that, a window listener is added by calling **addWindowListener( )**, passing a **WindowAdapter** object that overrides the **windowClosing( )** event handler. This handler calls the **actionExit( )** method when the window is closed. Next, a menu bar with a File menu is added to the window.

Similar to other applications in this book, the next several lines of the constructor initialize and lay out the interface controls. First, the button panel is set up. The button panel contains the Back, Forward, and Go buttons, along with the location text field. An **ActionListener** is added to each of the buttons so that the corresponding action method is called each time the button is clicked. Similarly, a **KeyAdapter** is added to the location text field so that the **actionGo( )** method is invoked each time the ENTER key is pressed inside the text field.

The editor pane for displaying pages is set up next. There are three things to take note of here. First, the editor's content type is set to "text/html", which causes the editor to display HTML pages. Second, the **setEditable( )** method is passed a **false** flag to indicate that the editor should not allow its contents to be edited, which enables the HTML tags to be rendered. Third, **displayEditorPane.addHyperlinkListener( )** is called to register the browser to receive **HyperlinkEvent**s.

The **MiniBrowser** constructor ends by adding the button panel and editor pane to the interface. Notice that the editor pane is wrapped in a **JScrollPane** instance. This makes the editor pane scrollable.

The actionBack( ) Method

The **actionBack( )** method, shown here, is invoked each time the Back button is clicked and is used for navigating back a page in the list of pages that have been visited in the browser:

```
// Go back to the page viewed before the current page.
private void actionBack() {
  URL currentUrl = displayEditorPane.getPage();
  int pageIndex = pageList.indexOf(currentUrl.toString());
  try {
    showPage(
      new URL((String) pageList.get(pageIndex - 1)), false);
  }
  catch (Exception e) {}
}
```

This method first retrieves the URL of the page currently being displayed in the browser by calling **displayEditorPane.getPage( )**. Next, the page's index in the page list is retrieved by using the **indexOf( )** method of **ArrayList**. It takes an object reference and returns the index for the object in the list. Finally, **showPage( )** is called to display the previous page, which is one page back from the current page. Notice that **false** is passed as the second argument to the **showPage( )** method. This specifies that the page being displayed should not be added to the page list, because it is not a new page and is already in the list. The **showPage( )** call is wrapped in a **try-catch** block because the **URL** constructor can throw an exception if something goes wrong in the creation of the URL from a string. Since all the pages in the page list have already been run through the **verifyUrl( )** method, the **catch** block is left empty.

The actionForward( ) Method

The **actionForward( )** method, shown here, is invoked each time the Forward button is clicked and is used for navigating forward a page in the list of pages that have been visited in the browser:

```
// Go forward to the page viewed after the current page.
private void actionForward() {
  URL currentUrl = displayEditorPane.getPage();
  int pageIndex = pageList.indexOf(currentUrl.toString());
  try {
    showPage(
      new URL((String) pageList.get(pageIndex + 1)), false);
  }
  catch (Exception e) {}
}
```

The same as **actionBack( )**, this method first retrieves the URL of the page currently being displayed in the browser by calling **displayEditorPane.getPage( )**. Next, the page's index in the page list is retrieved by using the **indexOf( )** method of **ArrayList**. It then takes an object reference and returns the index for the object in the list. Finally, **showPage( )** is called to display the next page, which is one page forward from the current page. Notice that **false** is passed as the second argument to the **showPage( )** method. This specifies that the page being displayed should not be added to the page list, because it is not a new page and is already in the list. The **showPage( )** call is wrapped in a **try-catch** block because the **URL** constructor can throw an exception if something goes wrong in the creation of the URL from a string. Since all the pages in the page list have already been run through the **verifyUrl( )** method, the **catch** block is left empty.

The actionGo( ) Method

Each time a page URL is entered into the location text field and the Go button is clicked, the **actionGo( )** method is invoked. Additionally, **actionGo( )** is invoked if the ENTER key is entered into the location text field. The **actionGo( )** method is shown here:

```
// Load and show the page specified in the location text field.
private void actionGo() {
```

```
URL verifiedUrl = verifyUrl(locationTextField.getText());
if (verifiedUrl != null) {
  showPage(verifiedUrl, true);
} else {
  showError("Invalid URL");
}
}
```

The **actionGo( )** method starts out by verifying the URL entered into the location text field by calling the **verifyUrl( )** method. The **verifyUrl( )** method returns a **URL** object that has been verified or returns **null** if the URL specified is invalid. If the URL entered is valid, **showPage( )** is called to display the page. Otherwise, an error is presented to the user with a call to **showError( )**.

The showError( ) Method

The **showError( )** method, shown here, displays an error dialog box on the screen with the given message. This method is invoked throughout **MiniBrowser** any time an error condition occurs:

```
// Show dialog box with error message.
private void showError(String errorMessage) {
  JOptionPane.showMessageDialog(this, errorMessage,
    "Error", JOptionPane.ERROR_MESSAGE);
}
```

The verifyUrl( ) Method

The **verifyUrl( )** method, shown here, is used by the **actionGo( )** method to verify the format of a URL. Additionally, this method serves to convert a string representation of a URL into a **URL** object:

```
// Verify URL format.
private URL verifyUrl(String url) {
  // Only allow HTTP URLs.
  if (!url.toLowerCase().startsWith("http://"))
    return null;

  // Verify format of URL.
  URL verifiedUrl = null;
  try {
    verifiedUrl = new URL(url);
  } catch (Exception e) {
    return null;
```

```
    }

    return verifiedUrl;
}
```

This method first verifies that the given URL is an HTTP URL since only HTTP URLs are supported by Mini Browser. Next, the URL being verified is used to construct a new **URL** object. If the URL is malformed, the **URL** class constructor will throw an exception resulting in **null** being returned from this method. A **null** return value indicates that the string passed to **url** is not valid or verified.

The showPage( ) Method

The **showPage( )** method loads and displays pages in Mini Browser's display editor pane. Because it handles much of the action, **showPage( )** is examined line by line. It begins with these lines of code:

```
private void showPage(URL pageUrl, boolean addToList)
{
    // Show hourglass cursor while crawling is under way.
    setCursor(Cursor.getPredefinedCursor(Cursor.WAIT_CURSOR));
```

The method is passed the URL of the page to display and a flag that indicates if the page is to be added to the page list. Next, the cursor is set to the **WAIT_CURSOR** to signify that the application is busy. On most operating systems, the **WAIT_CURSOR** is an hourglass.

After setting the cursor, the specified page is displayed in the editor pane, as shown here:

```
try {
    // Get URL of page currently being displayed.
    URL currentUrl = displayEditorPane.getPage();

    // Load and display specified page.
    displayEditorPane.setPage(pageUrl);

    // Get URL of new page being displayed.
    URL newUrl = displayEditorPane.getPage();
```

Before loading the new page in the editor pane, the URL of the page currently being displayed is recorded. The current page is recorded so that it can be used later in this method if the page being loaded is to be added to the page list. The new page is loaded next. After loading the new page, its URL is recorded so that it also can be used later in this method if it is to be added to the page list.

The next few lines of code check to see if the page passed to **showPage( )** should be added to the page list and, if so, add it to the list:

```
// Add page to list if specified.
if (addToList) {
```

```
    int listSize = pageList.size();
    if (listSize > 0) {
      int pageIndex =
        pageList.indexOf(currentUrl.toString());
      if (pageIndex < listSize - 1) {
        for (int i = listSize - 1; i > pageIndex; i--) {
          pageList.remove(i);
        }
      }
    }
    pageList.add(newUrl.toString());
}
```

If the **addToList** flag is set to **true**, the page being displayed is added to the page list. First, the page list's size is retrieved. If the list has at least one page in it, the index of the page last displayed is retrieved. If this index is less than the size of the list, then all pages in the list after the page last displayed are removed. This is so that there are no longer any more pages to go forward to.

Next, the user interface is updated, as shown here:

```
// Update location text field with URL of current page.
locationTextField.setText(newUrl.toString());

// Update buttons based on the page being displayed.
updateButtons();
```

First, the location text field is updated to reflect the current URL being displayed in the browser. Second, the **updateButtons( )** method is called to enable or disable the Back and Forward buttons based on the position of the current page in the page list.

If an exception is thrown while trying to load the new page, the **catch** block, shown in the following code, is executed:

```
}
catch (Exception e)
{
  // Show error message.
  showError("Unable to load page");
}
```

If an exception occurs, the **showError( )** method is called to display an error message to the user.

The **showPage( )** method wraps up by specifying a **finally** clause for the **try-catch** block. The **finally** clause is used to ensure that the application cursor gets set back to its default state:

```
finally
{
```

```
    // Return to default cursor.
    setCursor(Cursor.getDefaultCursor());
}
```

The updateButtons( ) Method

The **updateButtons( )** method, shown here, updates the state of the Back and Forward buttons
on the button panel based on the position inside the page list of the page currently being
displayed. This method is invoked by the **showPage( )** method each time a page is displayed:

```
/* Update Back and Forward buttons based on
   the page being displayed. */
private void updateButtons() {
  if (pageList.size() < 2) {
    backButton.setEnabled(false);
    forwardButton.setEnabled(false);
  } else {
    URL currentUrl = displayEditorPane.getPage();
    int pageIndex = pageList.indexOf(currentUrl.toString());
    backButton.setEnabled(pageIndex > 0);
    forwardButton.setEnabled(
      pageIndex < (pageList.size() - 1));
  }
}
```

If there are fewer than two pages in the page list, both the Back and Forward buttons are
disabled, giving them a grayed-out appearance. This is because there are no pages to go back
or forward to. However, if there are at least two pages in the page list, each button's state will
be set based on where the page currently being displayed is relative to its position in the page
list. If **pageIndex** is greater than 0, meaning that there are pages in the page list before the
current page, the Back button is enabled. If the **pageIndex** is less than the number of pages
in the page list minus 1 (since the index is 0-based), then the Forward button is enabled.

The hyperlinkUpdate( ) Method

The **hyperlinkUpdate ( )** method is shown next. It fulfills the **HyperlinkListener** interface
contract allowing the **MiniBrowser** class to receive notifications each time a hyperlink event,
such as a hyperlink being clicked, occurs in the display editor pane.

```
// Handle hyperlinks being clicked.
public void hyperlinkUpdate(HyperlinkEvent event) {
  HyperlinkEvent.EventType eventType = event.getEventType();
  if (eventType == HyperlinkEvent.EventType.ACTIVATED) {
    if (event instanceof HTMLFrameHyperlinkEvent) {
      HTMLFrameHyperlinkEvent linkEvent =
        (HTMLFrameHyperlinkEvent) event;
```

```
      HTMLDocument document =
         (HTMLDocument) displayEditorPane.getDocument();
      document.processHTMLFrameHyperlinkEvent(linkEvent);
    } else {
         showPage(event.getURL(), true);
    }
  }
}
```

The **hyperlinkUpdate( )** method is passed a **HyperlinkEvent** object that encapsulates all of the information related to the hyperlink event that has occurred. First, the event's type is checked to see if it is **ACTIVATED**, which specifies that the link has been clicked. Next, the event is checked to see if it is an instance of **HTMLFrameHyperlinkEvent**, which indicates that a link within an HTML frame was clicked. If so, the event is cast to **HTMLFrameHyperlinkEvent** and stored in **linkEvent**. Next, the call to **displayEditorPane .getDocument( )** obtains the document instance associated with the page. In this case, the document is of type **HTMLDocument**. Finally, **processHTMLFrameHyperlinkEvent( )** is called with **linkEvent** as an argument. This process allows links inside of HTML frames to be processed.

If the event is not an **HTMLFrameHyperlinkEvent**, the link is a standard link and its URL is obtained by calling **getURL( )**. The page associated with this URL is then displayed in the editor pane by calling **showPage( )**.

Compiling and Running the Mini Web Browser

Compile **MiniBrowser** like this:

```
javac MiniBrowser.java
```

Run **MiniBrowser** like this:

```
javaw MiniBrowser
```

NOTE

*You must compile and run **MiniBrowser** with a JDK other than 1.4.0. For example, JDK 1.4.2 works fine. Compiling with JDK 1.4.0 causes **JEditorPane** to exhibit erroneous behavior that prevents many Web sites from working with **MiniBrowser**.*

Using Mini Browser is similar to using a full-featured browser. First, enter the URL of the page you want to view and then click the Go button. This will load the specified page in the browser.

After visiting more than one page with Mini Browser, you'll notice that the Back and Forward buttons become enabled. Each of the buttons is independently enabled based on which page is being displayed in the browser relative to the current page's position in the page list. To go back to the previous page viewed, click the Back button. To go forward to the page viewed after the current page, click the Forward button. Figure 7-2 shows Mini Browser in action.

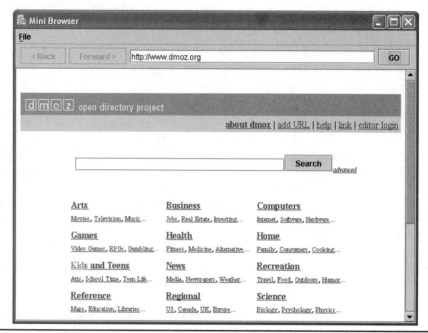

Figure 7-2   *Mini Browser in action*

HTML Renderer Possibilities

The ease with which HTML can be handled by **JEditorPane** opens the door to a number of interesting possibilities. As mentioned at the start of this chapter, representing Help information as HTML is especially useful. Online user documentation is also a good candidate for representation in HTML. For example, you might use HTML to display a tutorial that shows novices how to use an application that you created. Both the Help information and the tutorial can be displayed via **JEditorPane**. Here is one other idea. Try using HTML for error messages. The message could contain hyperlinks to further information.

Statistics, Graphing, and Java

by Herb Schildt

A main use of Java is to create small programs, such as applets or servlets, that process and display data. This data is often in the form of numeric values, such as stock prices, daily temperatures, customer traffic, and so on. It is frequently desirable to obtain and display various statistics relating to this data and to plot the data in a graphic form. For example, an applet might display the average price of a share of stock over the past month and plot the share prices using a bar graph. Because statistics and graphing in one form or another are so often required in Java programming, they are the subject of this chapter.

This chapter develops methods that find the following statistics:

▶   Mean

▶   Median

▶   Mode

▶   Standard deviation

▶   Regression equation (the line of best fit)

▶   Coefficient of correlation

The chapter also develops graphing methods that display the data in a bar graph or scatter graph. The examples found here can be used as is or tailored to fit your own specific needs.

This chapter also utilizes two important aspects of Java: its mathematical processing abilities and its GUI-based graphics abilities. Mathematical computation is not something for which Java was optimized, but it is an area for which Java provides extensive support. Although none of the computations in this chapter are very demanding, they still illustrate the ease with which Java handles number crunching.

Java was, however, designed from the start for GUI-based applications. Java provides a rich assortment of classes that support a window-based interface. As you probably know, Java supports GUIs in two ways: with the Abstract Window Toolkit (AWT) and with Swing. Because Swing is featured prominently in preceding chapters, the AWT is used here. You will see how the AWT can be used to create stand-alone windows and handle resizing, repainting, and other events. Because of features unique to Java, such as inner classes and adaptor classes, GUI-based code in Java is cleaner and smaller than similar code produced by other languages.

Samples, Populations, Distributions, and Variables

Before beginning, it is necessary to define a few key terms and concepts relating to statistics. Generally, statistical information is derived by taking a *sample* of specific data points and then making generalizations from them. Each sample comes from the universe of all possible outcomes for the situation under study, which is called the *population*. For example, you might measure the output of a box factory over the course of one year by generalizing from the Wednesday output figures. In this case, the sample would consist of a year's worth of Wednesday figures.

If the sample is exhaustive, then it equals the population. In the case of the box factory, if the sample included every day's output for a year, then the sample would equal the population.

Whenever the sample is less than the population, there is the possibility for error, and often the error factor can be known. For this chapter, we will be assuming that the sample equals the population, and we will not be concerned with issues surrounding sample errors.

Statistical information is affected by the way events are distributed in the population. Several distributions are possible, but the most common, and the only one we will be using, is the *normal distribution,* or "bell curve," with which you are undoubtedly familiar. In a bell curve, elements are symmetrically distributed around the middle (or peak) of the curve.

In any statistical process, there is a *dependent variable,* which is the number under study, and an *independent variable,* which is the quantity that determines the dependent variable. This chapter uses time for the independent variable—that is, the stepwise incremental passage of events as measured in whole number units. The use of time for the independent variable is quite common. For example, in watching a stock portfolio, you might monitor its value on a daily basis.

The Basic Statistics

At the core of most statistical analysis are three quantities: the *mean,* the *median,* and the *mode.* Each is useful on its own, but combined they paint a fairly clear picture of the characteristics of a sample.

The statistical methods in this chapter assume that the elements that comprise the sample are stored in an array of **double**. All of the statistical methods are **static** methods stored in a class called **Stats**, which is shown in its entirety later in the chapter. Because they are **static**, they can be called without having to create a **Stats** object.

The Mean

The mean is the most commonly used statistic because it is the arithmetic average of a set of values. Thus, the mean is the "center of gravity" of the data. To compute the mean, divide the sum of the elements in the sample by the number of the elements. For example, the sum of these values

   1 2 3 4 5 6 7 8 9 10

is 55. Dividing that value by the number of elements in the sample, which is 10, yields the mean, which is 5.5 in this example. Thus, the formula for finding the mean is

$$M = \frac{1}{N} \sum_{i=1}^{N} D_i$$

Here, D_i represents an element of data, and N is the number of elements in the sample.

The following method called **mean( )** computes the mean of the elements contained in the array referred to by its parameter. The mean is returned.

```
// Return the average of a set of values.
public static double mean(double[] vals) {
```

```
  double avg = 0.0;

  for(int i=0; i < vals.length; i++)
    avg += vals[i];

  avg /= vals.length;

  return avg;
}
```

To use **mean( )**, simply call it with a reference to an array containing a set of values, and the mean is returned.

The Median

The median of a sample is the middle value based on order of magnitude. For example, in the sample set

　　　1 2 3 4 5 6 7 8 9

the median is 5. For samples with an even number of elements, the median is the average of the two middle values. For example:

　　　1 2 3 4 5 6 7 8 9 10

Here, the median is 5.5. For a sample that has a normal distribution, the median and the mean will be similar. However, as the distribution of elements within a sample moves further away from a normal distribution curve, the difference between the median and the mean increases.

An easy way to obtain the median of a sample is first to sort the data and then take the middle value. This is the way the **median( )** method, shown here, works:

```
// Return the median of a set of values.
public static double median(double[] vals) {
  double temp[] = new double[vals.length];

  System.arraycopy(vals, 0, temp, 0, vals.length);

  Arrays.sort(temp); // sort the data

  // Return the middle value.
  if((vals.length)%2==0) {
    // If even number of values, find average
    return (temp[temp.length/2] +
            temp[(temp.length/2)-1]) /2;
  } else return
```

```
      temp[temp.length/2];
}
```

To use **median( )**, simply pass a reference to an array containing the values, and the middle value is returned.

Notice that a copy of the array is made by calling **System.arraycopy( )**. It is the copy that is sorted. The copy, not the original array, must be sorted to avoid changing the order of the original data. The original order is important for displaying the data in graphical form, as well as for certain other statistical measurements.

The Mode

The mode of a sample is the value of the most frequently occurring element. For example, given the sample

1 2 3 3 4 5 6 7 7 7 8 9

the mode is 7 because it occurs more than any other element. The mode may not be unique. For example, given

10 20 30 30 40 50 60 60 70

both 30 and 60 occur twice. Either could be the mode. Such a set is referred to as *bimodal*. A set that has only one mode is called *unimodal*. For the purposes of this book, when a set contains more than one mode, the first one found is used. If no value occurs more often than any other, the sample has no mode.

The following **mode( )** method finds the mode for a set of values:

```
/* Returns the mode of a set of values.
A NoModeException is thrown if no value
   occurs more frequently than any other.
   If two or more values occur with the
   same frequency, the first value is
   returned. */
public static double mode(double[] vals)
    throws NoModeException
{
  double m, modeVal = 0.0;
  int count, oldcount = 0;

  for(int i=0; i < vals.length; i++) {
    m = vals[i];
    count = 0;

    // Count how many times each value occurs.
    for(int j=i+1; j < vals.length; j++)
```

```
        if(m == vals[j]) count++;

    /* If this value occurs more frequently than
       the previous candidate, save it. */
    if(count > oldcount) {
      modeVal = m;
      oldcount = count;
    }
  }

  if(oldcount == 0)
    throw new NoModeException();
  else
    return modeVal;
}
```

The **mode( )** method works by counting the number of times a value occurs within the **vals** array. If it finds a value repeated more often than the previous candidate, that new value is stored in **modeVal**. After the process ends, the mode is contained in **modeVal**, and this is the value returned. For samples having more than one mode, **mode( )** returns the first mode. If the sample contains no mode, a **NoModeException** is thrown. The **NoModeException** class is shown here:

```
// This is the exception thrown by mode()
class NoModeException extends Exception {
  public String toString() {
    return "Set contains no mode.";
  }
}
```

Variance and Standard Deviation

Although a "one number" summary, such as the mean or median, is very convenient, it suffers from the fact that in certain circumstances, it can mislead rather than inform. For example, if a sample has values clustered on the extremes, then the mean and median do not fairly represent the set. Consider this sample:

> 10, 11, 9, 1, 0, 2, 3, 12, 11, 10

The mean is 6.9, but this value is hardly representative of the sample because no value is close to it. The problem with the mean in this case is that it does not convey any information about the variations or spread of the data. To illuminate the mean, it is necessary to know how close each element is to it. In essence, knowing the dispersion of the data helps you better interpret the mean, median, and mode.

To find the variability of a sample, you must compute its *standard deviation*. The standard deviation is derived from the *variance*. Both are values that represent the dispersion of the data. Of the two, the standard deviation is the most important because it can be thought of as the average of the distances between each value in the sample and the mean.

The variance is computed as shown here:

$$V = \frac{1}{N} \sum_{i=1}^{N} (D_i \text{-} M)^2$$

Here, N is the number of elements in the set, M is the mean, and D_i is an individual value from the sample. It is necessary to square the differences of the mean from each element to produce a positive outcome. If the difference were not squared, the result would always be zero.

The standard deviation is derived by finding the square root of the variance. Thus, the formula for the standard deviation is shown here:

$$std = \sqrt{\frac{1}{N} \sum_{i=1}^{N} (D_i \text{-} M)^2}$$

As mentioned, the standard deviation is usually more useful than the variance. Consider the following set:

11 20 40 30 99 30 50

The variance is computed by first finding the mean, which is 40. Next, the average distance each element is from the mean is computed, as shown here:

D_i	$D_i\text{-}M$	$(D_i\text{-}M)^2$
11	−29	841
20	−20	400
40	00	0
30	−10	100
99	59	3481
30	−10	100
50	10	100
	Sum:	5022
	Mean of sum:	717.43

As the chart shows, the average of the squared differences is 717.43. To derive the standard deviation, simply find the square root of that value. The result is approximately 26.78. To interpret the standard deviation, remember that it is the average distance from the mean of each element in the sample.

The standard deviation tells you how representative the mean is of the entire sample. For example, if you owned a candy bar factory and your plant foreman reported that the daily output averaged 2,500 bars last month but that the standard deviation was 2,000, you would have a pretty good idea that the production line needed better supervision!

Here is an important rule of thumb: assuming that the data you are using conforms to a normal distribution, about 68 percent of the data will be within one standard deviation from the mean, and about 95 percent will be within two standard deviations.

The **stdDev( )** method shown next computes the standard deviation of an array of values:

```
// Return the standard deviation of a set of values.
public static double stdDev(double[] vals) {
  double std = 0.0;
  double avg = mean(vals);

  for(int i=0; i < vals.length; i++)
    std += (vals[i]-avg) * (vals[i]-avg);

  std /= vals.length;
  std = Math.sqrt(std);

  return std;
}
```

The Regression Equation

One of the most common uses of statistical information is to make projections about the future. Even though past data does not necessarily predict future events, often such *trend analysis* is still useful. Perhaps the most widely used statistical tool for trend analysis is the *regression equation*. This is the equation of a straight line that best fits the data, and it is often referred to as the *regression line*, the *least square line*, or the *line of best fit*.

Before describing how to find the line of best fit, recall that a line in two-dimensional space has this equation:

$$Y = a + bX$$

Here, X is the independent variable, Y is the dependent variable, a is the Y-intercept, and b is the slope of the line. Therefore, to find a line that best fits a set of values, you must determine the values of a and b.

To find the regression equation, we will use *the method of least squares*. The general idea is to find the line that minimizes the sum of the squares of the deviations between the actual data and the line. To find this equation involves two steps. First, you compute b using the following formula:

$$b = \frac{\sum_{i=1}^{N} (X_i\text{-}M_x)(Y_i\text{-}M_y)}{\sum_{i=1}^{N} (X_i\text{-}M_x)^2}$$

Here, M_x is the mean of the X coordinate, and M_y is the mean of the Y coordinate. Having found b, a is computed by this formula:

$$a = M_y - bM_x$$

Given the regression equation, it is possible to plug in any value for X and find the projected value for Y.

To understand the significance and value of the regression line, consider this example. Assume that a study tracked the average price of a share of stock for XYZ Inc. over a period of ten years. The data collected is shown here:

Year	Price
0	68
1	75
2	74
3	80
4	81
5	85
6	82
7	87
8	91
9	94

The regression equation for this data is

$$Y = 70.22 + 2.55\ X$$

The data and the regression line are shown in Figure 8-1. As the figure shows, the regression line is sloping upward (positively). This indicates an upward trend in stock prices. Notice also that the line closely fits the data. Using this line, one might predict that in year 11 the share price will increase to 98.27. (This is found by substituting 11 for X in the equation and solving for Y.) Of course, such a prediction is only that: a prediction. There is no guarantee that the prediction will come true!

The Correlation Coefficient

Although the regression line in Figure 8-1 seems to indicate an upward trend, we don't know how well this line actually fits the data. If the line and data have only a slight correlation, the regression line is of little interest. If the line fits the data well, it is of much greater value.

The most common way to determine the correlation of the data to the regression line is to compute the *correlation coefficient*, which is a number between -1 and 1. The correlation coefficient represents the amount of deviation from the mean that is explained by the line. This may sound confusing, but it really isn't. The correlation coefficient is related to the

Figure 8-1 A graph of the average share price and regression line

distance each data point is from the line. If the correlation coefficient is 1, the data corresponds perfectly to the line. A coefficient of 0 means that there is no correlation between the line and the data. (In this case, any line would be about as good!) The sign of the correlation coefficient must be set according to the sign of the slope of the regression line, which is b. If the correlation coefficient is positive, it means that there is a direct relationship between the dependent variable and the independent variable. If the correlation coefficient is negative, then an inverse relationship exists.

The formula to find the correlation coefficient is

$$\text{cor} = \frac{\dfrac{1}{N}\sum\limits_{i=1}^{N}(X_i\text{-}M_x)(Y_i\text{-}M_y)}{\sqrt{\dfrac{1}{N}\sum\limits_{i=1}^{N}(X_i\text{-}M_x)^2}\ \sqrt{\dfrac{1}{N}\sum\limits_{i=1}^{N}(Y_i\text{-}M_y)^2}}$$

where M_x is the mean of X and M_y is the mean of Y. The sign is set based on the sign of the slope of the regression line. Generally, an absolute value of 0.81 or greater is considered a strong correlation. It means that about 66 percent of the data fits the regression line. To convert any correlation coefficient into a percentage, simply square it. This squared value is called the *coefficient of determination.*

The **regress( )** method, shown next, computes the regression equation and the correlation coefficient:

```
/* Compute the regression equation and coefficient
   of correlation for a set of values.   The
   values represent the Y coordinate.   The X
   coordinate is time (i.e., ascending increments
   of 1).  */
```

```
public static RegData regress(double[] vals) {
  double a, b, yAvg, xAvg, temp, temp2, cor;
  double vals2[] = new double[vals.length];

  // Create number format with 2 decimal digits.
  NumberFormat nf = NumberFormat.getInstance();
  nf.setMaximumFractionDigits(2);

  // Find mean of Y values.
  yAvg = mean(vals);

  // Find mean of X component.
  xAvg = 0.0;
  for(int i=0; i < vals.length; i++) xAvg += i;
  xAvg /= vals.length;

  // Find b.
  temp = temp2 = 0.0;
  for(int i=0; i < vals.length; i++) {
    temp += (vals[i]-yAvg) * (i-xAvg);
    temp2 += (i-xAvg) * (i-xAvg);
  }

  b = temp/temp2;

  // Find a.
  a = yAvg - (b*xAvg);

  // Compute the coefficient of correlation.
  for(int i=0; i < vals.length; i++) vals2[i] = i+1;
  cor = temp/vals.length;
  cor /= stdDev(vals) * stdDev(vals2);

  return new RegData(a, b, cor, "Y = " +
                     nf.format(a) +  " + " +
                     nf.format(b) + " * X");

  }
}
```

It is important to point out that **regress( )** assumes that the independent variable (X) is time—that is, the stepwise progression of events represented in units of one. The mean of the X values is computed using this sequence:

```
// Find mean of X component.
xAvg = 0.0;
```

```
for(int i=0; i < vals.length; i++) xAvg += i;
xAvg /= vals.length;
```

Here, the values from 0 to the number of elements in the set are summed and then divided by the number of the elements. This yields the average of X.

Because time is used for the X axis, **regress( )** performs what is sometimes called a *time-series analysis*. This is why only a single array of values need be passed. It would be possible to modify **regress( )** to accept two arrays, one containing the Y values and one containing the X values, but this was not necessary for the purposes of this chapter.

The **regress( )** method returns the values of *a* and *b*, a string representation of the regression equation, and the correlation coefficient, contained within a **RegData** object. **RegData** is shown here:

```
// This class holds the regression analysis data.
class RegData {
  public double a, b;
  public double cor;
  public String equation;

  public RegData(double i, double j, double k, String str) {
    a = i;
    b = j;
    cor = k;
    equation = str;
  }
}
```

The Entire Stats Class

All of the statistical methods can be assembled into a class called **Stats**, as shown next. The same file also makes a convenient place to store the **RegData** and **NoModeException** classes.

```
import java.util.*;
import java.text.*;

// This class holds the regression analysis data.
class RegData {
  public double a, b;
  public double cor;
  public String equation;

  public RegData(double i, double j, double k, String str) {
    a = i;
    b = j;
    cor = k;
```

```
    equation = str;
  }
}


// This is the exception thrown by mode()
class NoModeException extends Exception {
  public String toString() {
    return "Set contains no mode.";
  }
}


// A general-purpose statistics class.
public class Stats {
  // Return the average of a set of values.
  public static double mean(double[] vals) {
    double avg = 0.0;

    for(int i=0; i < vals.length; i++)
      avg += vals[i];

    avg /= vals.length;

    return avg;
  }

  // Return the median of a set of values.
  public static double median(double[] vals) {
    double temp[] = new double[vals.length];

    System.arraycopy(vals, 0, temp, 0, vals.length);

    Arrays.sort(temp); // sort the data

    // Return the middle value.
    if((vals.length)%2==0) {
      // If even number of values, find average.
      return (temp[temp.length/2] +
              temp[(temp.length/2)-1]) /2;
    } else return
      temp[temp.length/2];
  }

  /* Returns the mode of a set of values.
     A NoModeException is thrown if no value
     occurs more frequently than any other.
```

```
      If two or more values occur with the
      same frequency, the first value is
      returned. */
public static double mode(double[] vals)
      throws NoModeException
{
  double m, modeVal = 0.0;
  int count, oldcount = 0;

  for(int i=0; i < vals.length; i++) {
    m = vals[i];
    count = 0;

    // Count how many times each value occurs.
    for(int j=i+1; j < vals.length; j++)
      if(m == vals[j]) count++;

    /* If this value occurs more frequently than
       the previous candidate, save it. */
    if(count > oldcount) {
      modeVal = m;
      oldcount = count;
    }
  }

  if(oldcount == 0)
    throw new NoModeException();
  else
    return modeVal;
}

// Return the standard deviation of a set of values.
public static double stdDev(double[] vals) {
  double std = 0.0;
  double avg = mean(vals);

  for(int i=0; i < vals.length; i++)
    std += (vals[i]-avg) * (vals[i]-avg);

  std /= vals.length;
  std = Math.sqrt(std);

  return std;
}
```

```java
/* Compute the regression equation and coefficient
   of correlation for a set of values.  The
   values represent the Y coordinate.  The X
   coordinate is time (i.e., ascending increments
   of 1). */
public static RegData regress(double[] vals) {
  double a, b, yAvg, xAvg, temp, temp2, cor;
  double vals2[] = new double[vals.length];

  // Create number format with 2 decimal digits.
  NumberFormat nf = NumberFormat.getInstance();
  nf.setMaximumFractionDigits(2);

  // Find mean of Y values.
  yAvg = mean(vals);

  // Find mean of X component.
  xAvg = 0.0;
  for(int i=0; i < vals.length; i++) xAvg += i;
  xAvg /= vals.length;

  // Find b.
  temp = temp2 = 0.0;
  for(int i=0; i < vals.length; i++) {
    temp += (vals[i]-yAvg) * (i-xAvg);
    temp2 += (i-xAvg) * (i-xAvg);
  }

  b = temp/temp2;

  // Find a.
  a = yAvg - (b*xAvg);

  // Compute the coefficient of correlation.
  for(int i=0; i < vals.length; i++) vals2[i] = i+1;
  cor = temp/vals.length;
  cor /= stdDev(vals) * stdDev(vals2);

  return new RegData(a, b, cor, "Y = " +
                     nf.format(a) +  " + " +
                     nf.format(b) + " * X");
  }
}
```

Graphing Data

Although statistics are useful by themselves, they don't always give a complete feel for the data. In many cases, it is helpful to see the data displayed in some form of graph. Depicting data in a visual form enables one to spot both correlations and anomalies that might not be immediately apparent simply by reviewing the statistics. A graph also shows at a glance how the data is actually distributed and its variability. Because of the importance of graphs to statistics, three graphing methods are developed here.

In addition to displaying data in a visually useful form, the graphing methods provide a secondary benefit: they illustrate several techniques related to Java's AWT and event handling. As you know, the AWT is part of the core Java class library. It provides support for a graphically oriented, window-based environment—that is, a graphical user interface (GUI). A GUI-based application interacts with the user by handling events, which include everything from keystrokes, to menu selections, to repaint and resizing requests. In the process of developing the graphing methods, we will be dealing with several side issues relating to the GUI environment. For example, a graph must be dynamically scalable because a user might resize the window that contains it.

This chapter develops three types of graphs. The first is a bar graph, the second is a scatter graph, and the third is a scatter graph that includes the regression line. As you will see, much of the code, such as that which scales output, is common to all three.

Scaling Data

To make a plotting method handle arbitrarily sized units, it is necessary to scale the data appropriately. It is also necessary to adjust the scale based on the size of the window in which it is displayed. Furthermore, the data must be scaled dynamically each time the window is repainted because the user might have resized the window.

The process of scaling the data involves finding the ratio between the range of the data and the physical dimensions of the window. Once this ratio is known, data can be plotted by multiplying each element by the ratio, the result of which yields a coordinate within the window. For example, the formula for scaling the Y coordinate is

$$Y' = Y * (\text{width-of-window} / (max - min))$$

where Y' is the scaled value that describes a location within the window.

Although the preceding formula is quite simple, there are complications that occur that relate to the GUI-based environment. For example, the width of the window must be obtained each time the graph is redisplayed because the size of the window might change. Furthermore, the width of the window's border must be subtracted from the overall width of the window. Also, the height and width of the digits used to display the range need to be obtained and accounted for. Thus, the process of scaling data for output requires several steps, but none are particularly complicated.

The Graphs Class

The graphing methods are contained within the **Graphs** class. The **Graphs** class extends **Frame**. Thus, graphs are contained within top-level frame windows. This makes the window resizable and somewhat independent from the application that uses one. For example, you can display a graph and then minimize its window without minimizing the rest of the application.

The **Graphs** class is shown here. Each portion of **Graphs** is examined in detail by the following sections.

```java
import java.awt.*;
import java.awt.event.*;
import java.applet.*;
import java.util.*;

// A general-purpose graph class.
public class Graphs extends Frame {
  // Constants for type of graph.
  public final static int BAR = 0;
  public final static int SCATTER = 1;
  public final static int REGPLOT = 2;

  private int graphStyle;

  /* These specify the amount of space to
     leave between data and borders. */
  private final int leftGap = 2;
  private final int topGap = 2;
  private final int bottomGap = 2;
  private int rightGap; // this value is computed

  // These hold the min and max values of the data.
  private double min, max;

  // Refers to the data.
  private double[] data;

  // Colors used by the graph.
  Color gridColor = new Color(0, 150, 150);
  Color dataColor = new Color(0, 0, 0);

  // Various values used to scale and display data.
  private int hGap;    // space between data points
  private int spread; // distance between min and max data
  private double scale; // scaling factor
  private int baseline; // vertical coordinate of baseline
```

```java
// Location of data area within the window.
private int top, bottom, left, right;

public Graphs(double[] vals, int style) {
  // Handle window-closing events.
  addWindowListener(new WindowAdapter() {
    public void windowClosing(WindowEvent we) {
      setVisible(false);
      dispose();
    }
  });

  // Handle resize events.
  addComponentListener(new ComponentAdapter() {
    public void componentResized(ComponentEvent ce) {
      repaint();
    }
  });

  graphStyle = style;

  data = vals;

  // Sort the data to find min and max values.
  double t[] = new double[vals.length];
  System.arraycopy(vals, 0, t, 0, vals.length);
  Arrays.sort(t);
  min = t[0];
  max = t[t.length-1];

  setSize(new Dimension(200, 120));

  switch(graphStyle) {
    case BAR:
      setTitle("Bar Graph");
      setLocation(25, 250);
      break;
    case SCATTER:
      setTitle("Scatter Graph");
      setLocation(250, 250);
      break;
    case REGPLOT:
      setTitle("Regression Plot");
      setLocation(475, 250);
      break;
```

```
    }

    setVisible(true);
}

public void paint(Graphics g) {

    Dimension winSize = getSize(); // size of window
    Insets ins = getInsets(); // size of borders

    // Get the size of the currently selected font.
    FontMetrics fm = g.getFontMetrics();

    // Compute right gap.
    rightGap = fm.stringWidth("" + data.length);

    // Compute the total insets for the data region.
    left = ins.left + leftGap + fm.charWidth('0');
    top = ins.top + topGap + fm.getAscent();
    bottom = ins.bottom + bottomGap + fm.getAscent();
    right = ins.right + rightGap;

    /* If minimum value positive, then use 0
       as the starting point for the graph.
       If maximum value is negative, use 0. */
    if(min > 0) min = 0;
    if(max < 0) max = 0;

    /* Compute the distance between the minimum
       and maximum values. */
    spread = (int) (max - min);

    // Compute the scaling factor.
    scale = (double) (winSize.height - bottom - top) / spread;

    // Find where the baseline goes.
    baseline = (int) (winSize.height - bottom + min * scale);

    // Compute the spacing between data.
    hGap = (winSize.width - left - right) / (data.length-1);

    // Set the grid color.
    g.setColor(gridColor);

    // Draw the baseline.
```

```
    g.drawLine(left, baseline,
               left + (data.length-1) * hGap, baseline);

    // Draw the Y axis.
    if(graphStyle != BAR)
      g.drawLine(left, winSize.height-bottom, left, top);

    // Display the min, max, and 0 values.
    g.drawString("0", ins.left, baseline+fm.getAscent()/2);

    if(max != 0)
      g.drawString("" + max, ins.left, baseline -
                   (int) (max*scale) - 4);
    if(min != 0)
      g.drawString("" + min, ins.left, baseline -
                   (int) (min*scale)+fm.getAscent());

    // Display number of values.
    g.drawString("" + data.length,
                 (data.length-1) * (hGap) + left,
                 baseline + fm.getAscent());

    // Set the data color.
    g.setColor(dataColor);

    // Display the data.
    switch(graphStyle) {
      case BAR:
        bargraph(g);
        break;
      case SCATTER:
        scatter(g);
        break;
      case REGPLOT:
        regplot(g);
        break;
    }
  }

  // Display a bar graph.
  private void bargraph(Graphics g) {
    int v;

    for(int i=0; i < data.length; i++) {
      v = (int) (data[i] * scale);
```

```
        g.drawLine(i*hGap+left, baseline,
                i*hGap+left, baseline - v);
    }
  }

  // Display a scatter graph.
  private void scatter(Graphics g) {
    int v;

    for(int i=0; i < data.length; i++) {
      v = (int) (data[i] * scale);
      g.drawRect(i*hGap+left, baseline - v, 1, 1);
    }
  }

  // Display a scatter graph with regression line.
  private void regplot(Graphics g) {
    int v;

    RegData rd = Stats.regress(data);

    for(int i=0; i < data.length; i++) {
      v = (int) (data[i] * scale);
      g.drawRect(i*hGap+left, baseline - v, 1, 1);
    }

    // Draw the regression line.
    g.drawLine(left, baseline - (int) ((rd.a)*scale),
            hGap*(data.length-1)+left+1,
            baseline - (int) ((rd.a+(rd.b*(data.length-1)))*scale));
  }
}
```

The Graphs final and Instance Variables

Graphs begins by declaring the following variables:

```
// Constants for type of graph.
public final static int BAR = 0;
public final static int SCATTER = 1;
public final static int REGPLOT = 2;

private int graphStyle;
```

The first three **final static** variables are called **BAR**, **SCATTER**, and **REGPLOT**. These values are used to specify which type of graph you want to display. The style of the graph is stored in **graphStyle**.

Next, variables that hold the width of the gap between the window borders and the start of the area in which data is displayed are declared, as shown here:

```
/* These specify the amount of space to
   leave between data and borders. */
private final int leftGap = 2;
private final int topGap = 2;
private final int bottomGap = 2;
private int rightGap; // this value is computed
```

Three are **final**, but **rightGap** is not because its value depends on the current character width and the number of data items being displayed.

Next the following variables are declared:

```
// These hold the min and max values of the data.
private double min, max;

// Refers to the data.
private double[] data;
```

The **min** and **max** variables hold the minimum and maximum values of the data. The array holding the data is referred to by **data**.

The colors used by the graph are stored in **gridColor** and **dataColor**, shown next:

```
// Colors used by the graph.
Color gridColor = new Color(0, 150, 150);
Color dataColor = new Color(0, 0, 0);
```

The grid color is light green, and the data color is black, but you can change these colors if you want.

Next, variables that hold various scaling-related values are declared, as shown here:

```
// Various values used to scale and display data.
private int hGap;   // space between data points
private int spread; // distance between min and max data
private double scale; // scaling factor
private int baseline; // vertical coordinate of baseline
```

The distance between data points along the X-axis is stored in **hGap**. The number of units between the minimum and maximum values in the data is stored in **spread**. The scaling factor is held by **scale**. The vertical location of the baseline (i.e., the X axis) is stored in **baseline**.

Finally, **top**, **bottom**, **left**, and **right** are declared:

```
// Location of data area within the window.
private int top, bottom, left, right;
```

These variables will define the data area within the window.

The Graphs Constructor

The **Graphs** constructor takes two arguments. The first specifies a reference to the data being displayed. The second is a value that indicates the style of the graph. This value must be **Graph.BAR**, **Graph.SCATTER**, or **Graph.REGPLOT**.

Graphs( ) begins by adding an event listener for the window-closing event, as shown here:

```
// Handle window-closing events.
addWindowListener(new WindowAdapter() {
  public void windowClosing(WindowEvent we) {
    setVisible(false);
    dispose();
  }
});
```

The listener is added by calling **addWindowListener( )**, passing a **WindowAdapter** object that overrides the **windowClosing( )** event handler. Recall that an adapter class provides an empty implementation for all the methods in its corresponding event listener interface. In this specific case, **WindowAdapter** implements the **WindowListener** interface. Because empty implementations for all of the methods specified by **WindowListener** are provided by **WindowAdapter**, we need override only the one in which we are interested, which is **windowClosing( )**.

When the window is closed, the graph window is removed from view by calling **setVisible(false)** and then removed from the system by calling **dispose( )**. These are methods defined by the AWT for **Frame** windows.

Next, an event listener is added that handles window-resize events. This is done by calling **addComponentListener( )**, passing a **ComponentAdapter** object that overrides the **componentResized( )** event handler, as shown here:

```
// Handle resize events.
addComponentListener(new ComponentAdapter() {
  public void componentResized(ComponentEvent ce) {
    repaint();
  }
});
```

When the window is resized, **componetResized( )** calls **repaint( )**, which causes the **paint( )** method to be called. As you will see, **paint( )** dynamically scales the output based on the current window size. Thus, when the window is resized, **paint( )** simply redisplays the graph using the new dimensions.

Next, **graphStyle** is assigned the graph style, and **data** is assigned a reference to the array of data. Then, a temporary copy of the data is created and sorted. From this sorted array, the minimum and maximum values are obtained. The lines of code that accomplish these actions are shown here:

```
graphStyle = style;

data = vals;

// Sort the data to find min and max values.
double t[] = new double[vals.length];
System.arraycopy(vals, 0, t, 0, vals.length);
Arrays.sort(t);
min = t[0];
max = t[t.length-1];
```

The **Graphs** constructor ends with these lines of code:

```
setSize(new Dimension(200, 120));

switch(graphStyle) {
  case BAR:
    setTitle("Bar Graph");
    setLocation(25, 250);
    break;
  case SCATTER:
    setTitle("Scatter Graph");
    setLocation(250, 250);
    break;
  case REGPLOT:
    setTitle("Regression Plot");
    setLocation(475, 250);
    break;
}

setVisible(true);
```

The initial size of the graph window is set to 200 by 120 by calling **setSize( )**. Then, based on **graphStyle**, the title bar is assigned an appropriate title by calling **setTitle( )**, and a screen location is set by calling **setLocation( )**. Finally, the graph window is displayed by calling **setVisible(true)**. This causes **paint( )** to be called to display the window.

The paint( ) method

Much of the work related to displaying a graph takes place in **paint( )**. It performs the following main activities:

▶   Determines the size of the window and the size of the border

- ▶ Obtains the size of the currently selected text font
- ▶ Computes the size of the data area within the window, which is the size of the window less the regions occupied by the window border and insets
- ▶ Computes the scaling factor
- ▶ Computes the Y coordinate of the baseline, which is the X axis
- ▶ Determines the spacing between data points
- ▶ Draws the baseline and the Y axis
- ▶ Displays the maximum and minimum X and Y values
- ▶ Calls the appropriate method to actually plot the data

The comments in **paint( )** describe the action in detail, and much is self-explanatory. However, because of its importance, we will walk through its operation line by line.

The **paint( )** method begins with these two declarations:

```
Dimension winSize = getSize(); // size of window
Insets ins = getInsets(); // size of borders
```

A **Frame** window consists of two general parts: the border, including the title bar and menu bar (if one exists), and the area in which data can be displayed. The size of a window is obtained by calling **getSize( )**. It returns the overall dimensions of the window in the form of a **Dimension** object. A reference to this object is stored in **winSize**. **Dimension** has two fields: **width** and **height**. Thus, the overall size of the window is found in **winSize.width** and **winSize.height**.

To find that part of the window in which data can be displayed, you must subtract the portion of the window that is allocated to the border. To do this, you must call **getInsets( )**. It returns the size of the border in an **Insets** object, which contains these fields: **left**, **right**, **top**, and **bottom**. A reference to this object is stored in **ins**. Recall that the coordinates of the upper-left corner of a window are 0, 0. Thus, the location of the top-left corner of the data area is **ins.left**, **ins.top**, and the location of the bottom-right corner is **winSize.width–right**, **winSize.height–bottom**.

Next, **paint( )** obtains the metrics for the currently selected font, as shown here:

```
// Get the size of the currently selected font.
FontMetrics fm = g.getFontMetrics();
```

The information in **fm** will be used to compute the height and width of the characters used to display the range of the data.

Although the insets determine the maximum region in which data can be displayed, not all is necessarily usable for aesthetic reasons. Often it is more pleasing to leave a small gap between the data and the border. To accomplish this, the data region is further reduced by the values **leftGap**, **topGap**, **bottomGap**, and **rightGap**. The first three of these contain the value 2, but the value of **rightGap** is computed based on the width of the string that contains the number of elements in the set, as shown here:

```
// Compute right gap.
rightGap = fm.stringWidth("" + data.length);
```

Because the string that displays the number of elements is on the far-right side of the baseline, room must be left for it. This is why the font metrics must be obtained by calling **getFontMetrics( )**. Using this object, the method **stringWidth( )** returns the width of the string, which is assigned to **rightGap**.

Next, the total inset for each side is computed by using all the previously obtained values, and the results are stored in **left**, **top**, **right**, and **bottom**, as shown here:

```
// Compute the total insets for the data region.
left = ins.left + leftGap + fm.charWidth('0');
top = ins.top + topGap + fm.getAscent();
bottom = ins.bottom + bottomGap + fm.getAscent();
right = ins.right + rightGap;
```

Notice that room is left for displaying the range of the data.

The next few lines of code compute the scaling factor:

```
/* If minimum value positive, then use 0
   as the starting point for the graph.
   If maximum value is negative, use 0. */
if(min > 0) min = 0;
if(max < 0) max = 0;

/* Compute the distance between the minimum
   and maximum values. */
spread = (int) (max - min);

// Compute the scaling factor.
scale = (double) (winSize.height - bottom - top) / spread;
```

The process begins first by normalizing the values in **min** and **max**. All graphs will set the origin at 0, 0. So, if the minimum value is greater than 0, **min** is set to 0. If the maximum value is less than 0, **max** is set to zero. Next, the spread between **min** and **max** is computed. This value is then used to compute the scaling factor, which is stored in **scale**.

After computing the scaling factor, the location of the baseline can be found by scaling the value of **min**, as shown here:

```
// Find where the baseline goes.
baseline = (int) (winSize.height - bottom + min * scale);
```

If **min** is zero, the baseline is on the lower edge of the window. Otherwise, it is somewhere in the middle, or if all values are negative, the baseline is at the top.

The spacing between data is determined by dividing the width of data area by the number of elements, as shown here:

```
// Compute the spacing between data.
hGap = (winSize.width - left - right) / (data.length-1);
```

Next, the current color is set to **gridColor**, and the X and Y axis and ranges are displayed. The code that accomplishes these tasks is shown here:

```
// Set the grid color.
g.setColor(gridColor);

// Draw the baseline.
g.drawLine(left, baseline,
           left + (data.length-1) * hGap, baseline);

// Draw the Y axis.
if(graphStyle != BAR)
  g.drawLine(left, winSize.height-bottom, left, top);

// Display the min, max, and 0 values.
g.drawString("0", ins.left, baseline+fm.getAscent()/2);

if(max != 0)
  g.drawString("" + max, ins.left, baseline -
               (int) (max*scale) - 4);
if(min != 0)
  g.drawString("" + min, ins.left, baseline -
               (int) (min*scale)+fm.getAscent());

// Display number of values.
g.drawString("" + data.length,
             (data.length-1) * (hGap) + left,
             baseline + fm.getAscent());
```

Notice that the Y axis is not displayed for a bar graph. Also, notice that the maximum range is displayed only if it is not zero, and the minimum range is displayed only if it is not zero. Also notice that the height of a character affects the precise location at which the range of the data is displayed.

Finally, the code shown next sets the color to **dataColor** and calls the appropriate graphing method to actually display the data:

```
// Set the data color.
g.setColor(dataColor);

// Display the data.
switch(graphStyle) {
```

```
case BAR:
  bargraph(g);
  break;
case SCATTER:
  scatter(g);
  break;
case REGPLOT:
  regplot(g);
  break;
}
```

The bargraph( ) Method

The **bargraph( )** method scales each element in the array referred to by **data** and then displays a line whose length is proportional to that data. The line is drawn from the baseline. The **bargraph( )** method is shown here:

```
// Display a bar graph.
private void bargraph(Graphics g) {
  int v;

  for(int i=0; i < data.length; i++) {
    v = (int) (data[i] * scale);

    g.drawLine(i*hGap+left, baseline,
               i*hGap+left, baseline - v);
  }
}
```

Because so much of the work has already been done by **paint( )**, there is nothing for **bargraph( )** to do other than scale each element using the scaling factor and then draw the line. The line begins at the baseline, which is the X axis. The end point is computed by subtracting the scaled value from the **baseline**. Remember, the upper-left corner of a window is 0, 0. Thus, smaller Y values are located higher in the window than are larger Y values. Therefore, the value in **v** is subtracted from **baseline**. The spacing between bars is specified by **hGap**. The X location of each bar is found by multiplying the index of the element by the gap and then adding the offset from the left edge (found in **left**).

The scatter( ) Method

The **scatter( )** method works much like **bargraph( )** except that it plots points rather than lines. It is shown here:

```
// Display a scatter graph.
private void scatter(Graphics g) {
```

```
    int v;

    for(int i=0; i < data.length; i++) {
      v = (int) (data[i] * scale);
      g.drawRect(i*hGap+left, baseline - v, 1, 1);
    }
  }
}
```

The **scatter( )** method scales each element in the array referred to by **data** and then displays a point at the Y position that is proportional to that data.

The regplot( ) Method

Like **scatter( )**, the **regplot( )** method, shown next, plots a scatter graph. The difference is that it then draws the regression line using the regression data by calling **regress( )**:

```
// Display a scatter graph with regression line.
private void regplot(Graphics g) {
  int v;

  RegData rd = Stats.regress(data);

  for(int i=0; i < data.length; i++) {
    v = (int) (data[i] * scale);
    g.drawRect(i*hGap+left, baseline - v, 1, 1);
  }

  // Draw the regression line.
  g.drawLine(left, baseline - (int) ((rd.a)*scale),
             hGap*(data.length-1)+left+1,
             baseline - (int) ((rd.a+(rd.b*(data.length-1)))*scale));
}
```

Notice how the regression line is drawn. In the call to **drawLine( )**, the end points of the line are computed based on the value of **rd.a** and **rd.b**, which correspond to the Y intercept (*a*) and slope of the line (*b*) in the regression equation.

A Statistics Application

With the **Stats** and **Graphs** classes, it is possible to build a simple, yet effective graphics application. The main window of the application is created by the **StatsWin** class, shown here:

```
import java.awt.*;
import java.awt.event.*;
import java.util.*;
```

```java
import java.text.*;

// Process and display statistical data.
public class StatsWin extends Frame
    implements ItemListener, ActionListener  {

  NumberFormat nf = NumberFormat.getInstance();

  TextArea statsTA;
  Checkbox bar = new Checkbox("Bar Graph");
  Checkbox scatter = new Checkbox("Scatter Graph");
  Checkbox regplot = new Checkbox("Regression Line Plot");
  Checkbox datawin = new Checkbox("Show Data");

  double[] data;

  Graphs bg;
  Graphs sg;
  Graphs rp;
  DataWin da;

  RegData rd;

  public StatsWin(double vals[]) {
    data = vals; // save reference to data

    addWindowListener(new WindowAdapter() {
      public void windowClosing(WindowEvent we) {
        shutdown();
      }
    });

    // Create the File menu.
    createMenu();

    // Change to flow layout, centering components.
    setLayout(new FlowLayout(FlowLayout.CENTER));

    setSize(new Dimension(300, 240));
    setTitle("Statistical Data");

    rd = Stats.regress(data);

    // Set the number format to 2 decimal digits.
```

```
      nf.setMaximumFractionDigits(2);


      // Construct output.
      String mstr;
      try {
        // Obtain mode, if there is one.
        mstr = nf.format(Stats.mode(data));
      } catch(NoModeException exc) {
        mstr = exc.toString();
      }

      String str = "Mean: " +
                   nf.format(Stats.mean(data)) + "\n" +
                  "Median: " +
                   nf.format(Stats.median(data)) + "\n" +
                  "Mode: " + mstr + "\n" +
                  "Standard Deviation: " +
                   nf.format(Stats.stdDev(data)) + "\n\n" +
                  "Regression equation: " + rd.equation +
                  "\nCorrelation coefficient: " +
                   nf.format(rd.cor);

      // Put output in text area.
      statsTA = new TextArea(str, 6, 38, TextArea.SCROLLBARS_NONE);
      statsTA.setEditable(false);

      // Add components to window.
      add(statsTA);
      add(bar);
      add(scatter);
      add(regplot);
      add(datawin);

      // Add component listeners.
      bar.addItemListener(this);
      scatter.addItemListener(this);
      regplot.addItemListener(this);
      datawin.addItemListener(this);

      setVisible(true);
   }

   // Handle the Close menu option.
   public void actionPerformed(ActionEvent ae) {
```

```java
    String arg = (String)ae.getActionCommand();

    if(arg == "Close") {
      shutdown();
    }
  }


  // User changed a check box.
  public void itemStateChanged(ItemEvent ie) {
    if(bar.getState()) {
      if(bg == null) {
        bg = new Graphs(data, Graphs.BAR);
        bg.addWindowListener(new WindowAdapter() {
          public void windowClosing(WindowEvent we) {
            bar.setState(false);
            bg = null;
          }
        });
      }
    }
    else {
      if(bg != null) {
        bg.dispose();
        bg = null;
      }
    }

    if(scatter.getState()) {
      if(sg == null) {
        sg = new Graphs(data, Graphs.SCATTER);
        sg.addWindowListener(new WindowAdapter() {
          public void windowClosing(WindowEvent we) {
            scatter.setState(false);
            sg = null;
          }
        });
      }
    }
    else {
      if(sg != null) {
        sg.dispose();
        sg = null;
      }
    }
```

```java
    if(regplot.getState()) {
      if(rp == null) {
        rp = new Graphs(data, Graphs.REGPLOT);
        rp.addWindowListener(new WindowAdapter() {
          public void windowClosing(WindowEvent we) {
            regplot.setState(false);
            rp = null;
          }
        });
      }
    }
    else {
      if(rp != null) {
        rp.dispose();
        rp = null;
      }
    }

    if(datawin.getState()) {
      if(da == null) {
        da = new DataWin(data);
        da.addWindowListener(new WindowAdapter() {
          public void windowClosing(WindowEvent we) {
            datawin.setState(false);
            da = null;
          }
        });
      }
    }
    else {
      if(da != null) {
        da.dispose();
        da = null;
      }
    }
}

// Create the File menu.
private void createMenu()
{
  MenuBar mbar = new MenuBar();
  setMenuBar(mbar);

  Menu file = new Menu("File");
  MenuItem close = new MenuItem("Close");
```

```
    file.add(close);
    mbar.add(file);
    close.addActionListener(this);
  }


  // Shut down the windows.
  private void shutdown() {
    if(bg != null) bg.dispose();
    if(sg != null) sg.dispose();
    if(rp != null) rp.dispose();
    if(da != null) da.dispose();
    setVisible(false);
    dispose();
  }
}
```

The **StatsWin** class extends **Frame** to create a top-level window in which statistical information is displayed. It also includes check boxes that allow the user to display the data in the various graphic formats and to display a window that shows the data. **StatsWin** implements the **ItemListener** and **ActionListener** interfaces.

StatsWin begins by obtaining a **NumberFormat** object. **NumberFormat** is a class that helps format numeric data. **StatsWin** uses it to specify the number of decimal digits that will be displayed for the various statistics.

StatsWin continues by declaring several instance variables that hold references to the various GUI objects used by the class. This includes a text area, four check boxes, and three **Graphs** objects. A reference to a **DataWin** object is stored in **da**. **DataWin** is a window class that displays the data as numerical values and is described later. A reference to the data being analyzed is stored in **data**, and a reference to the regression data is stored in **rd**.

The methods in **StatsWin** are described in turn.

The StatsWin Constructor

StatsWin( ) must be passed a reference to the data being analyzed. It then constructs an object that performs statistical analysis on that data. Most of the code in the constructor is straightforward, but we will briefly walk through its operation.

StatsWin( ) begins by saving a reference to the data. It then adds a window listener that handles window-closing events. When such an event occurs, the **shutdown( )** method is called, which removes all windows opened by **StatsWin**.

Next, **StatsWin( )** creates the File menu by calling **CreateMenu( )**. The file menu contains only one entry: Close. When Close is selected, the application is terminated.

StatsWin( ) then changes the layout manager to centering, flow layout. This is necessary because **Frame** uses border layout by default.

Next, the size and title of the window are set and the regression data is obtained. Then, the number format that will be used to display the statistics is set to two decimal places using this line of code:

```
nf.setMaximumFractionDigits(2);
```

As mentioned earlier, **nf** refers to a **NumberFormat** object. This is an object that can be used to describe the display format of numeric values. The **setMaximumFractionDigits( )** method sets the maximum number of digits displayed after the decimal point. **StatsWin** uses **nf** to format all numeric output. If you want to see more decimal places, simply change the value in the call to **setMaximumFractionDigits( )**.

The next few lines of code create a string that contains the results of the various statistics for the data:

```
// Construct output.
String mstr;
try {
  // Obtain mode, if there is one.
  mstr = nf.format(Stats.mode(data));
} catch(NoModeException exc) {
  mstr = exc.toString();
}

String str = "Mean: " +
             nf.format(Stats.mean(data)) + "\n" +
             "Median: " +
             nf.format(Stats.median(data)) + "\n" +
             "Mode: " + mstr + "\n" +
             "Standard Deviation: " +
              nf.format(Stats.stdDev(data)) + "\n\n" +
             "Regression equation: " + rd.equation +
             "\nCorrelation coefficient: " +
             nf.format(rd.cor);
```

Notice how the string for the mode is obtained. Recall that **mode( )** throws an exception when the sample has no mode. Thus, **mstr** will contain either a string containing the mode or a message signifying that no mode exists.

Once the output string, **str**, has been fully constructed, it is then put into a **TextArea** object referred to by **statsTA**. This object is then set to read-only by calling **setEditable(false)**. Thus, the text area displays the data, but does not allow it to be altered.

The various GUI objects are then added to the window along with their component listeners. Because the text area is read-only, it does not require a listener. Finally, the window is made visible.

The itemStateChanged( ) Handler

Much of the action in **StatsWin** occurs in **itemStateChanged( )**. This method handles changes to the four check boxes. Each time the user checks a box, the window associated with that box is displayed. Each time the user clears a box, the window associated with that box is removed. To understand how this process works, we will examine the code sequence that handles changes to the Bar Graph check box. It is shown here:

```
if(bar.getState()) {
if(bg == null) {
    bg = new Graphs(data, Graphs.BAR);
    bg.addWindowListener(new WindowAdapter() {
      public void windowClosing(WindowEvent we) {
        bar.setState(false);
        bg = null;
      }
    });
  }
}
else {
  if(bg != null) {
    bg.dispose();
    bg = null;
  }
}
```

The state of **bar**, which holds a reference to the Bar Graph check box, is obtained by calling **getState( )**. If the return value is true, then the box is checked; otherwise it is cleared. If the box is checked and if **bg** is **null**, it means that no bar graph window is currently being displayed. In this case, **bg** is assigned a reference to a new **Graphs** object that displays the bar graph. Otherwise, if **bg** is not **null**, then a bar graph window is already being displayed and no other action takes place.

If a new bar graph window is created, a window listener is added that monitors the bar graph window. This listener handles the window-closing event generated by the bar graph window. This means that a **StatsWin** object will receive a notification when the bar graph window is closed. When a close notification is received, the state of the Bar Graph check box is cleared and **bg** is set to **null**.

If the state of **bar** is cleared when an item change event occurs, and if **bg** is not **null**, the window holding the bar graph is removed by calling **dispose( )** and **bg** is set to **null**. This same basic mechanism is used by all four check boxes.

The actionPerformed( ) Method

The **actionPerformed( )** method handles the selection of the Close menu item from the File menu. It simply calls **shutdown( )** to terminate the program.

The shutdown( ) Method

When a **StatsWin** window is closed, the **shutdown( )** method is called. It removes all open windows created by a **StatsWin** object, including the main window and any graph or data windows. Therefore, even though the graphs are displayed in top-level windows, they are removed when the main application is terminated.

The createMenu( ) Method

The **createMenu( )** method constructs the File menu. It begins by creating a **MenuBar** object called **mbar**. It then creates a **Menu** object called **file** to which a **MenuItem** object called **close** is added. Then, the **file** is added to **mbar**. Finally, the **StatsWin** object is added as an action listener for the menu. Thus, the action event generated when the user selects the Close menu item is handled by the **actionPerformed( )** method described earlier.

The DataWin Class

StatsWin uses an object of type **DataWin** to display the raw numeric data that is being analyzed. The **DataWin** class is shown here:

```
import java.awt.event.*;
import java.awt.*;

// Display an array of numeric data.
class DataWin extends Frame {
  TextArea dataTA;

  DataWin(double[] data) {
    addWindowListener(new WindowAdapter() {
      public void windowClosing(WindowEvent we) {
        setVisible(false);
        dispose();
      }
    });

    dataTA = new TextArea(10, 10);
    dataTA.setEditable(false);

    for(int i=0; i < data.length; i++)
      dataTA.append(data[i]+"\n");

    setSize(new Dimension(100, 140));
    setLocation(320, 100);

    setTitle("Data");
    setResizable(false);

    add(dataTA);
```

```
    setVisible(true);
  }
}
```

DataWin extends **Frame** and is also a top-level window. The **DataWin** constructor is passed a reference to the array of data to display. It then constructs a **TextArea** to display the data. The text area is set to read-only and is not resizable. However, it can be minimized.

Putting Together the Pieces

The following program demonstrates **Stats** and **Graphs**:

```
// Demonstrate the Stats and Graphs.
import java.io.*;
import java.awt.*;

class DemoStat {
  public static void main(String args[])
    throws IOException
  {
    double nums[] = { 10, 10, 11, 9, 8, 8, 9,
                      10, 10, 13, 11, 11, 11,
                      11, 12, 13, 14, 16, 17,
                      15, 15, 16, 14, 16 };

    new StatsWin(nums);
  }
}
```

To compile the program, use this command line:

```
javac DemoStat.java DataWin.java StatsWin.java Stats.java Graphs.java
```

To run the program, type

```
javaw DemoStat
```

Notice that **javaw** (rather than **java**) is used to run the application. **javaw** runs the application without requiring a console window. Using **javaw** ensures that the application will shut down correctly when the main window is closed. For Java 2, version 1.4 and later, you could also use **java**, but for earlier versions of Java, such as version 1.3, **javaw** is needed. Figures 8-2 through 8-4 show the statistic classes in action.

One thing that makes this application interesting is the use of resizable, top-level windows to hold the graphs. This technique enables the graphs to be resized dynamically by the user, with the scale of the data automatically adjusted. Also, a graph window can be minimized. This allows it to be removed from the screen but not entirely removed from the system.

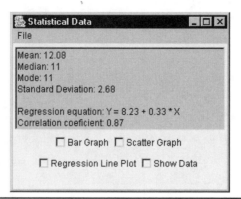

Figure 8-2   *The main StatsWin window*

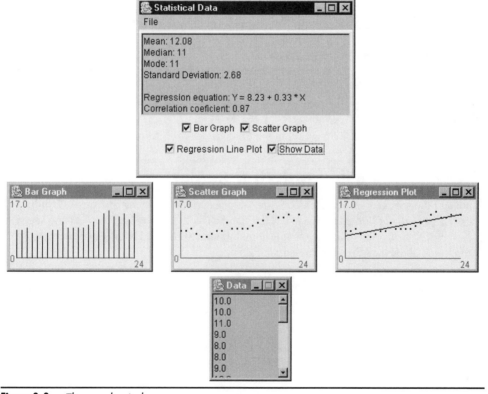

Figure 8-3   *The graph windows*

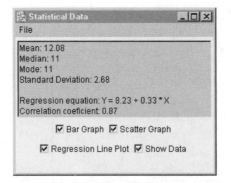

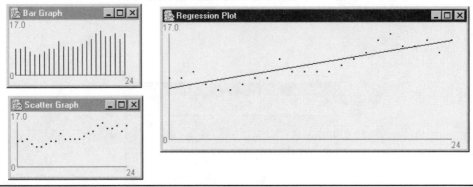

Figure 8-4   *The effects of resizing a graph window*

Creating a Simple Statistical Applet

Although the previous section created a stand-alone application using **Stats** and **Graphs**, these classes are not limited to this use. They can be easily used by both applets and servlets. To see how, consider the following simple applet. It uses **Stats** and **Graphs** to display statistical information about data that it is passed.

```
// A demonstration applet that uses Stats and Graphs.
import java.awt.*;
import java.awt.event.*;
import java.applet.*;
import java.util.*;
/*
  <applet code="StatApplet" width=120 height=50>
  <param name=data value="1.2, 3.6, 5.7, 4.4, 7.1, 4.4,
                          6.89, 8.9, 10.3, 9.45">
  </applet>
*/
```

```java
public class StatApplet extends Applet implements ActionListener {
  StatsWin sw;
  Button show;

  ArrayList al = new ArrayList();

  public void init() {
    StringTokenizer st = new
      StringTokenizer(getParameter("data"), ", \n\r");

    String v;

    // Get the values from the HTML.
    while(st.hasMoreTokens()) {
      v = st.nextToken();
      al.add(v);
    }

    show = new Button("Display Statistics");
    add(show);

    show.addActionListener(this);
  }

  public void actionPerformed(ActionEvent ae) {

    if(sw == null) {
      double nums[] = new double[al.size()];
      try {
        for(int i=0; i<al.size(); i++)
          nums[i] = Double.parseDouble((String)al.get(i));
      } catch(NumberFormatException exc) {
        System.out.println("Error reading data.");
        return;
      }

      sw = new StatsWin(nums);
      show.setEnabled(false);

      sw.addWindowListener(new WindowAdapter() {
        public void windowClosing(WindowEvent we) {
          sw = null;
          show.setEnabled(true);
        }
      });
    }
  }
}
```

Notice that the data is passed to **StatApplet** through an HTML parameter called **data**. This string contains a comma-separated list of values. **StatApplet** uses a **StringTokenizer** to retrieve each individual value in its **String** form. As each value is read, it is added to an **ArrayList** object referred to by **al**. **ArrayList** is a collection class that supports a dynamic array that grows as needed.

When the user presses the Display Statistics button, the **actionPerformed( )** method is executed. Because a **StatsWin** object requires an array of type **double**, not an **ArrayList**, as a parameter, the strings in **al** must be converted into **double** values and copied into an array. After this has been done, a **StatsWin** object is created and the statistics are displayed.

Sample output as produced by the Applet Viewer is shown in Figure 8-5. An applet like this would make a great addition to many Web sites.

Some Things to Try

Here are some ideas that you might want to try. As explained, the graphing methods and the **regress( )** method operate on only one set of data that corresponds to the Y values. The X values are time. You might want to create a second set of these methods that takes two arrays as arguments, with the second array specifying the X values.

You might find it interesting to allow the user to rotate the axes of the graphs, perhaps in real time. You might want to allow the user to specify the width of the bars in the bar graph or the shapes of the points in the scatter graph.

Finally, you might want to experiment with embedding a graph window within the **StatsWin** window instead of making them stand-alone windows. In this approach, you could use the check boxes to determine which type of graph was displayed within the dedicated graph window.

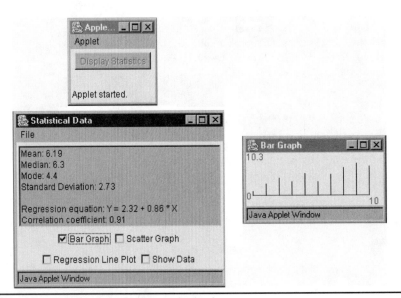

Figure 8-5   *Sample output from the StatApplet applet*

Financial Applets
and Servlets

by Herb Schildt

Despite all the large, sophisticated applications, such as word processors, databases, and accounting packages that dominate much of the computing landscape, there has remained a class of programs that are both popular and small. These perform various financial calculations, such as the regular payments on a loan, the future value of an investment, or the remaining balance on a loan. None of these calculations are very complicated or require much code, yet they yield information that is quite useful.

As most readers will know, Java was initially designed to support the creation of small, portable programs. Originally, these programs took the form of applets, but a few years later servlets were added. (Recall that applets run on the local machine, inside the browser, and servlets execute on the server.) Because of their small size, many of the common financial calculations are right-sized for applets and servlets. Furthermore, including a financial applet/servlet in a Web page is an amenity that many users will appreciate. A user will return again and again to a page that offers the calculation that he or she desires.

This chapter develops a number of applets that perform the financial calculations shown here:

- ▶ Regular payments on a loan
- ▶ Remaining balance on a loan
- ▶ Future value of an investment
- ▶ Initial investment needed to attain a desired future value
- ▶ Annuity from an investment
- ▶ Investment necessary for a desired annuity

These applets can be used as is or tweaked to fit your specific need. The chapter ends by showing how to convert the financial applets into servlets.

Finding the Payments for a Loan

Perhaps the most popular financial calculation is the one that computes the regular payments on a loan, such as a car or house loan. The payments on a loan are found by using the following formula:

$$\text{Payment} = \frac{(\text{intRate} * (\text{principal} / \text{payPerYear}))}{(1 - ((\text{intRate} / \text{payPerYear}) + 1)^{-\text{payPerYear} * \text{numYears}})}$$

where *intRate* specifies the interest rate, *principal* contains the starting balance, *payPerYear* specifies the number of payments per year, and *numYears* specifies the length of the loan in years.

The following applet called **RegPay** uses the preceding formula to compute the payments on a loan given the information entered by the user. Notice that the **RegPay** class extends **Applet** and implements **ActionListener**.

```
// A simple loan calculator applet.
import java.awt.*;
import java.awt.event.*;
import java.applet.*;
import java.text.*;
/*
  <applet code="RegPay" width=280 height=200>
  </applet>
*/

public class RegPay extends Applet
  implements ActionListener {

  TextField amountText, paymentText, periodText,
            rateText;
  Button doIt;

  double principal; // original princial
  double intRate;   // interest rate
  double numYears;  // length of loan in years

  /* Number of payments per year.  You could
     allow this value to be set by the user. */
  final int payPerYear = 12;

  NumberFormat nf;

  public void init() {
    // Use a grid bag layout.
    GridBagLayout gbag = new GridBagLayout();
    GridBagConstraints gbc = new GridBagConstraints();
    setLayout(gbag);

    Label heading = new
          Label("Compute Monthly Loan Payments");

    Label amountLab = new Label("Principal");
    Label periodLab = new Label("Years");
    Label rateLab = new Label("Interest Rate");
    Label paymentLab = new Label("Monthly Payments");

    amountText = new TextField(16);
    periodText = new TextField(16);
    paymentText = new TextField(16);
    rateText = new TextField(16);
```

```
     // Payment field for display only.
     paymentText.setEditable(false);

     doIt = new Button("Compute");

     // Define the grid bag.
     gbc.weighty = 1.0; // use a row weight of 1
     gbc.gridwidth = GridBagConstraints.REMAINDER;
     gbc.anchor = GridBagConstraints.NORTH;
     gbag.setConstraints(heading, gbc);

     // Anchor most components to the right.
     gbc.anchor = GridBagConstraints.EAST;

     gbc.gridwidth = GridBagConstraints.RELATIVE;
     gbag.setConstraints(amountLab, gbc);
     gbc.gridwidth = GridBagConstraints.REMAINDER;
     gbag.setConstraints(amountText, gbc);

     gbc.gridwidth = GridBagConstraints.RELATIVE;
     gbag.setConstraints(periodLab, gbc);
     gbc.gridwidth = GridBagConstraints.REMAINDER;
     gbag.setConstraints(periodText, gbc);

     gbc.gridwidth = GridBagConstraints.RELATIVE;
     gbag.setConstraints(rateLab, gbc);
     gbc.gridwidth = GridBagConstraints.REMAINDER;
     gbag.setConstraints(rateText, gbc);

     gbc.gridwidth = GridBagConstraints.RELATIVE;
     gbag.setConstraints(paymentLab, gbc);
     gbc.gridwidth = GridBagConstraints.REMAINDER;
     gbag.setConstraints(paymentText, gbc);

     gbc.anchor = GridBagConstraints.CENTER;
     gbag.setConstraints(doIt, gbc);

     // Add all the components.
     add(heading);
     add(amountLab);
     add(amountText);
     add(periodLab);
     add(periodText);
     add(rateLab);
     add(rateText);
```

```
    add(paymentLab);
    add(paymentText);
    add(doIt);

    // Register to receive action events.
    amountText.addActionListener(this);
    periodText.addActionListener(this);
    rateText.addActionListener(this);
    doIt.addActionListener(this);

    nf = NumberFormat.getInstance();
    nf.setMinimumFractionDigits(2);
    nf.setMaximumFractionDigits(2);
  }

/* User pressed Enter on a text field or
   pressed Compute. */
public void actionPerformed(ActionEvent ae) {
  repaint();
}

// Display the result if all fields are completed.
public void paint(Graphics g) {
  double result = 0.0;

  String amountStr = amountText.getText();
  String periodStr = periodText.getText();
  String rateStr = rateText.getText();

  try {
    if(amountStr.length() != 0 &&
       periodStr.length() != 0 &&
       rateStr.length() != 0) {

      principal = Double.parseDouble(amountStr);
      numYears = Double.parseDouble(periodStr);
      intRate = Double.parseDouble(rateStr) / 100;

      result = compute();

      paymentText.setText(nf.format(result));
    }

    showStatus(""); // erase any previous error message
```

```java
    } catch (NumberFormatException exc) {
      showStatus("Invalid Data");
      paymentText.setText("");
    }
  }

  // Compute the loan payment.
  double compute() {
    double numer;
    double denom;
    double b, e;

    numer = intRate * principal / payPerYear;

    e = -(payPerYear * numYears);
    b = (intRate / payPerYear) + 1.0;

    denom = 1.0 - Math.pow(b, e);

    return numer / denom;
  }
}
```

The applet produced by this program is shown in Figure 9-1. To use the applet, simply enter the loan principal, the length of the loan in years, and the interest rate. The payments are assumed to be monthly. Once the information is entered, press Compute to calculate the monthly payment.

The following sections examine the code to **RegPay** in detail. Because all the applets in this chapter use the same basic framework, much of the explanation presented here applies to the other applets presented in this chapter.

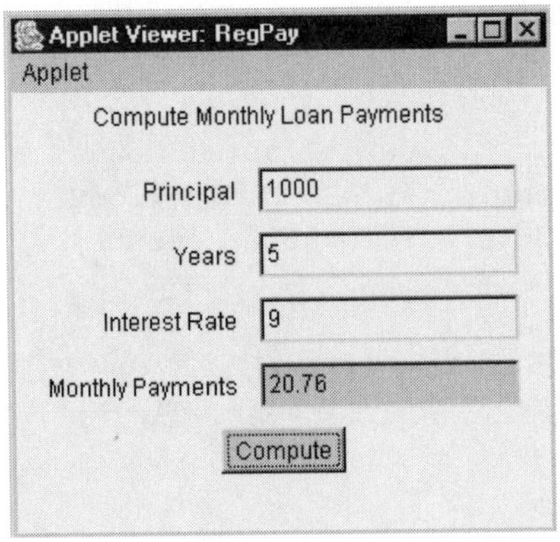

Figure 9-1   *The RegPay applet*

The RegPay Fields

RegPay begins by declaring a number of instance variables that hold references to the text fields into which the user will enter the loan information. Next, it declares the **doIt** variable that will hold a reference to the Compute button.

    RegPay then declares three **double** variables that hold the loan values. The original principal is stored in **principal**, the interest rate is stored in **intRate**, and the length of the loan in years is stored in **numYears**. These values are entered by the user through the text fields. Next, the **final** integer variable **payPerYear** is declared and initialized to 12. Thus, the number of payments per year is hard coded to monthly because this is the way that most loans are paid. As the comments suggest, you could allow the user to enter this value, but doing so will require another text field.

    The last instance variable declared by **RegPay** is **nf**, a reference to an object of type **NumberFormat**, which will describe the number format used for output.

The init( ) Method

Like all applets, the **init( )** method is called when the applet first starts execution. This method performs four main tasks:

1. It changes the layout manager to **GridBagLayout**.
2. It instantiates the various GUI components.
3. It adds the components to the grid bag.
4. It adds action listeners for the components.

    Let's now look at **init( )** line by line. The **init( )** method begins with these lines of code:

```
// Use a grid bag layout.
GridBagLayout gbag = new GridBagLayout();
GridBagConstraints gbc = new GridBagConstraints();
setLayout(gbag);
```

    For many small applets, the default flow layout is perfectly acceptable. However, because the financial applets require the user to enter several values, it is necessary to take a bit more control over how the components are arranged within the applet window. A good way to do this is to use a grid bag layout, which is specified by the **GridBagLayout** class. What makes the grid bag useful is that you can specify the relative placement of components by specifying their positions in a grid. The key to the grid bag is that each component can be a different size, and each row in the grid can have a different number of columns. This is why the layout is called a *grid bag*. It's a collection of small grids joined together.

    The location and size of each component in a grid bag are determined by a set of constraints that are linked to it. The constraints are contained in an object of type **GridBagConstraints**. Constraints include the height and width of a component, its alignment, and its anchor point.

Next, **init( )** creates the label components, text fields, and Compute button, as shown here:

```
Label heading = new
      Label("Compute Monthly Loan Payments");

Label amountLab = new Label("Principal");
Label periodLab = new Label("Years");
Label rateLab = new Label("Interest Rate");
Label paymentLab = new Label("Monthly Payments");

amountText = new TextField(16);
periodText = new TextField(16);
paymentText = new TextField(16);
rateText = new TextField(16);

// Payment field for display only.
paymentText.setEditable(false);

doIt = new Button("Compute");
```

Notice that the text field that displays the monthly payment is set to read-only by calling **setEditable(false)**. This causes the field to be grayed.

Next, the grid bag constraints for each component are set by the following code sequence:

```
// Define the grid bag.
gbc.weighty = 1.0; // use a row weight of 1
gbc.gridwidth = GridBagConstraints.REMAINDER;
gbc.anchor = GridBagConstraints.NORTH;
gbag.setConstraints(heading, gbc);

// Anchor most components to the right.
gbc.anchor = GridBagConstraints.EAST;

gbc.gridwidth = GridBagConstraints.RELATIVE;
gbag.setConstraints(amountLab, gbc);
gbc.gridwidth = GridBagConstraints.REMAINDER;
gbag.setConstraints(amountText, gbc);

gbc.gridwidth = GridBagConstraints.RELATIVE;
gbag.setConstraints(periodLab, gbc);
gbc.gridwidth = GridBagConstraints.REMAINDER;
gbag.setConstraints(periodText, gbc);

gbc.gridwidth = GridBagConstraints.RELATIVE;
gbag.setConstraints(rateLab, gbc);
```

```
gbc.gridwidth = GridBagConstraints.REMAINDER;
gbag.setConstraints(rateText, gbc);

gbc.gridwidth = GridBagConstraints.RELATIVE;
gbag.setConstraints(paymentLab, gbc);
gbc.gridwidth = GridBagConstraints.REMAINDER;
gbag.setConstraints(paymentText, gbc);

gbc.anchor = GridBagConstraints.CENTER;
gbag.setConstraints(doIt, gbc);
```

Although this seems a bit complicated at first glance, it really isn't. Just remember that each row in the grid is specified separately. Here is how the sequence works. First, the weight of each row, contained in **gbc.weighty**, is set to 1. This tells the grid bag to distribute extra space evenly when there is more vertical space than needed to hold the components. Next, the **gbc.gridwidth** is set to **REMAINDER**, and **gbc.anchor** is set to **NORTH**. The label referred to by **heading** is added by calling **setConstraints( )** on **gbag**. This sequence sets the location of **heading** to the top of the grid (north) and gives it the remainder of the row. Thus, after this sequence executes, the heading will be at the top of the window and on a row by itself.

Next, the four text fields and their labels are added. First, **gbc.anchor** is set to **EAST**. This causes each component to be aligned to the right. Next, **gbc.gridWidth** is set to **RELATIVE**, and the label is added. Then, **gbc.gridWidth** is set to **REMAINDER**, and the text field is added. Thus, each text field and label pair occupies one row. This process repeats until all four text field and label pairs have been added. Finally, the Compute button is added in the center.

After the grid bag constraints have been set, the components are actually added to the window by the following code:

```
// Add all the components.
add(heading);
add(amountLab);
add(amountText);
add(periodLab);
add(periodText);
add(rateLab);
add(rateText);
add(paymentLab);
add(paymentText);
add(doIt);
```

Next, action listeners are registered for the three input text fields and the Compute button, as shown here:

```
// Register to receive action events.
amountText.addActionListener(this);
periodText.addActionListener(this);
```

```
rateText.addActionListener(this);
doIt.addActionListener(this);
```

Finally, the number format is set to two decimal digits:

```
nf = NumberFormat.getInstance();
nf.setMinimumFractionDigits(2);
nf.setMaximumFractionDigits(2);
```

The actionPerformed( ) Method

The **actionPerformed( )** method is called whenever the user presses ENTER when in a text field or presses the Compute button. This method simply calls **repaint( )**, which eventually causes **paint( )** to be called.

The paint( ) Method

The **paint( )** method performs three main functions: it obtains the loan information entered by the user, it calls **compute( )** to find the loan payments, and it displays the result. Let's now examine **paint( )** line by line.

After declaring the **result** variable, **paint( )** begins by obtaining the strings from the three user-input text fields using the following sequence:

```
String amountStr = amountText.getText();
String periodStr = periodText.getText();
String rateStr = rateText.getText();
```

Next, it begins a **try** block and then verifies that all three fields actually contain information, as shown here:

```
try {
  if(amountStr.length() != 0 &&
     periodStr.length() != 0 &&
     rateStr.length() != 0) {
```

Recall that the user must enter the original loan amount, the number of years for the loan, and the interest rate. If all three text fields contain information, then the length of each string will be greater than zero.

If the user has entered all the loan data, then the numeric values corresponding to those strings are obtained and stored in the appropriate instance variable. Next, **compute( )** is called to compute the loan payment, and the result is displayed in the read-only text field referred to by **paymentText**, as shown here:

```
principal = Double.parseDouble(amountStr);
numYears = Double.parseDouble(periodStr);
intRate = Double.parseDouble(rateStr) / 100;
```

```
result = compute();

paymentText.setText(nf.format(result));
```

If the user has entered a nonnumeric value into one of the text fields, then
Double.parseDouble( ) will throw a **NumberFormatException**. If this happens, an
error message will be displayed on the status line and the Payment text field will be
emptied, as shown here:

```
  showStatus(""); // erase any previous error message
} catch (NumberFormatException exc) {
  showStatus("Invalid Data");
  paymentText.setText("");
}
```

Otherwise, any previously reported error is removed.

The compute( ) Method

The calculation of the loan payment takes place in **compute( )**. It implements the formula
shown earlier and operates on the values in **principal**, **intRate**, **numYears**, and **payPerYear**.
It returns the result.

NOTE

*The basic skeleton used by **RegPay** is used by all the applets shown in this chapter.*

Finding the Future Value of an Investment

Another popular financial calculation finds the future value of an investment given the initial
investment, the rate of return, the number of compounding periods per year, and the number
of years the investment is held. For example, you might want to know what your retirement
account will be worth in 12 years if it currently contains $98,000 and has an average annual
rate of return of 6 percent. The **FutVal** applet developed here will supply the answer.

To compute the future value, use the following formula:

$$\text{Future Value} = \text{principal} * ((\text{rateOfRet} / \text{compPerYear}) + 1)^{\text{compPerYear} * \text{numYears}}$$

where *rateOfRet* specifies the rate of return, *principal* contains the initial value of the investment,
compPerYear specifies the number of compounding periods per year, and *numYears* specifies
the length of the investment in years. If you use an annualized rate of return for *rateOfRet,*
then the number of compounding periods is 1.

The following applet called **FutVal** uses the preceding formula to compute the future
value of an investment. The applet produced by this program is shown in Figure 9-2.

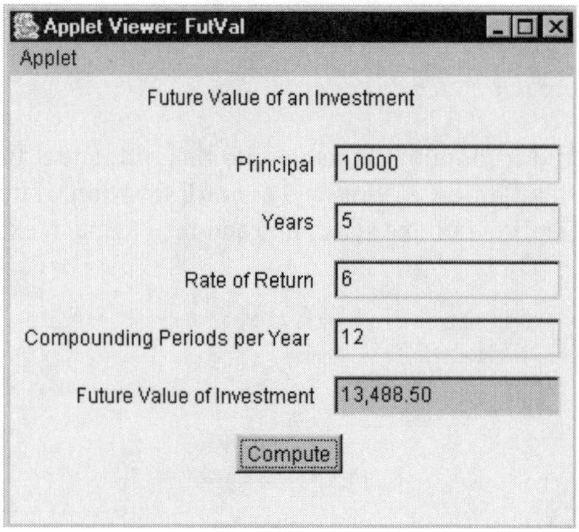

Figure 9-2 *The FutVal applet*

Aside from the computational differences within the **compute( )** method, the applet is similar in operation to the **RegPay** applet described in the preceding section.

```java
// Compute the future value of an investment.
import java.awt.*;
import java.awt.event.*;
import java.applet.*;
import java.text.*;
/*
  <applet code="FutVal" width=340 height=240>
  </applet>
*/

public class FutVal extends Applet
  implements ActionListener {

  TextField amountText, futvalText, periodText,
            rateText, compText;
  Button doIt;

  double principal; // original principal
  double rateOfRet; // rate of return
  double numYears;  // length of investment in years
  int compPerYear;  // number of compoundings per year

  NumberFormat nf;

  public void init() {
```

```
// Use a grid bag layout.
GridBagLayout gbag = new GridBagLayout();
GridBagConstraints gbc = new GridBagConstraints();
setLayout(gbag);

Label heading = new
      Label("Future Value of an Investment");

Label amountLab = new Label("Principal");
Label periodLab = new Label("Years");
Label rateLab = new Label("Rate of Return");
Label futvalLab =
        new Label("Future Value of Investment");
Label compLab =
        new Label("Compounding Periods per Year ");

amountText = new TextField(16);
periodText = new TextField(16);
futvalText = new TextField(16);
rateText = new TextField(16);
compText = new TextField(16);

// Future value field for display only.
futvalText.setEditable(false);

doIt = new Button("Compute");

// Define the grid bag.
gbc.weighty = 1.0; // use a row weight of 1
gbc.gridwidth = GridBagConstraints.REMAINDER;
gbc.anchor = GridBagConstraints.NORTH;
gbag.setConstraints(heading, gbc);

// Anchor most components to the right.
gbc.anchor = GridBagConstraints.EAST;

gbc.gridwidth = GridBagConstraints.RELATIVE;
gbag.setConstraints(amountLab, gbc);
gbc.gridwidth = GridBagConstraints.REMAINDER;
gbag.setConstraints(amountText, gbc);

gbc.gridwidth = GridBagConstraints.RELATIVE;
gbag.setConstraints(periodLab, gbc);
gbc.gridwidth = GridBagConstraints.REMAINDER;
gbag.setConstraints(periodText, gbc);
```

```
        gbc.gridwidth = GridBagConstraints.RELATIVE;
        gbag.setConstraints(rateLab, gbc);
        gbc.gridwidth = GridBagConstraints.REMAINDER;
        gbag.setConstraints(rateText, gbc);

        gbc.gridwidth = GridBagConstraints.RELATIVE;
        gbag.setConstraints(compLab, gbc);
        gbc.gridwidth = GridBagConstraints.REMAINDER;
        gbag.setConstraints(compText, gbc);

        gbc.gridwidth = GridBagConstraints.RELATIVE;
        gbag.setConstraints(futvalLab, gbc);
        gbc.gridwidth = GridBagConstraints.REMAINDER;
        gbag.setConstraints(futvalText, gbc);

        gbc.anchor = GridBagConstraints.CENTER;
        gbag.setConstraints(doIt, gbc);

        add(heading);
        add(amountLab);
        add(amountText);
        add(periodLab);
        add(periodText);
        add(rateLab);
        add(rateText);
        add(compLab);
        add(compText);
        add(futvalLab);
        add(futvalText);
        add(doIt);

        // Register to receive action events.
        amountText.addActionListener(this);
        periodText.addActionListener(this);
        rateText.addActionListener(this);
        compText.addActionListener(this);
        doIt.addActionListener(this);

        nf = NumberFormat.getInstance();
        nf.setMinimumFractionDigits(2);
        nf.setMaximumFractionDigits(2);
    }

    /* User pressed Enter on a text field or
       pressed Compute. */
```

```java
public void actionPerformed(ActionEvent ae) {
  repaint();
}

public void paint(Graphics g) {
  double result = 0.0;

  String amountStr = amountText.getText();
  String periodStr = periodText.getText();
  String rateStr = rateText.getText();
  String compStr = compText.getText();

  try {
    if(amountStr.length() != 0 &&
       periodStr.length() != 0 &&
       rateStr.length() != 0 &&
       compStr.length() != 0) {

      principal = Double.parseDouble(amountStr);
      numYears = Double.parseDouble(periodStr);
      rateOfRet = Double.parseDouble(rateStr) / 100;
      compPerYear = Integer.parseInt(compStr);

      result = compute();

      futvalText.setText(nf.format(result));
    }

    showStatus(""); // erase any previous error message
  } catch (NumberFormatException exc) {
    showStatus("Invalid Data");
    futvalText.setText("");
  }
}

// Compute the future value.
double compute() {
  double b, e;

  b = (1 + rateOfRet/compPerYear);
  e = compPerYear * numYears;

  return principal * Math.pow(b, e);
}
}
```

Finding the Initial Investment Required to Achieve a Future Value

Sometimes you will want to know how large an initial investment is required to achieve some future value. For example, if you are saving for your child's college education and you know that you will need $75,000 in five years, how much money do you need to invest at 7 percent to reach that goal? The **InitInv** applet developed here can answer that question.

The formula to compute an initial investment is shown here:

$$\text{Initial Investment} = \text{targetValue} / (((\text{rateOfRet} / \text{compPerYear}) + 1)^{\text{compPerYear} * \text{numYears}})$$

where *rateOfRet* specifies the rate of return, *targetValue* contains the starting balance, *compPerYear* specifies the number of compounding periods per year, and *numYears* specifies the length of the investment in years. If you use an annualized rate of return for *rateOfRet*, then the number of compounding periods is 1.

The following applet called **InitInv** uses the preceding formula to compute the initial investment require to reach a desired future value. The applet produced by this program is shown in Figure 9-3.

```java
/* Compute the initial investment necessary for
   a specified future value.  */
import java.awt.*;
import java.awt.event.*;
import java.applet.*;
import java.text.*;
/*
  <applet code="InitInv" width=340 height=240>
  </applet>
*/

public class InitInv extends Applet
  implements ActionListener {

  TextField targetText, initialText, periodText,
            rateText, compText;
  Button doIt;

  double targetValue; // original target value
  double rateOfRet;   // rate of return
  double numYears;    // length of loan in years
  int compPerYear;    // number of compoundings per year

  NumberFormat nf;

  public void init() {
    // Use a grid bag layout.
```

```
GridBagLayout gbag = new GridBagLayout();
GridBagConstraints gbc = new GridBagConstraints();
setLayout(gbag);

Label heading = new
      Label("Initial Investment Needed for " +
            "Future Value");

Label targetLab = new Label("Desired Future Value ");
Label periodLab = new Label("Years");
Label rateLab = new Label("Rate of Return");
Label compLab =
        new Label("Compounding Periods per Year");
Label initialLab =
        new  Label("Initial Investment Required");

targetText = new TextField(16);
periodText = new TextField(16);
initialText = new TextField(16);
rateText = new TextField(16);
compText = new TextField(16);

// Initial value field for display only.
initialText.setEditable(false);

doIt = new Button("Compute");

// Define the grid bag.
gbc.weighty = 1.0; // use a row weight of 1

gbc.gridwidth = GridBagConstraints.REMAINDER;
gbc.anchor = GridBagConstraints.NORTH;
gbag.setConstraints(heading, gbc);

// Anchor most components to the right.
gbc.anchor = GridBagConstraints.EAST;

gbc.gridwidth = GridBagConstraints.RELATIVE;
gbag.setConstraints(targetLab, gbc);
gbc.gridwidth = GridBagConstraints.REMAINDER;
gbag.setConstraints(targetText, gbc);

gbc.gridwidth = GridBagConstraints.RELATIVE;
gbag.setConstraints(periodLab, gbc);
gbc.gridwidth = GridBagConstraints.REMAINDER;
gbag.setConstraints(periodText, gbc);
```

```java
    gbc.gridwidth = GridBagConstraints.RELATIVE;
    gbag.setConstraints(rateLab, gbc);
    gbc.gridwidth = GridBagConstraints.REMAINDER;
    gbag.setConstraints(rateText, gbc);

    gbc.gridwidth = GridBagConstraints.RELATIVE;
    gbag.setConstraints(compLab, gbc);
    gbc.gridwidth = GridBagConstraints.REMAINDER;
    gbag.setConstraints(compText, gbc);

    gbc.gridwidth = GridBagConstraints.RELATIVE;
    gbag.setConstraints(initialLab, gbc);
    gbc.gridwidth = GridBagConstraints.REMAINDER;
    gbag.setConstraints(initialText, gbc);

    gbc.anchor = GridBagConstraints.CENTER;
    gbag.setConstraints(doIt, gbc);

    // Add all the components.
    add(heading);
    add(targetLab);
    add(targetText);
    add(periodLab);
    add(periodText);
    add(rateLab);
    add(rateText);
    add(compLab);
    add(compText);
    add(initialLab);
    add(initialText);
    add(doIt);

    // Register to receive action events
    targetText.addActionListener(this);
    periodText.addActionListener(this);
    rateText.addActionListener(this);
    compText.addActionListener(this);
    doIt.addActionListener(this);

    nf = NumberFormat.getInstance();
    nf.setMinimumFractionDigits(2);
    nf.setMaximumFractionDigits(2);
  }

  /* User pressed Enter on a text field
     or pressed Compute. */
```

```java
  public void actionPerformed(ActionEvent ae) {
    repaint();
  }

  public void paint(Graphics g) {
    double result = 0.0;

    String targetStr = targetText.getText();
    String periodStr = periodText.getText();
    String rateStr = rateText.getText();
    String compStr = compText.getText();

    try {
      if(targetStr.length() != 0 &&
         periodStr.length() != 0 &&
         rateStr.length() != 0 &&
         compStr.length() != 0) {

        targetValue = Double.parseDouble(targetStr);
        numYears = Double.parseDouble(periodStr);
        rateOfRet = Double.parseDouble(rateStr) / 100;
        compPerYear = Integer.parseInt(compStr);

        result = compute();

        initialText.setText(nf.format(result));
      }

      showStatus(""); // erase any previous error message
    } catch (NumberFormatException exc) {
      showStatus("Invalid Data");
      initialText.setText("");
    }
  }

  // Compute the required initial investment.
  double compute() {
    double b, e;

    b = (1 + rateOfRet/compPerYear);
    e = compPerYear * numYears;

    return targetValue / Math.pow(b, e);
  }

}
```

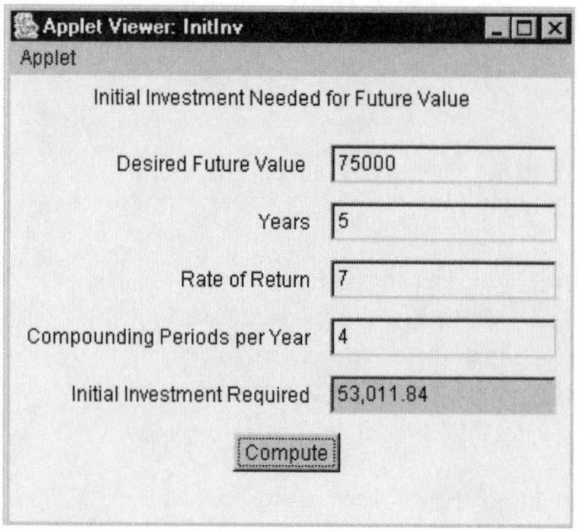

Figure 9-3   *The InitInv applet*

Finding the Initial Investment Needed for a Desired Annuity

Another common financial calculation computes the amount of money that one must invest so that a desired annuity, in terms of a regular withdrawal, can be paid. For example, you might decide that you need $5,000 per month at retirement and that you will need that amount for 20 years. The question is how much will you need to invest to secure that annuity? The answer can be found using the following formula:

$$\text{Initial Investment} = ((\text{regWD} * \text{wdPerYear}) / \text{rateOfRet}) * \\ (1 - (1 / (\text{rateOfRet} / \text{wdPerYear} + 1)^{\text{wdPerYear} * \text{numYears}}))$$

where *rateOfRet* specifies the rate of return, *regWD* contains the desired regular withdrawal, *wdPerYear* specifies the number of withdrawals per year, and *numYears* specifies the length of the annuity in years.

The **Annuity** applet shown here computes the initial investment required to produce the desired annuity. The applet produced by this program is shown in Figure 9-4.

```
/* Compute the initial investment necessary for
   a desired annuity. In other words, find
   the initial amount needed to allow the regular
   withdrawals of a desired amount over a period
   of time.  */
import java.awt.*;
import java.awt.event.*;
import java.applet.*;
import java.text.*;
```

```
/*
   <applet code="Annuity" width=340 height=260>
   </applet>
*/

public class Annuity extends Applet
   implements ActionListener {

   TextField regWDText, initialText, periodText,
               rateText, numWDText;
   Button doIt;

   double regWDAmount; // amount of each withdrawal
   double rateOfRet;   // rate of return
   double numYears;    // length of time in years
   int numPerYear;     // number of withdrawals per year

   NumberFormat nf;

   public void init() {
      // Use a grid bag layout.
      GridBagLayout gbag = new GridBagLayout();
      GridBagConstraints gbc = new GridBagConstraints();
      setLayout(gbag);

      Label heading = new
            Label("Initial Investment Needed for " +
                  "Regular Withdrawals");

      Label regWDLab = new Label("Desired Withdrawal");
      Label periodLab = new Label("Years");
      Label rateLab = new Label("Rate of Return");
      Label numWDLab =
            new Label("Number of Withdrawals per Year ");
      Label initialLab =
            new Label("Initial Investment Required");

      regWDText = new TextField(16);
      periodText = new TextField(16);
      initialText = new TextField(16);
      rateText = new TextField(16);
      numWDText = new TextField(16);

      // Initial investment field for display only.
      initialText.setEditable(false);
```

```
    doIt = new Button("Compute");

    // Define the grid bag.

    gbc.weighty = 1.0; // use a row weight of 1

    gbc.gridwidth = GridBagConstraints.REMAINDER;
    gbc.anchor = GridBagConstraints.NORTH;
    gbag.setConstraints(heading, gbc);

    // Anchor most components to the right.
    gbc.anchor = GridBagConstraints.EAST;

    gbc.gridwidth = GridBagConstraints.RELATIVE;
    gbag.setConstraints(regWDLab, gbc);
    gbc.gridwidth = GridBagConstraints.REMAINDER;
    gbag.setConstraints(regWDText, gbc);

    gbc.gridwidth = GridBagConstraints.RELATIVE;
    gbag.setConstraints(periodLab, gbc);
    gbc.gridwidth = GridBagConstraints.REMAINDER;
    gbag.setConstraints(periodText, gbc);

    gbc.gridwidth = GridBagConstraints.RELATIVE;
    gbag.setConstraints(rateLab, gbc);
    gbc.gridwidth = GridBagConstraints.REMAINDER;
    gbag.setConstraints(rateText, gbc);

    gbc.gridwidth = GridBagConstraints.RELATIVE;
    gbag.setConstraints(numWDLab, gbc);
    gbc.gridwidth = GridBagConstraints.REMAINDER;
    gbag.setConstraints(numWDText, gbc);

    gbc.gridwidth = GridBagConstraints.RELATIVE;
    gbag.setConstraints(initialLab, gbc);
    gbc.gridwidth = GridBagConstraints.REMAINDER;
    gbag.setConstraints(initialText, gbc);

    gbc.anchor = GridBagConstraints.CENTER;
    gbag.setConstraints(doIt, gbc);

    // Add all the components.
    add(heading);
    add(regWDLab);
    add(regWDText);
```

```java
    add(periodLab);
    add(periodText);
    add(rateLab);
    add(rateText);
    add(numWDLab);
    add(numWDText);
    add(initialLab);
    add(initialText);
    add(doIt);

    // Register to receive text field action events.
    regWDText.addActionListener(this);
    periodText.addActionListener(this);
    rateText.addActionListener(this);
    numWDText.addActionListener(this);
    doIt.addActionListener(this);

    nf = NumberFormat.getInstance();
    nf.setMinimumFractionDigits(2);
    nf.setMaximumFractionDigits(2);
  }

  // User pressed Enter on a text field.
  public void actionPerformed(ActionEvent ae) {
    repaint();
  }

  public void paint(Graphics g) {
    double result = 0.0;

    String regWDStr = regWDText.getText();
    String periodStr = periodText.getText();
    String rateStr = rateText.getText();
    String numWDStr = numWDText.getText();

    try {
      if(regWDStr.length() != 0 &&
         periodStr.length() != 0 &&
         rateStr.length() != 0 &&
         numWDStr.length() != 0) {

        regWDAmount = Double.parseDouble(regWDStr);
        numYears = Double.parseDouble(periodStr);
        rateOfRet = Double.parseDouble(rateStr) / 100;
        numPerYear = Integer.parseInt(numWDStr);
```

```
        result = compute();

        initialText.setText(nf.format(result));
      }

      showStatus(""); // erase any previous error message
    } catch (NumberFormatException exc) {
      showStatus("Invalid Data");
      initialText.setText("");
    }
  }

  // Compute the required initial investment.
  double compute() {
    double b, e;
    double t1, t2;

    t1 = (regWDAmount * numPerYear) / rateOfRet;

    b = (1 + rateOfRet/numPerYear);
    e = numPerYear * numYears;

    t2 = 1 - (1 / Math.pow(b, e));

    return t1 * t2;
  }
}
```

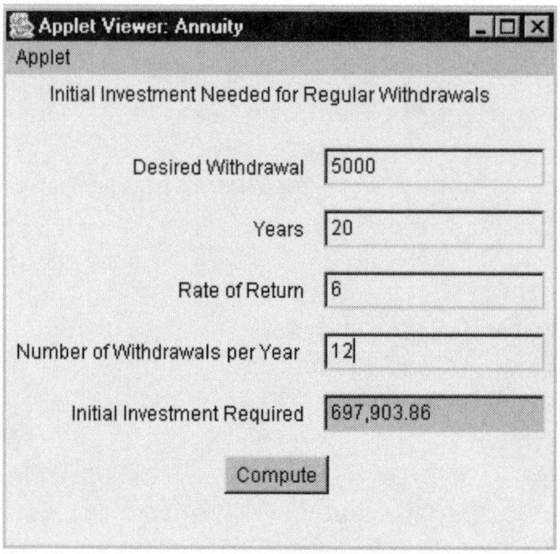

Figure 9-4   *The Annuity applet*

Finding the Maximum Annuity for a Given Investment

Another annuity calculation computes the maximum annuity (in terms of a regular withdrawal) available from a given investment over a specified period of time. For example, if you have $500,000 in a retirement account, how much can you take out each month for 20 years, assuming a 6 percent rate of return? The formula that computes the maximum withdrawal is shown here:

$$\text{Maximum Withdrawal} = principal * (\,(\,(rateOfRet\,/\,wdPerYear)\,/\, (-1 + ((rateOfRet\,/\,wdPerYear) + 1)^{wdPerYear * numYears})\,) + (rateOfRet\,/\,wdPerYear)\,)$$

where *rateOfRet* specifies the rate of return, *principal* contains the value of the initial investment, *wdPerYear* specifies the number of withdrawals per year, and *numYears* specifies the length of the annuity in years.

The **MaxWD** applet shown here computes the maximum periodic withdrawals that can be made over a specified length of time for an assumed rate of return. The applet produced by this program is shown in Figure 9-5.

```java
/* Compute the maximum annuity that can
   be withdrawn from an investment over
   a period of time.  */
import java.awt.*;
import java.awt.event.*;
import java.applet.*;
import java.text.*;
/*
  <applet code="MaxWD" width=340 height=260>
  </applet>
*/

public class MaxWD extends Applet
  implements ActionListener {

  TextField maxWDText, orgPText, periodText,
            rateText, numWDText;
  Button doIt;

  double principal; // initial principal
  double rateOfRet; // annual rate of return
  double numYears;  // length of time in years
  int numPerYear;   // number of withdrawals per year

  NumberFormat nf;

  public void init() {
    // Use a grid bag layout.
```

```java
GridBagLayout gbag = new GridBagLayout();
GridBagConstraints gbc = new GridBagConstraints();
setLayout(gbag);

Label heading = new
      Label("Maximum Regular Withdrawals");

Label orgPLab = new Label("Original Principal");
Label periodLab = new Label("Years");
Label rateLab = new Label("Rate of Return");
Label numWDLab =
        new Label("Number of Withdrawals per Year");
Label maxWDLab = new Label("Maximum Withdrawal");

maxWDText = new TextField(16);
periodText = new TextField(16);
orgPText = new TextField(16);
rateText = new TextField(16);
numWDText = new TextField(16);

// Max withdrawal field for display only.
maxWDText.setEditable(false);

doIt = new Button("Compute");

// Define the grid bag.
gbc.weighty = 1.0; // use a row weight of 1

gbc.gridwidth = GridBagConstraints.REMAINDER;
gbc.anchor = GridBagConstraints.NORTH;
gbag.setConstraints(heading, gbc);

// Anchor most components to the right.
gbc.anchor = GridBagConstraints.EAST;

gbc.gridwidth = GridBagConstraints.RELATIVE;
gbag.setConstraints(orgPLab, gbc);
gbc.gridwidth = GridBagConstraints.REMAINDER;
gbag.setConstraints(orgPText, gbc);

gbc.gridwidth = GridBagConstraints.RELATIVE;
gbag.setConstraints(periodLab, gbc);
gbc.gridwidth = GridBagConstraints.REMAINDER;
gbag.setConstraints(periodText, gbc);

gbc.gridwidth = GridBagConstraints.RELATIVE;
gbag.setConstraints(rateLab, gbc);
```

```
    gbc.gridwidth = GridBagConstraints.REMAINDER;
    gbag.setConstraints(rateText, gbc);

    gbc.gridwidth = GridBagConstraints.RELATIVE;
    gbag.setConstraints(numWDLab, gbc);
    gbc.gridwidth = GridBagConstraints.REMAINDER;
    gbag.setConstraints(numWDText, gbc);

    gbc.gridwidth = GridBagConstraints.RELATIVE;
    gbag.setConstraints(maxWDLab, gbc);
    gbc.gridwidth = GridBagConstraints.REMAINDER;
    gbag.setConstraints(maxWDText, gbc);

    gbc.anchor = GridBagConstraints.CENTER;
    gbag.setConstraints(doIt, gbc);

    // Add all the components.
    add(heading);
    add(orgPLab);
    add(orgPText);
    add(periodLab);
    add(periodText);
    add(rateLab);
    add(rateText);
    add(numWDLab);
    add(numWDText);
    add(maxWDLab);
    add(maxWDText);
    add(doIt);

    // Register to receive action events.
    orgPText.addActionListener(this);
    periodText.addActionListener(this);
    rateText.addActionListener(this);
    numWDText.addActionListener(this);
    doIt.addActionListener(this);

    nf = NumberFormat.getInstance();
    nf.setMinimumFractionDigits(2);
    nf.setMaximumFractionDigits(2);
  }

  /* User pressed Enter on a text field or
     pressed Compute. */
  public void actionPerformed(ActionEvent ae) {
    repaint();
  }
```

```java
public void paint(Graphics g) {
  double result = 0.0;

  String orgPStr = orgPText.getText();
  String periodStr = periodText.getText();
  String rateStr = rateText.getText();
  String numWDStr = numWDText.getText();

  try {
    if(orgPStr.length() != 0 &&
       periodStr.length() != 0 &&
       rateStr.length() != 0 &&
       numWDStr.length() != 0) {

      principal = Double.parseDouble(orgPStr);
      numYears = Double.parseDouble(periodStr);
      rateOfRet = Double.parseDouble(rateStr) / 100;
      numPerYear = Integer.parseInt(numWDStr);

      result = compute();

      maxWDText.setText(nf.format(result));
    }

    showStatus(""); // erase any previous error message
  } catch (NumberFormatException exc) {
    showStatus("Invalid Data");
    maxWDText.setText("");
  }
}

// Compute the maximum regular withdrawals.
double compute() {
  double b, e;
  double t1, t2;

  t1 = rateOfRet / numPerYear;

  b = (1 + t1);
  e = numPerYear * numYears;

  t2 = Math.pow(b, e) - 1;

  return principal * (t1/t2 + t1);
}
}
```

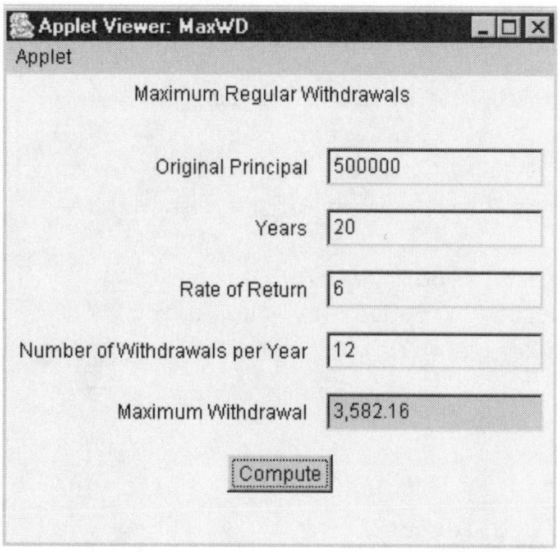

Figure 9-5   *The MaxWD applet*

Finding the Remaining Balance on a Loan

Often you will want to know the remaining balance on a loan. This is easily calculated if you know the original principal, the interest rate, the loan length, and the number of payments made. To find the remaining balance, you must sum the payments, subtracting from each payment the amount allocated to interest, and then subtract that result from the principal.

The **RemBal** applet, shown here, finds the remaining balance of a loan. The applet produced by this program is shown in Figure 9-6.

```
// Find the remaining balance on a loan.
import java.awt.*;
import java.awt.event.*;
import java.applet.*;
import java.text.*;
/*
  <applet code="RemBal" width=340 height=260>
  </applet>
*/

public class RemBal extends Applet
  implements ActionListener {

  TextField orgPText, paymentText, remBalText,
            rateText, numPayText;
```

```java
Button doIt;

double orgPrincipal; // original principal
double intRate;      // interest rate
double payment;      // amount of each payment
double numPayments;  // number of payments made

/* Number of payments per year.  You could
   allow this value to be set by the user. */
final int payPerYear = 12;

NumberFormat nf;

public void init() {
  // Use a grid bag layout.
  GridBagLayout gbag = new GridBagLayout();
  GridBagConstraints gbc = new GridBagConstraints();
  setLayout(gbag);

  Label heading = new
        Label("Find Loan Balance ");

  Label orgPLab = new Label("Original Principal");
  Label paymentLab = new Label("Amount of Payment");
  Label numPayLab = new Label("Number of Payments Made");
  Label rateLab = new Label("Interest Rate");
  Label remBalLab = new Label("Remaining Balance");

  orgPText = new TextField(16);
  paymentText = new TextField(16);
  remBalText = new TextField(16);
  rateText = new TextField(16);
  numPayText = new TextField(16);

  // Payment field for display only.
  remBalText.setEditable(false);

  doIt = new Button("Compute");

  // Define the grid bag.

  gbc.weighty = 1.0; // use a row weight of 1
```

```
gbc.gridwidth = GridBagConstraints.REMAINDER;
gbc.anchor = GridBagConstraints.NORTH;
gbag.setConstraints(heading, gbc);

// Anchor most components to the right.
gbc.anchor = GridBagConstraints.EAST;

gbc.gridwidth = GridBagConstraints.RELATIVE;
gbag.setConstraints(orgPLab, gbc);
gbc.gridwidth = GridBagConstraints.REMAINDER;
gbag.setConstraints(orgPText, gbc);

gbc.gridwidth = GridBagConstraints.RELATIVE;
gbag.setConstraints(paymentLab, gbc);
gbc.gridwidth = GridBagConstraints.REMAINDER;
gbag.setConstraints(paymentText, gbc);

gbc.gridwidth = GridBagConstraints.RELATIVE;
gbag.setConstraints(rateLab, gbc);
gbc.gridwidth = GridBagConstraints.REMAINDER;
gbag.setConstraints(rateText, gbc);

gbc.gridwidth = GridBagConstraints.RELATIVE;
gbag.setConstraints(numPayLab, gbc);
gbc.gridwidth = GridBagConstraints.REMAINDER;
gbag.setConstraints(numPayText, gbc);

gbc.gridwidth = GridBagConstraints.RELATIVE;
gbag.setConstraints(remBalLab, gbc);
gbc.gridwidth = GridBagConstraints.REMAINDER;
gbag.setConstraints(remBalText, gbc);

gbc.anchor = GridBagConstraints.CENTER;
gbag.setConstraints(doIt, gbc);

// Add all the components.
add(heading);
add(orgPLab);
add(orgPText);
add(paymentLab);
add(paymentText);
add(numPayLab);
add(numPayText);
```

```java
      add(rateLab);
      add(rateText);
      add(remBalLab);
      add(remBalText);
      add(doIt);

      // Register to receive action events.
      orgPText.addActionListener(this);
      numPayText.addActionListener(this);
      rateText.addActionListener(this);
      paymentText.addActionListener(this);
      doIt.addActionListener(this);

      nf = NumberFormat.getInstance();
      nf.setMinimumFractionDigits(2);
      nf.setMaximumFractionDigits(2);
    }

    /* User pressed Enter on a text field
       or pressed Compute. */
    public void actionPerformed(ActionEvent ae) {
      repaint();
    }

    public void paint(Graphics g) {
      double result = 0.0;

      String orgPStr = orgPText.getText();
      String numPayStr = numPayText.getText();
      String rateStr = rateText.getText();
      String payStr = paymentText.getText();

      try {
        if(orgPStr.length() != 0 &&
           numPayStr.length() != 0 &&
           rateStr.length() != 0 &&
           payStr.length() != 0) {

          orgPrincipal = Double.parseDouble(orgPStr);
          numPayments = Double.parseDouble(numPayStr);
          intRate = Double.parseDouble(rateStr) / 100;
          payment = Double.parseDouble(payStr);
```

```
      result = compute();

      remBalText.setText(nf.format(result));
    }

    showStatus(""); // erase any previous error message
  } catch (NumberFormatException exc) {
    showStatus("Invalid Data");
    remBalText.setText("");
  }
}

// Compute the loan balance.
double compute() {
  double bal = orgPrincipal;
  double rate = intRate / payPerYear;

  for(int i = 0; i < numPayments; i++)
    bal -= payment - (bal * rate);

  return bal;
}
}
```

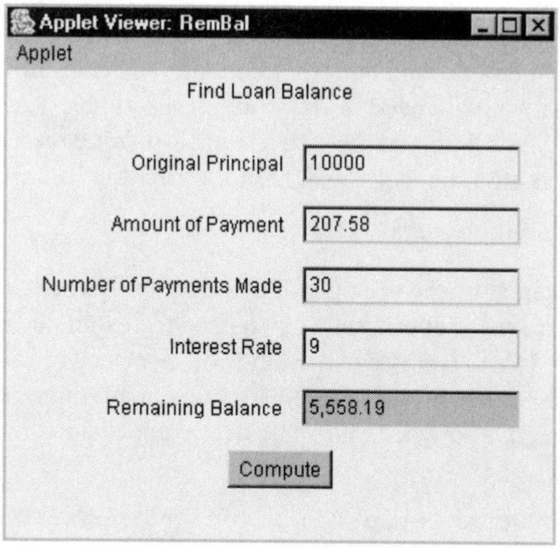

Figure 9-6   *The RemBal applet*

Creating Financial Servlets

Although applets are easy to create and use, they are only one half of the Java Internet equation. The other half is servlets. Servlets execute on the server side of the connection, and they are more appropriate for some applications. Because many readers may want to use servlets rather than applets in their commercial applications, the remainder of this chapter shows how to convert the financial applets into servlets.

Because all the financial applets use the same basic skeleton, we will walk through the conversion of only one applet: **RegPay**. You can then apply the same basic process to convert any of the other applets into servlets on your own. As you will see, it's not hard to do.

One other point: This book assumes that you understand the basic architecture and life cycle of a servlet. If you need to refresh your understanding of servlets, an overview can be found in *Java 2: The Complete Reference* by Herbert Schildt (Berkeley, CA: McGraw-Hill/ Osborne, 2002).

Using Tomcat

Before developing a servlet, it will be useful to review the procedure needed to compile and run one. Servlets require a bit more work on your part than do applets.

To compile and test the servlet developed here, you must have installed a servlet development environment. The one currently recommended by Sun is Tomcat. At the time of this writing, the current release version of Tomcat is 4.1, which supports servlet specification 2.3. (The complete servlet specification is available for download by linking through **java.sun.com**. Both the current release of Tomcat and the servlet specification may have been updated by the time you read this book.) Tomcat replaces the old Java Servlet Development Kit (JSDK) that was previously provided by Sun. Tomcat is an open-source product maintained by the Jakarta Project of the Apache Software Foundation. It contains the class libraries, documentation, and runtime support that you will need to create and test servlets. You can download Tomcat by linking through the Sun Microsystems web site at **java.sun.com**.

Assuming a Windows environment, the default location for Tomcat 4.1 is

```
C:\Program Files\Apache Group\Tomcat 4.1\
```

This is the location assumed by the example in this chapter. If you load Tomcat in a different location, you will need to make appropriate changes to the example. You may need to set the environmental variable **JAVA_HOME** to the top-level directory in which the Java Software Developers Kit is installed. For Java 2, version 1.4, the default directory is **C:\j2sdk1.4.0**, but you will need to confirm this for your environment and adjust accordingly.

The directory

```
C:\Program Files\Apache Group\Tomcat 4.1\common\lib\
```

contains **servlet.jar**. This JAR file contains the classes and interfaces that are needed to build servlets. To make this file accessible, update your CLASSPATH environment variable so that it includes:

```
C:\Program Files\Apache Group\Tomcat 4.1\common\lib\servlet.jar
```

Alternatively, you can specify this class file when you compile the servlets. For example, the following command compiles a servlet called **MyServlet**:

```
javac MyServlet.java -classpath "C:\Program Files\Apache Group\
                        Tomcat 4.1\common\lib\servlet.jar"
```

Once you have compiled a servlet, you must copy the class file onto the server that you will be using or use Tomcat to test the servlet, as described next.

Test Running a Servlet

For the purposes of testing or experimenting, you can use Tomcat to run a servlet directly from the host computer without having to connect to the Internet. To do this, you must copy the servlet's **.class** file into the directory that Tomcat uses for example servlet class files, which for the purposes of this chapter, is shown here:

```
C:\Program Files\Apache Group\Tomcat 4.1\webapps\examples\WEB-INF\classes
```

Once you have the servlet copied into the proper directory, you must start Tomcat. You can either select Start Tomcat in the Start | Programs menu or run **startup.bat** from the following directory:

```
C:\Program Files\Apache Group\Tomcat 4.1\bin\
```

When you are done testing servlets, you can stop Tomcat by selecting Stop Tomcat in the Start | Programs menu or by running **shutdown.bat**.

To test the servlet, start a web browser and enter a URL that is similar to that shown here:

```
http://localhost:8080/examples/servlet/MyServlet
```

Of course, you must substitute the real name of the servlet for **MyServlet.** By specifying **localhost:8080**, you are specifying the host computer.

Converting the RegPay Applet into a Servlet

It is fairly easy to convert the **RegPay** loan calculating applet into a servlet. First, the servlet must import the **javax.servlet** and **javax.servlet.http** packages. It must also extend **HttpServlet**, not **Applet**. Next, you must remove all the GUI code. Then, you must add the code that obtains the parameters passed to the servlet by the HTML that calls the servlet. Finally, the servlet must send the HTML that displays the results. The basic financial calculations remain the same. It is only the way data is obtained and displayed that changes.

The RegPayS Servlet

The following **RegPayS** class is the servlet version of the **RegPay** applet:

```
// A simple loan calculator servlet.
import javax.servlet.*;
import javax.servlet.http.*;
```

```java
import java.io.*;
import java.text.*;

public class RegPayS extends HttpServlet {
  double principal; // original principal
  double intRate;   // interest rate
  double numYears;  // length of loan in years

  /* Number of payments per year.  You could
     allow this value to be set by the user. */
  final int payPerYear = 12;

  NumberFormat nf;

  public void doGet(HttpServletRequest request,
                    HttpServletResponse response)
    throws ServletException, IOException {
    String payStr = "";

    nf = NumberFormat.getInstance();
    nf.setMinimumFractionDigits(2);
    nf.setMaximumFractionDigits(2);

    // Get the parameters.
    String amountStr = request.getParameter("amount");
    String periodStr = request.getParameter("period");
    String rateStr = request.getParameter("rate");

    try {
      if(amountStr != null && periodStr != null &&
         rateStr != null) {
        principal = Double.parseDouble(amountStr);
        numYears = Double.parseDouble(periodStr);
        intRate = Double.parseDouble(rateStr) / 100;

        payStr = nf.format(compute());
      }
      else { // one or more parameters missing
        amountStr = "";
        periodStr = "";
        rateStr = "";
      }
    } catch (NumberFormatException exc) {
```

```
    // No action required for this exception.
  }

  // Set the content type.
  response.setContentType("text/html");

  // Get the output stream.
  PrintWriter pw = response.getWriter();

  // Display the necessary HTML.
  pw.print("<html><body> <left>" +
           "<form name=\"Form1\"" +
           " action=\"http://localhost:8080/" +
           "examples/servlet/RegPayS\">" +
           "<B>Enter amount to finance:</B>" +
           " <input type=textbox name=\"amount\"" +
           " size=12 value=\"");
  pw.print(amountStr + "\">");
  pw.print("<BR><B>Enter term in years:</B>" +
           " <input type=textbox name=\"period\""+
           " size=12 value=\"");
  pw.println(periodStr + "\">");
  pw.print("<BR><B>Enter interest rate:</B>" +
           " <input type=textbox name=\"rate\"" +
           " size=12 value=\"");
  pw.print(rateStr + "\">");
  pw.print("<BR><B>Monthly Payment:</B>" +
           " <input READONLY type=textbox" +
           " name=\"payment\" size=12 value=\"");
  pw.print(payStr + "\">");
  pw.print("<BR><P><input type=submit value=\"Submit\">");
  pw.println("</form> </body> </html>");
}

// Compute the loan payment.
double compute() {
  double numer;
  double denom;
  double b, e;

  numer = intRate * principal / payPerYear;

  e = -(payPerYear * numYears);
```

```
    b = (intRate / payPerYear) + 1.0;

    denom = 1.0 - Math.pow(b, e);

    return numer / denom;
  }
}
```

The first thing to notice about **RegPayS** is that it has only two methods: **doGet( )** and **compute( )**. The **compute( )** method is the same as that used by the applet. The **doGet( )** method is defined by the **HttpServlet** class, which **RegPayS** extends. This method is called by the server when the servlet must respond to a GET request. Notice that it is passed a reference to the **HttpServletRequest** and **HttpServletResponse** objects associated with the request.

From the **request** parameter, the servlet obtains the arguments associated with the request. It does this by calling **getParameter( )**. The parameter is returned in its string form. Thus, a numeric value must be manually converted into its binary format. If no parameter is available, a **null** is returned.

From the **response** object, the servlet obtains a stream to which response information can be written. The response is then returned to the browser by outputting to that stream. Prior to obtaining a **PrintWriter** to the response stream, the output type should be set to text/html by calling **setContentType( )**.

RegPayS can be called with or without parameters. If called without parameters, the servlet responds with the necessary HTML to display an empty loan calculator form. Otherwise, if called with all needed parameters, then **RegPayS** calculates the loan payment and redisplays the form, with the payment field filled in. Figure 9-7 shows the **RegPayS** servlet in action.

The simplest way to invoke **RegPayS** is to link to its URL without passing any parameters. For example, if you are using Tomcat, you can use this line:

```
<A HREF = "http://localhost:8080/examples/servlet/RegPayS">Loan Calculator</A>
```

This displays a link called Loan Calculator that links to the **RegPayS** servlet in the Tomcat example servlets directory. Notice that no parameters are passed. This causes **RegPayS** to return the complete HTML that displays an empty loan calculator page.

You can also invoke **RegPayS** by first displaying an empty form manually, if you like. This approach is shown here, again using the Tomcat directory:

```
<html>
<body>
<form name="Form1"
  action="http://localhost:8080/examples/servlet/RegPayS">
<B>Enter amount to finance:</B>
```

```
<input type=textbox name="amount" size=12 value="">
<BR>
<B>Enter term in years:</B>
<input type=textbox name="period" size=12 value="">
<BR>
<B>Enter interest rate:</B>
<input type=textbox name="rate" size=12 value="">
<BR>
<B>Monthly Payment:</B>
<input READONLY type=textbox name="payment"
  size=12 value="">
<BR><P>
<input type=submit value="Submit">
</form>
</body>
</html>
```

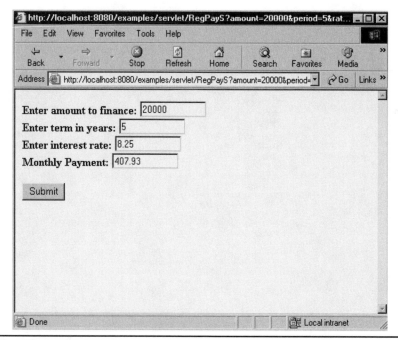

Figure 9-7   *The RegPayS servlet in action*

Some Things to Try

The first thing you might want to try is converting the other financial applets into servlets. Because all the financial applets are built on the same skeleton, simply follow the same approach as used by **RegPayS**.

There are many other financial calculations that you might find useful to implement as applets or servlets, such as the rate of return of an investment or the amount of a regular deposit needed over time to reach a future value. You could also print a loan amortization chart.

You might want to try creating a larger application that offers all the calculations presented in this chapter, allowing the user to select the desired calculation from a menu.

AI-Based
Problem Solving

by Herb Schildt

To conclude this book, we will examine a topic from an interesting discipline of programming: artificial intelligence (AI). As explained earlier, the goal of this book is to show the richness and power of the Java language. Perhaps nothing demonstrates that better than its application to the demanding realm of artificial intelligence. Java's powerful string-handling capabilities and **Stack** class streamline many types of AI-based code. Java's object model keeps the code clean, as does its garbage collection facility. As this final chapter shows, Java is a language well suited to the AI developer.

The field of artificial intelligence is comprised of several fascinating areas, but fundamental to many AI-based applications is problem solving. Essentially, there are two types of problems. The first type can be solved through the use of some sort of deterministic procedure that is guaranteed success, such as the computation of the sine of an angle or the square root of a value. These types of problems are easily translated into algorithms that a computer can execute. In the real world, however, few problems lend themselves to such straightforward solutions. Instead, many problems can be solved only by searching for a solution. It is this type of problem solving with which AI is concerned. It is also the type of searching that is explored in this chapter.

To understand why searching is so important to AI, consider the following. One of the early goals of AI research was the creation of a general problem solver. A *general problem solver* is a program that can produce solutions to all sorts of different problems about which it has no specific, designed-in knowledge. It is an understatement to say that such a program would be highly desirable. Unfortunately, a general problem solver is as difficult to realize as it is tantalizing. One complication is the sheer size and complexity of many real-world situations. Because a general problem solver must search for a solution through what might be a very large, mazelike universe of possibilities, finding ways to search such an environment is a priority. Although we won't attempt something as ambitious as a general problem solver in this chapter, we will explore several AI-based search techniques that are applicable to a wide variety of problems.

Representation and Terminology

Imagine that you have lost your car keys. You know that they are somewhere in your house, which looks like this:

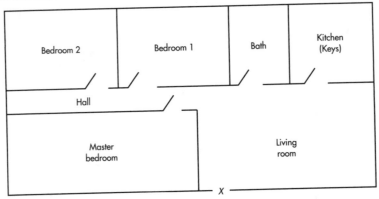

You are standing at the front door (where the *X* is). As you begin your search, you check the living room. Then you go down the hall to the first bedroom, through the hall to the second bedroom, back to the hall, and to the master bedroom. Not having found your keys, you backtrack further by going back through the living room. Finally, you find your keys in the kitchen. This situation is easily represented by a graph, as shown in Figure 10-1. Representing search problems in graphical form is helpful because it provides a convenient way to depict the way a solution was found.

With the preceding discussion in mind, consider the following terms, which will be used throughout this chapter:

Node	A discrete point
Terminal node	A node that ends a path
Search space	The set of all nodes
Goal	The node that is the object of the search
Heuristics	Information about whether any specific node is a better next choice than another
Solution path	A directed graph of the nodes visited en route to the goal

In the example of the lost keys, each room in the house is a node; the entire house is the search space; the goal, as it turns out, is the kitchen; and the solution path is shown in Figure 10-1. The bedrooms, kitchen, and the bath are terminal nodes because they lead nowhere. Heuristics are not represented on a graph. Rather, they are techniques that you might employ to help you better choose a path.

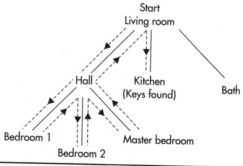

Figure 10-1   *The solution path to find the missing keys*

Combinatorial Explosions

Given the preceding example, you may think that searching for a solution is easy—you start at the beginning and work your way to the conclusion. In the extremely simple case of the lost keys, this is not a bad approach because the search space is so small. But for many problems (especially those for which you would want to use a computer) the number of nodes in the search space is very large, and as the search space grows, so does the number of possible paths to the goal. The trouble is that often, adding another node to the search space adds more than one path. That is, the number of potential pathways to the goal can increase in a nonlinear fashion as the size of the search space grows. In a nonlinear situation, the number of possible paths can quickly become very large.

For instance, consider the number of ways three objects—A, B, and C—can be arranged on a table. The six possible permutations are

A	B	C
A	C	B
B	C	A
B	A	C
C	B	A
C	A	B

You can quickly prove to yourself that these six are the only ways that A, B, and C can be arranged. However, you can derive the same number by using a theorem from the branch of mathematics called *combinatorics*—the study of the way things can be combined. According to the theorem, the number of ways that N objects can be arranged is equal to $N!$ (N factorial). The factorial of a number is the product of all whole numbers equal to or less than itself down to 1. Therefore, 3! is $3 \times 2 \times 1$, or 6. If you had four objects to arrange, there would be 4!, or 24, permutations. With five objects, the number is 120, and with six it is 720. With 1000 objects the number of possible permutations is huge! The graph in Figure 10-2 gives you a visual feel for what is sometimes referred to as a *combinatoric explosion*. Once there are more than a handful of possibilities, it very quickly becomes difficult to examine (indeed, even to enumerate) all the arrangements.

This same sort of combinatorial explosion can occur in paths through search spaces. Because of this, only the simplest of problems lend themselves to exhaustive searches. An *exhaustive search* is one that examines all nodes. Thus, it is a "brute-force" technique. Brute force always works but is not often practical for large problems because it consumes too much time, too many computing resources, or both. For this reason, AI-based search techniques were developed.

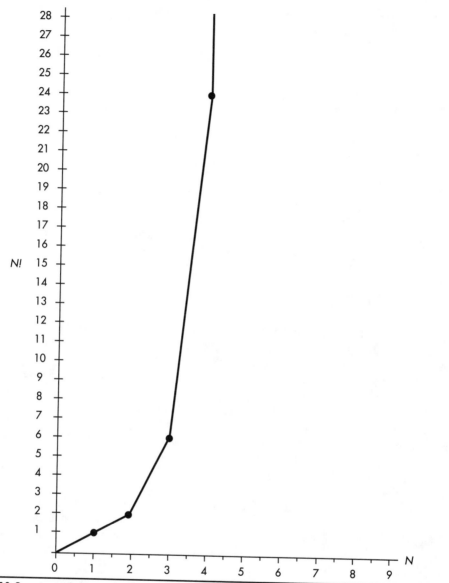

Figure 10-2   *A combinatoric explosion with factorials*

Search Techniques

There are several ways to search for a solution. The four most fundamental are

- ▶ Depth first
- ▶ Breadth first
- ▶ Hill climbing
- ▶ Least cost

In the course of this chapter, each of these searches is examined.

Evaluating a Search

Evaluating the performance of an AI-based search technique can be complicated. Fortunately, for our purposes we are concerned only with these two measurements:

- ▶ How quickly a solution is found
- ▶ How good the solution is

There are several types of problems for which all that matters is that a solution, any solution, be found with the minimum effort. For these problems, the first measurement is especially important. In other situations, the quality of the solution is more important.

The speed of a search is affected both by the size of the search space and by the number of nodes actually traversed in the process of finding the solution. Because backtracking from dead ends is wasted effort, you want a search that seldom retraces its steps.

In AI-based searching, there is a difference between finding the best solution and finding a good solution. Finding the best solution can require an exhaustive search because sometimes this is the only way to know that the best solution has been found. Finding a good solution, in contrast, means finding a solution that is within a set of constraints—it does not matter if a better solution might exist.

As you will see, the search techniques described in this chapter all work better in certain situations than in others, so it is difficult to say whether one search method is *always* superior to another. But some search techniques have a greater probability of being better for the average case. In addition, the way a problem is defined can sometimes help you choose an appropriate search method.

The Problem

Now let us consider the problem that we will use various searches to solve. Imagine that you are a travel agent and a rather quarrelsome customer wants you to book a flight from New York to Los Angeles with XYZ Airlines. You try to tell the customer that XYZ does not have a direct flight from New York to Los Angeles, but the customer insists that XYZ is the only airline that he will fly. Thus, you must find connecting flights between New York and Los Angeles. You consult XYZ's scheduled flights, shown here:

Flight	Distance
New York to Chicago	900 miles
Chicago to Denver	1000 miles
New York to Toronto	500 miles
New York to Denver	1800 miles
Toronto to Calgary	1700 miles
Toronto to Los Angeles	2500 miles
Toronto to Chicago	500 miles
Denver to Urbana	1000 miles
Denver to Houston	1000 miles
Houston to Los Angeles	1500 miles
Denver to Los Angeles	1000 miles

Quickly you see that there are connections that enable your customer to fly from New York to Los Angeles. The problem is to write a Java program that does the same thing that you just did in your head!

A Graphic Representation

The flight information in XYZ's schedule can be translated into the directed graph shown in Figure 10-3. A *directed graph* is simply a graph in which the lines connecting each node

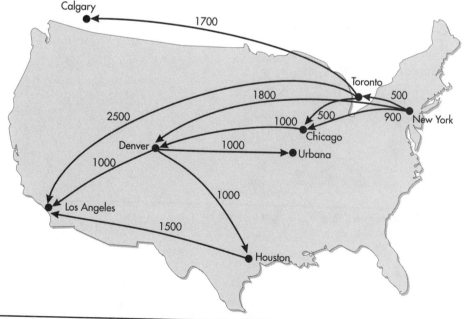

Figure 10-3 *A directed graph of XYZ's flight schedule*

include an arrow to indicate the direction of motion. In a directed graph, you cannot travel against the direction of the arrow.

To make things easier to understand, we can redraw this graph in a treelike fashion, as shown in Figure 10-4. Refer to this version for the rest of this chapter. The goal, Los Angeles, is circled. Notice also that various cities appear more than once to simplify the construction of the graph. Thus, the treelike representation *does not* depict a binary tree. It is simply a visual convenience.

Now we are ready to develop the various search programs that will find paths from New York to Los Angeles.

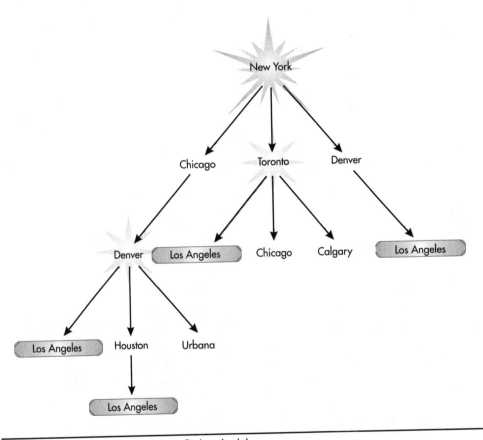

Figure 10-4 *A tree version of XYZ's flight schedule*

The FlightInfo Class

Writing a program to find a route from New York to Los Angeles requires a database that contains the information about XYZ's flights. Each entry in the database must contain the departure and destination cities, the distance between them, and a flag that aids in backtracking. This information is held in a class called **FlightInfo**, shown here:

```
// Flight information.
class FlightInfo {
  String from;
  String to;
  int distance;
  boolean skip; // used in backtracking

  FlightInfo(String f, String t, int d) {
    from = f;
    to = t;
    distance = d;
    skip = false;
  }
}
```

This class will be used by all the search techniques described in the remainder of the chapter.

The Depth-First Search

The *depth-first search* explores each possible path to its conclusion before another path is tried. To understand exactly how this works, consider the tree that follows. F is the goal.

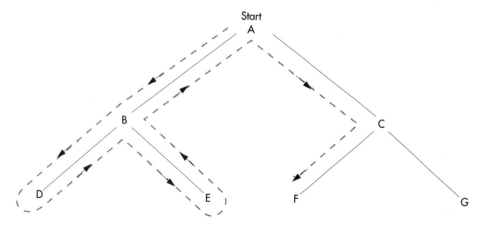

A depth-first search traverses the graph in the following order: ABDBEBACF. If you are familiar with trees, you recognize this type of search as an inorder tree traversal. That is, the path goes left until a terminal node is reached or the goal is found. If a terminal node is reached, the path backs up one level, goes right, and then left until either the goal or a terminal node is encountered. This procedure is repeated until the goal is found or the last node in the search space has been examined.

As you can see, a depth-first search is certain to find the goal because in the worst case it degenerates into an exhaustive search. In this example, an exhaustive search would result if G were the goal.

The depth-first approach is encapsulated within the **Depth** class, which begins like this:

```java
class Depth {
  final int MAX = 100; // maximum number of connections

  // This array holds the flight information.
  FlightInfo flights[] = new FlightInfo[MAX];

  int numFlights = 0; // number of entries in flight array

  Stack btStack = new Stack(); // backtrack stack

  public static void main(String args[])
  {
    String to, from;
    Depth ob = new Depth();
    BufferedReader br = new
      BufferedReader(new InputStreamReader(System.in));

    ob.setup();

    try {
      System.out.print("From? ");
      from = br.readLine();
      System.out.print("To? ");
      to = br.readLine();

      ob.isflight(from, to);

      if(ob.btStack.size() != 0)
        ob.route(to);
    } catch (IOException exc) {
      System.out.println("Error on input.");
    }
  }
```

An array of **FlightInfo** objects called **flights** is created, which holds the flight information. The size of this array is set by use of the **final** variable **MAX**. The number of flights actually stored in the array is held in **numFlights**. Note that it would have been possible to store the flight information in one of Java Collections classes, such as in an **ArrayList**. Doing so would allow arbitrarily sized lists of information. However, because we are storing information about only a few flights, an array is used for the sake of simplicity and clarity.

The **Stack** object that will be used for backtracking is created, and a reference to it is stored in **btStack**. As you will see, the backtrack stack is very important to all the search techniques.

Inside **main( )**, the **setup( )** method is called, which initializes the flight information. Next, the user is prompted for the departure and destination cities. Then, **isflight( )** is called to find a flight or a set of connecting flights between the two cities, which in this example are New York and Los Angeles. Finally, if a route between the two cities is found, it is displayed. Now, let's look at the various pieces.

The **setup( )** method works by repeatedly calling the **addFlight( )** method, which adds a flight to the **flights** array. The value of **numFlights** is incremented with each added flight. Thus, when **setup( )** returns, **numFlights** is equal to the number of flights in the database. The **setup( )** and **addFlight( )** methods are shown here:

```
// Initialize the flight database.
void setup()
{
  addFlight("New York", "Chicago", 900);
  addFlight("Chicago", "Denver", 1000);
  addFlight("New York", "Toronto", 500);
  addFlight("New York", "Denver", 1800);
  addFlight("Toronto", "Calgary", 1700);
  addFlight("Toronto", "Los Angeles", 2500);
  addFlight("Toronto", "Chicago", 500);
  addFlight("Denver", "Urbana", 1000);
  addFlight("Denver", "Houston", 1000);
  addFlight("Houston", "Los Angeles", 1500);
  addFlight("Denver", "Los Angeles", 1000);
}


// Put flights into the database.
void addFlight(String from, String to, int dist)
{
  if(numFlights < MAX) {
    flights[numFlights] =
      new FlightInfo(from, to, dist);

    numFlights++;
  }
  else System.out.println("Flight database full.\n");
}
```

To find a route between New York and Los Angeles, several support methods are needed. The first is **match( )**, which determines if there is a flight between two cities. If no such flight exists, it returns zero; or if there is a flight, it returns the distance between the two cities. This method is shown here:

```
/* If there is a flight between from and to,
   return the distance of flight;
   otherwise, return 0. */
int match(String from, String to)
{
  for(int i=numFlights-1; i > -1; i--) {
    if(flights[i].from.equals(from) &&
       flights[i].to.equals(to) &&
       !flights[i].skip)
    {
      flights[i].skip = true; // prevent reuse
      return flights[i].distance;
    }
  }


  return 0; // not found
}
```

The next support method is **find( )**. Given a departure city, **find( )** searches the database for any connection. If a connection is found, the **FlightInfo** object associated with that connection is returned. Otherwise, **null** is returned. Thus, the difference between **match( )** and **find( )** is that **match( )** determines if there is a flight between two specific cities, whereas **find( )** determines if there is a flight from a given city to *any other* city. The **find( )** method follows:

```
// Given from, find any connection.
FlightInfo find(String from)
{
  for(int i=0; i < numFlights; i++) {
    if(flights[i].from.equals(from) &&
       !flights[i].skip)
    {
      FlightInfo f = new FlightInfo(flights[i].from,
                                    flights[i].to,
                                    flights[i].distance);
      flights[i].skip = true; // prevent reuse

      return f;
    }
  }
}
```

```
    return null;
  }
```

In both **match( )** and **find( )**, connections that have the **skip** field set to 1 are bypassed. Also, if a connection is found, its **skip** field is set. This manages backtracking from dead ends, preventing the same connections from being tried over and over again.

Now consider the code that actually finds the connecting flights. It is contained in the **isflight( )** method, the key routine in finding a route between two cities. It is called with the names of the departure and destination cities.

```
// Determine if there is a route between from and to.
void isflight(String from, String to)
{
  int dist;
  FlightInfo f;

  // See if at destination.
  dist = match(from, to);
  if(dist != 0) {
    btStack.push(new FlightInfo(from, to, dist));
    return;
  }

  // Try another connection.
  f = find(from);
  if(f != null) {
    btStack.push(new FlightInfo(from, to, f.distance));
    isflight(f.to, to);
  }
  else if(btStack.size() > 0) {
    // Backtrack and try another connection.
    f = (FlightInfo) btStack.pop();
    isflight(f.from, f.to);
  }
}
```

Let's examine this method closely. First, the flight database is checked by **match( )** to see if there is a flight between **from** and **to**. If there is, the goal has been reached, the connection is pushed onto the stack, and the method returns. Otherwise, it uses **find( )** to find a connection between **from** and *any place else*. The **find( )** method returns the **FlightInfo** object describing the connection, if one is found, or **null** if no connecting flights are available. If there is such a flight, this connection is stored in **f**, the current flight is pushed onto the backtrack stack, and **isflight( )** is called recursively, with the city in **f.to** becoming the new departure city. Otherwise, backtracking takes place. The previous node is removed from the stack and **isflight( )** is called recursively. This process continues until the goal is found.

For example, if **isflight( )** is called with New York and Chicago, the first **if** would succeed and **isflight( )** would terminate because there is a direct flight from New York to Chicago. The situation is more complex when **isflight( )** is called with New York and Calgary. In this case, the first **if** would fail because there is no direct flight connecting these two cities. Next, the second **if** is tried by attempting to find a connection between New York and any other city. In this case, **find( )** first finds the New York to Chicago connection, this connection is pushed onto the backtrack stack, and **isflight( )** is called recursively with Chicago as the starting point. Unfortunately, there is no path from Chicago to Calgary and several false paths are followed. Eventually, after several recursive calls to **isflight( )** and substantial backtracking, the connection from New York to Toronto is found, and Toronto connects to Calgary. This causes **isflight( )** to return, unraveling all recursive calls in the process. Finally, the original call to **isflight( )** returns. You might want to try adding **println( )** statements in **isflight( )** to see precisely how it works with various departure and destination cities.

It is important to understand that **isflight( )** does not actually *return* the solution—it *generate*s it. Upon exit from **isflight( )**, the backtrack stack contains the route between New York and Calgary. That is, the solution is contained in **btStack**. Furthermore, the success or failure of **isflight( )** is determined by the state of the stack. An empty stack indicates failure; otherwise, the stack holds a solution.

In general, backtracking is a crucial ingredient in AI-based search techniques. Backtracking is accomplished through the use of recursion and a backtrack stack. Almost all backtracking situations are stack-like in operation—that is, they are first in, last out. As a path is explored, nodes are pushed onto the stack as they are encountered. At each dead end, the last node is popped off the stack and a new path, from that point, is tried. This process continues until either the goal is reached or all paths have been exhausted.

You need one more method, called **route( )**, to complete the entire program. It displays the path and the total distance. The **route( )** method is shown here:

```
// Show the route and total distance.
void route(String to)
{
  Stack rev = new Stack();
  int dist = 0;
  FlightInfo f;
  int num = btStack.size();

  // Reverse the stack to display route.
  for(int i=0; i < num; i++)
    rev.push(btStack.pop());

  for(int i=0; i < num; i++) {
    f = (FlightInfo) rev.pop();
    System.out.print(f.from + " to ");
    dist += f.distance;
  }
```

```
   System.out.println(to);
   System.out.println("Distance is " + dist);
}
```

Notice the use of a second stack called **rev**. The solution stored in **btStack** is in reverse order, with the top of the stack holding the last connection and the bottom of the stack holding the first connection. Thus, it must be reversed in order to display the connection in the proper sequence. To put the solution into its proper order, the connections are popped from **btStack** and pushed onto **rev**.

The entire depth-first search program follows:

```
// Find connections using a depth-first search.
import java.util.*;
import java.io.*;

// Flight information.
class FlightInfo {
  String from;
  String to;
  int distance;
  boolean skip; // used in backtracking

  FlightInfo(String f, String t, int d) {
    from = f;
    to = t;
    distance = d;
    skip = false;
  }
}

class Depth {
  final int MAX = 100; // maximum number of connections

  // This array holds the flight information.
  FlightInfo flights[] = new FlightInfo[MAX];

  int numFlights = 0; // number of entries in flight array

  Stack btStack = new Stack(); // backtrack stack

  public static void main(String args[])
  {
    String to, from;
    Depth ob = new Depth();
    BufferedReader br = new
```

```
      BufferedReader(new InputStreamReader(System.in));

    ob.setup();

    try {
      System.out.print("From? ");
      from = br.readLine();
      System.out.print("To? ");
      to = br.readLine();

      ob.isflight(from, to);

      if(ob.btStack.size() != 0)
        ob.route(to);
    } catch (IOException exc) {
      System.out.println("Error on input.");
    }
  }

  // Initialize the flight database.
  void setup()
  {
    addFlight("New York", "Chicago", 900);
    addFlight("Chicago", "Denver", 1000);
    addFlight("New York", "Toronto", 500);
    addFlight("New York", "Denver", 1800);
    addFlight("Toronto", "Calgary", 1700);
    addFlight("Toronto", "Los Angeles", 2500);
    addFlight("Toronto", "Chicago", 500);
    addFlight("Denver", "Urbana", 1000);
    addFlight("Denver", "Houston", 1000);
    addFlight("Houston", "Los Angeles", 1500);
    addFlight("Denver", "Los Angeles", 1000);
  }

  // Put flights into the database.
  void addFlight(String from, String to, int dist)
  {
    if(numFlights < MAX) {
      flights[numFlights] =
        new FlightInfo(from, to, dist);

      numFlights++;
    }
    else System.out.println("Flight database full.\n");
```

```java
  }

  // Show the route and total distance.
  void route(String to)
  {
    Stack rev = new Stack();
    int dist = 0;
    FlightInfo f;
    int num = btStack.size();

    // Reverse the stack to display route.
    for(int i=0; i < num; i++)
      rev.push(btStack.pop());

    for(int i=0; i < num; i++) {
      f = (FlightInfo) rev.pop();
      System.out.print(f.from + " to ");
      dist += f.distance;
    }

    System.out.println(to);
    System.out.println("Distance is " + dist);
  }

  /* If there is a flight between from and to,
     return the distance of flight;
     otherwise, return 0. */
  int match(String from, String to)
  {
    for(int i=numFlights-1; i > -1; i--) {
      if(flights[i].from.equals(from) &&
         flights[i].to.equals(to) &&
         !flights[i].skip)
      {
        flights[i].skip = true; // prevent reuse
        return flights[i].distance;
      }
    }

    return 0; // not found
  }

  // Given from, find any connection.
  FlightInfo find(String from)
  {
```

```
    for(int i=0; i < numFlights; i++) {
      if(flights[i].from.equals(from) &&
         !flights[i].skip)
      {
        FlightInfo f = new FlightInfo(flights[i].from,
                                      flights[i].to,
                                      flights[i].distance);
        flights[i].skip = true; // prevent reuse

        return f;
      }
    }

    return null;
  }

  // Determine if there is a route between from and to.
  void isflight(String from, String to)
  {
    int dist;
    FlightInfo f;

    // See if at destination.
    dist = match(from, to);
    if(dist != 0) {
      btStack.push(new FlightInfo(from, to, dist));
      return;
    }

    // Try another connection.
    f = find(from);
    if(f != null) {
      btStack.push(new FlightInfo(from, to, f.distance));
      isflight(f.to, to);
    }
    else if(btStack.size() > 0) {
      // Backtrack and try another connection.
      f = (FlightInfo) btStack.pop();
      isflight(f.from, f.to);
    }
  }
}
```

Notice that **main( )** prompts you for both the city of origin and the city of destination. This means that you can use the program to find routes between any two cities. However, the rest of this chapter assumes that New York is the origin and Los Angeles is the destination.

When run with New York as the origin and Los Angeles as the destination, the following solution is displayed. As Figure 10-5 shows, this is indeed the first solution that would be found by a depth-first search. It is also a fairly good solution.

```
From? New York
To? Los Angeles
New York to Chicago to Denver to Los Angeles
Distance is 2900
```

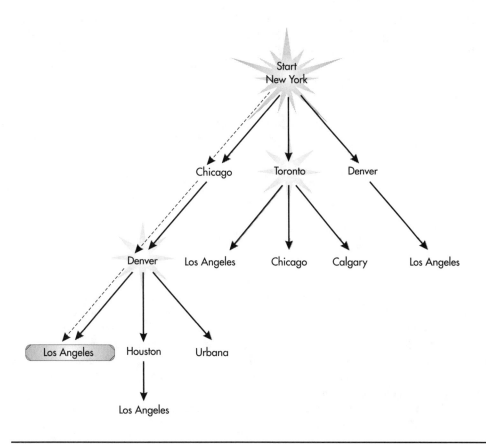

Figure 10-5   *The depth-first path to a solution*

An Analysis of the Depth-First Search

The depth-first approach found a good solution. Also, relative to this specific problem, depth-first searching found this solution on its first try with no backtracking—this is very good; but had the data been organized differently, finding a solution might have involved considerable backtracking. Thus, the outcome of this example cannot be generalized. Moreover, the performance of depth-first searches can be quite poor when a particularly long branch with no solution at the end is explored. In this case, a depth-first search wastes time not only exploring this chain but also backtracking to the goal.

The Breadth-First Search

The opposite of the depth-first search is the *breadth-first search*. In this method, each node on the same level is checked before the search proceeds to the next deeper level. This traversal method is shown here with C as the goal:

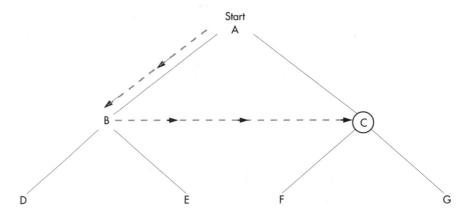

Although thinking in terms of a binary tree–structured search space makes it easy to describe the actions of a breadth-first search, many search spaces, including our flight example, are not binary trees. So precisely what constitutes "breadth" is a bit subjective in that it is defined by the problem at hand. As it relates to our flight example, the breadth-first approach is implemented by checking if any flight leaving the departure city connects to a flight that reaches the destination. In other words, before advancing to another level, the destinations of all connections of connecting flights are checked.

To make the route-seeking program perform a breadth-first search, you need to make an alteration to **isflight( )**, as shown here:

```
/* Determine if there is a route between from and to using
   breadth-first search. */
void isflight(String from, String to)
```

```
{
  int dist, dist2;
  FlightInfo f;

  // This stack is needed by the breadth-first search.
  Stack resetStck = new Stack();

  // See if at destination.
  dist = match(from, to);
  if(dist != 0) {
    btStack.push(new FlightInfo(from, to, dist));
    return;
  }

  /* Following is the first part of the breadth-first
     modification.  It checks all connecting flights
     from a specified node. */
  while((f = find(from)) != null) {
    resetStck.push(f);
    if((dist = match(f.to, to)) != 0) {
      resetStck.push(f.to);
      btStack.push(new FlightInfo(from, f.to, f.distance));
      btStack.push(new FlightInfo(f.to, to, dist));
      return;
    }
  }

  /* The following code resets the skip fields set by
     preceding while loop. This is also part of the
     breadth-first modification. */
  int i = resetStck.size();
  for(; i!=0; i--)
    resetSkip((FlightInfo) resetStck.pop());

  // Try another connection.
  f = find(from);
  if(f != null) {
    btStack.push(new FlightInfo(from, to, f.distance));
    isflight(f.to, to);
  }
  else if(btStack.size() > 0) {
    // Backtrack and try another connection.
```

```
      f = (FlightInfo) btStack.pop();
      isflight(f.from, f.to);
  }
}
```

Two changes have been made. First, the **while** loop checks all flights leaving from the departure city (**from**) to see if they connect with flights that arrive at the destination city. Second, if the destination is not found, the **skip** fields of those connecting flights are cleared by calling **resetSkip( )**. The connections that need to be reset are stored on their own stack, called **resetStck**, which is local to **isflight( )**. Resetting the **skip** flags is necessary to enable alternative paths that might involve those connections.

The **resetSkip( )** method is shown here:

```
// Reset skip field of specified flight.
void resetSkip(FlightInfo f) {
  for(int i=0; i< numFlights; i++)
    if(flights[i].from.equals(f.from) &&
       flights[i].to.equals(f.to))
         flights[i].skip = false;
}
```

To try the breadth-first search, substitute the new version of **isflight( )** into the preceding search program and then add the **resetSkip( )** method. When run, it produces the following solution:

```
From? New York
To? Los Angeles
New York to Toronto to Los Angeles
Distance is 3000
```

Figure 10-6 shows the breadth-first path to the solution.

An Analysis of the Breadth-First Search

In this example, the breadth-first search performed fairly well, finding a reasonable solution. As before, this result cannot be generalized because the first path to be found depends on the physical organization of the information. The example does illustrate, however, how depth-first and breadth-first searches often find different paths through the same search space.

Breadth-first searching works well when the goal is not buried too deeply in the search space. It works poorly when the goal is several layers deep. In this case, a breadth-first search expends substantial effort during the backtrack stage.

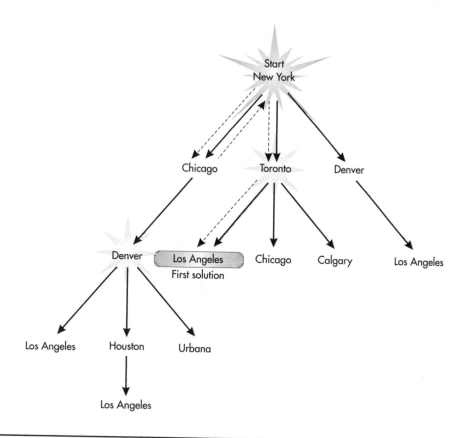

Figure 10-6   *The breadth-first path to a solution*

Adding Heuristics

Neither the depth-first nor the breadth-first search attempts to make any educated guesses about whether one node in the search space is closer to the goal than another. Instead, they simply move from one node to the next using a prescribed pattern until the goal is finally found. This may be the best you can do for some situations, but often a search space contains information that you can use to increase the probability that a search will reach its goal faster. To take advantage of such information, you must add heuristic capabilities to the search.

Heuristics are simply rules that increase the likelihood that a search will proceed in the correct direction. For example, imagine that you are lost in the woods and need a drink of water. The woods are so thick that you cannot see far ahead, and the trees are too big to climb to get a look around. However, you know that rivers, streams, and ponds are most likely in valleys; that animals frequently make paths to their watering places; that when you are near water it is possible to "smell" it; and that you can hear running water. So, you begin by moving downhill because water is unlikely to be uphill. Next, you come across a deer trail that also runs downhill. Knowing that this may lead to water, you follow it. You begin to hear a slight rushing off to your left. Knowing that this may be water, you cautiously move in that direction. As you move, you begin to detect the increased humidity in the air; you can smell the water. Finally, you find a stream and have your drink. In this situation, the heuristic information used to find the water did not guarantee success, but it did increase the probability of an early success. In general, heuristics improve the odds in favor of quickly finding a goal.

Most often, heuristic search methods are based on maximizing or minimizing some constraint. In the problem of scheduling a flight from New York to Los Angeles, there are two possible constraints that a passenger may want to minimize. The first is the number of connections that have to be made. The second is the length of the route. Remember, the shortest route does not necessarily imply the fewest connections, or vice versa. In this section, two heuristic searches are developed. The first minimizes the number of connections. The second minimizes the length of the route. Both heuristic searches are built on the depth-first search framework.

The Hill-Climbing Search

A search algorithm that attempts to find a route that minimizes the number of connections uses the heuristic that the longer the length of the flight, the greater the likelihood that it takes the traveler closer to the destination; therefore, the number of connections is minimized. In the language of AI, this is an example of *hill climbing*.

The hill-climbing algorithm chooses as its next step the node that appears to place it closest to the goal (that is, farthest away from the current position). It derives its name from the analogy of a hiker being lost in the dark, halfway up a mountain. Assuming that the hiker's camp is at the top of the mountain, even in the dark the hiker knows that each step that goes up is a step in the right direction.

Working only with the information contained in the flight-scheduling database, here is how to incorporate the hill-climbing heuristic into the routing program: Choose the connecting flight that is as far away as possible from the current position in the hope that it will be closer to the destination. To do this, modify the **find( )** routine, as shown here:

```java
// Given from, find the farthest away connection.
FlightInfo find(String from)
{
  int pos = -1;
  int dist = 0;

  for(int i=0; i < numFlights; i++) {
    if(flights[i].from.equals(from) &&
       !flights[i].skip)
    {
      // Use the longest flight.
```

```
        if(flights[i].distance > dist) {
          pos = i;
          dist = flights[i].distance;
        }
      }
    }

    if(pos != -1) {
      flights[pos].skip = true; // prevent reuse
      FlightInfo f = new FlightInfo(flights[pos].from,
                           flights[pos].to,
                           flights[pos].distance);
      return f;
    }

    return null;
}
```

The **find( )** routine now searches the entire database, looking for the connection that is farthest away from the departure city.

The entire hill-climbing program follows:

```
// Find connections using hill climbing.
import java.util.*;
import java.io.*;

// Flight information.
class FlightInfo {
  String from;
  String to;
  int distance;
  boolean skip; // used in backtracking

  FlightInfo(String f, String t, int d) {
    from = f;
    to = t;
    distance = d;
    skip = false;
  }
}

class Hill {
  final int MAX = 100;

  // This array holds the flight information.
```

```java
FlightInfo flights[] = new FlightInfo[MAX];

int numFlights = 0; // number of entries in flight array

Stack btStack = new Stack(); // backtrack stack

public static void main(String args[])
{

  String to, from;
  Hill ob = new Hill();
  BufferedReader br = new
    BufferedReader(new InputStreamReader(System.in));

  ob.setup();

  try {
    System.out.print("From? ");
    from = br.readLine();
    System.out.print("To? ");
    to = br.readLine();

    ob.isflight(from, to);

    if(ob.btStack.size() != 0)
      ob.route(to);

  } catch (IOException exc) {
    System.out.println("Error on input.");
  }
}

// Initialize the flight database.
void setup()
{
  addFlight("New York", "Chicago", 900);
  addFlight("Chicago", "Denver", 1000);
  addFlight("New York", "Toronto", 500);
  addFlight("New York", "Denver", 1800);
  addFlight("Toronto", "Calgary", 1700);
  addFlight("Toronto", "Los Angeles", 2500);
  addFlight("Toronto", "Chicago", 500);
  addFlight("Denver", "Urbana", 1000);
  addFlight("Denver", "Houston", 1000);
  addFlight("Houston", "Los Angeles", 1500);
```

```
    addFlight("Denver", "Los Angeles", 1000);
  }

  // Put flights into the database.
  void addFlight(String from, String to, int dist)
  {
    if(numFlights < MAX) {
      flights[numFlights] =
        new FlightInfo(from, to, dist);

      numFlights++;
    }
    else System.out.println("Flight database full.\n");
  }

  // Show the route and total distance.
  void route(String to)
  {
    Stack rev = new Stack();
    int dist = 0;
    FlightInfo f;
    int num = btStack.size();

    // Reverse the stack to display route.
    for(int i=0; i < num; i++)
      rev.push(btStack.pop());

    for(int i=0; i < num; i++) {
      f = (FlightInfo) rev.pop();
      System.out.print(f.from + " to ");
      dist += f.distance;
    }

    System.out.println(to);
    System.out.println("Distance is " + dist);
  }

  /* If there is a flight between from and to,
     return the distance of flight;
     otherwise, return 0. */
  int match(String from, String to)
  {
    for(int i=numFlights-1; i > -1; i--) {
      if(flights[i].from.equals(from) &&
         flights[i].to.equals(to) &&
```

```
        !flights[i].skip)
    {
      flights[i].skip = true; // prevent reuse
      return flights[i].distance;
    }
  }

  return 0; // not found
}

// Given from, find the farthest away connection.
FlightInfo find(String from)
{
  int pos = -1;
  int dist = 0;

  for(int i=0; i < numFlights; i++) {
    if(flights[i].from.equals(from) &&
       !flights[i].skip)
    {
      // Use the longest flight.
      if(flights[i].distance > dist) {
        pos = i;
        dist = flights[i].distance;
      }
    }
  }

  if(pos != -1) {
    flights[pos].skip = true; // prevent reuse
    FlightInfo f = new FlightInfo(flights[pos].from,
                       flights[pos].to,
                       flights[pos].distance);
    return f;
  }

  return null;
}

// Determine if there is a route between from and to.
void isflight(String from, String to)
{
  int dist;
  FlightInfo f;
```

```
    // See if at destination.
    dist = match(from, to);
    if(dist != 0) {
      btStack.push(new FlightInfo(from, to, dist));
      return;
    }

    // Try another connection.
    f = find(from);
    if(f != null) {
      btStack.push(new FlightInfo(from, to, f.distance));
      isflight(f.to, to);
    }
    else if(btStack.size() > 0) {
      // Backtrack and try another connection.
      f = (FlightInfo) btStack.pop();
      isflight(f.from, f.to);
    }
  }
}
```

When the program is run, the solution is

```
From? New York
To? Los Angeles
New York to Denver to Los Angeles
Distance is 2800
```

This is quite good! The route contains the minimal number of stops on the way (only one), and it is the shortest route. Thus, it found the best possible route.

However, if the Denver to Los Angeles connection did not exist, the solution would not be quite so good. It would be New York to Denver to Houston to Los Angeles—a distance of 4300 miles! In this case, the solution would climb a "false peak," because the connection to Houston would not take us closer to the goal of Los Angeles. Figure 10-7 shows the first solution as well as the path to the false peak.

An Analysis of Hill Climbing

Actually, hill climbing provides fairly good solutions in many circumstances because it tends to reduce the number of nodes that need to be visited before a solution is found. However, it can suffer from three maladies. First, there is the problem of false peaks, as just described. In this case, extensive backtracking may result. The second problem relates to *plateaus,* a situation in which all next steps look equally good (or bad). In this case, hill climbing is no better than depth-first searching. The final problem is that of a ridge. In this case, hill climbing really performs poorly because the algorithm causes the ridge to be crossed several times as

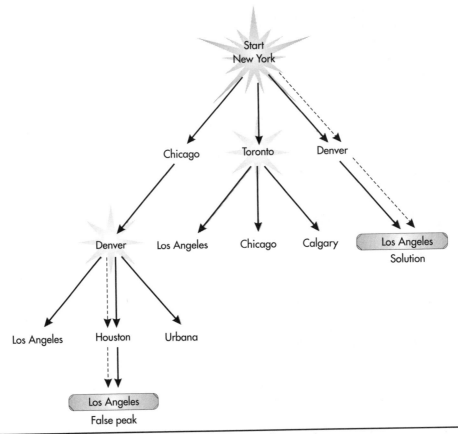

Figure 10-7   *The hill-climbing path to a solution and to a false peak*

backtracking occurs. In spite of these potential troubles, hill climbing often increases the probability of finding a good solution.

The Least-Cost Search

The opposite of a hill-climbing search is a *least-cost search*. This strategy is similar to standing in the middle of a street on a big hill while wearing roller skates. You have the definite feeling that it's a lot easier to go down rather than up! In other words, a least-cost search takes the path of least resistance.

Applying a least-cost search to the flight-scheduling problem implies that the shortest connecting flight is taken in all cases so that the route found has a good chance of covering the shortest distance. Unlike hill climbing, which attempts to minimize the number of connections, a least-cost search attempts to minimize the number of miles.

To use a least-cost search, you must again alter **find( )**, as shown here:

```
// Given from, find closest connection.
FlightInfo find(String from)
{
  int pos = -1;
  int dist = 10000; // longer than longest route

  for(int i=0; i < numFlights; i++) {
    if(flights[i].from.equals(from) &&
       !flights[i].skip)
    {
      // Use the shortest flight.
      if(flights[i].distance < dist) {
        pos = i;
        dist = flights[i].distance;
      }
    }
  }

  if(pos != -1) {
    flights[pos].skip = true; // prevent reuse
    FlightInfo f = new FlightInfo(flights[pos].from,
                        flights[pos].to,
                        flights[pos].distance);
    return f;
  }

  return null;
}
```

Using this version of **find( )**, the solution is

```
From? New York
To? Los Angeles
New York to Toronto to Los Angeles
Distance is 3000
```

As you can see, the search found a good route—not the best, but acceptable. Figure 10-8 shows the least-cost path to the goal.

An Analysis of the Least-Cost Search

Least-cost searches and hill climbing have the same advantages and disadvantages, but in reverse. There can be false valleys, lowlands, and gorges. In this specific case, the least-cost search worked about as well as the hill-climbing search.

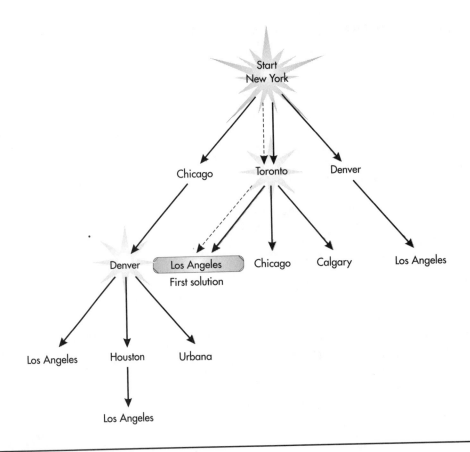

Figure 10-8   *The least-cost path to a solution*

Finding Multiple Solutions

Sometimes it is valuable to find several solutions to the same problem. This is not the same as finding all solutions (an exhaustive search). Instead, multiple solutions offer a representative sample of the solutions present in the search space.

There are several ways to generate multiple solutions, but only two are examined here. The first is path removal, and the second is node removal. As their names imply, generating multiple solutions without redundancy requires that solutions already found be removed from the system. Remember that neither of these techniques attempts to find all solutions. Finding all solutions is a different problem that usually is not attempted because it implies an exhaustive search.

Path Removal

The *path-removal* method of generating multiple solutions removes all nodes from the database that form the current solution and then attempts to find another solution. In essence, path removal prunes limbs from the tree. To find multiple solutions by using path removal, you just need to alter **main( )** in the depth-first search, as shown here, and change the name of the search class to **PathR**:

```
public static void main(String args[])
{
  String to, from;
  PathR ob = new PathR();
  BufferedReader br = new
    BufferedReader(new InputStreamReader(System.in));
  boolean done = false;

  ob.setup();

  try {
    System.out.print("From? ");
    from = br.readLine();
    System.out.print("To? ");
    to = br.readLine();
    do {
      ob.isflight(from, to);

      if(ob.btStack.size() == 0) done = true;
      else {
        ob.route(to);
        ob.btStack = new Stack();
      }
    } while(!done);
  } catch (IOException exc) {
    System.out.println("Error on input.");
  }
}
```

Here, a **do** loop is added that iterates until the backtrack stack is empty. Recall that when the backtrack stack is empty, no solution (in this case, no additional solution) has been found. No other modifications are needed because any connection that is part of a solution will have its **skip** field marked. Consequently, such a connection can no longer be found by **find( )** and cannot be part of the next solution, nor can it be refound. Of course, a new backtrack stack must be obtained to hold the next solution.

The path-removal method finds the following solutions:

```
From? New York
To? Los Angeles
New York to Chicago to Denver to Los Angeles
Distance is 2900
New York to Toronto to Los Angeles
Distance is 3000
New York to Denver to Houston to Los Angeles
Distance is 4300
```

The search found the three solutions. Notice, however, that none are the best solution.

Node Removal

The second way to force the generation of additional solutions, *node removal*, simply removes the last node in the current solution path and tries again. To do this, **main( )** is changed so that it removes the last connection from the flight database, clears all the **skip** fields, and obtains a new, empty stack that is used to hold the next solution. The last connection of the previous solution is removed from the flight database by using a new method called **remove( )**. All the **skip** fields are reset by using another new method called **resetAllSkip( )**. The updated **main( )** method, along with **resetAllSkip( )** and **remove( )**, are shown here:

```java
public static void main(String args[])
{
  String to, from;
  NodeR ob = new NodeR();
  BufferedReader br = new
    BufferedReader(new InputStreamReader(System.in));
  boolean done = false;
  FlightInfo f;

  ob.setup();

  try {
    System.out.print("From? ");
    from = br.readLine();
    System.out.print("To? ");
    to = br.readLine();
    do {
      ob.isflight(from, to);

      if(ob.btStack.size() == 0) done = true;
      else {
        // Save the flight on top-of-stack.
        f = (FlightInfo) ob.btStack.peek();
```

```
          ob.route(to); // display current route

          ob.resetAllSkip(); // reset all skip fields

          /* Remove last flight in previous route
             from the flight database. */
          ob.remove(f);

          // Reset the backtrack stack.
          ob.btStack = new Stack();
        }
      } while(!done);
    } catch (IOException exc) {
      System.out.println("Error on input.");
    }
  }
}

// Reset all skip fields.
void resetAllSkip() {
  for(int i=0; i< numFlights; i++)
    flights[i].skip = false;
}

// Remove a connection.
void remove(FlightInfo f) {
  for(int i=0; i< numFlights; i++)
    if(flights[i].from.equals(f.from) &&
       flights[i].to.equals(f.to))
         flights[i].from = "";
}
```

As you can see, removing a connection is accomplished by assigning a zero-length string to the name of the departure city. Because so many changes are required, the entire node-removal program is shown here for the sake of clarity:

```
// Find multiple connections using node removal.
import java.util.*;
import java.io.*;

// Flight information.
class FlightInfo {
  String from;
  String to;
  int distance;
```

```java
    boolean skip; // used in backtracking

    FlightInfo(String f, String t, int d) {
      from = f;
      to = t;
      distance = d;
      skip = false;
    }
  }

class NodeR {
  final int MAX = 100;

  // This array holds the flight information.
  FlightInfo flights[] = new FlightInfo[MAX];

  int numFlights = 0; // number of entries in flight array

  Stack btStack = new Stack(); // backtrack stack

  public static void main(String args[])
  {
    String to, from;
    NodeR ob = new NodeR();
    BufferedReader br = new
      BufferedReader(new InputStreamReader(System.in));
    boolean done = false;
    FlightInfo f;

    ob.setup();

    try {
      System.out.print("From? ");
      from = br.readLine();
      System.out.print("To? ");
      to = br.readLine();
      do {
        ob.isflight(from, to);

        if(ob.btStack.size() == 0) done = true;
        else {
          // Save the flight on top-of-stack.
          f = (FlightInfo) ob.btStack.peek();
```

```
          ob.route(to); // display current route

          ob.resetAllSkip(); // reset all skip fields

          /* Remove last flight in previous route
             from the flight database. */
          ob.remove(f);

          // Reset the backtrack stack.
          ob.btStack = new Stack();
        }
      } while(!done);
    } catch (IOException exc) {
      System.out.println("Error on input.");
    }
  }

// Initialize the flight database.
void setup()
{
  addFlight("New York", "Chicago", 900);
  addFlight("Chicago", "Denver", 1000);
  addFlight("New York", "Toronto", 500);
  addFlight("New York", "Denver", 1800);
  addFlight("Toronto", "Calgary", 1700);
  addFlight("Toronto", "Los Angeles", 2500);
  addFlight("Toronto", "Chicago", 500);
  addFlight("Denver", "Urbana", 1000);
  addFlight("Denver", "Houston", 1000);
  addFlight("Houston", "Los Angeles", 1500);
  addFlight("Denver", "Los Angeles", 1000);
}

// Put flights into the database.
void addFlight(String from, String to, int dist)
{
  if(numFlights < MAX) {
    flights[numFlights] =
      new FlightInfo(from, to, dist);

    numFlights++;
  }
  else System.out.println("Flight database full.\n");
}
```

```
// Show the route and total distance.
void route(String to)
{
  Stack rev = new Stack();
  int dist = 0;
  FlightInfo f;
  int num = btStack.size();

  // Reverse the stack to display route.
  for(int i=0; i < num; i++)
    rev.push(btStack.pop());

  for(int i=0; i < num; i++) {
    f = (FlightInfo) rev.pop();
    System.out.print(f.from + " to ");
    dist += f.distance;
  }

  System.out.println(to);
  System.out.println("Distance is " + dist);
}

/* If there is a flight between from and to,
   return the distance of flight;
   otherwise, return 0. */
int match(String from, String to)
{
  for(int i=numFlights-1; i > -1; i--) {
    if(flights[i].from.equals(from) &&
       flights[i].to.equals(to) &&
       !flights[i].skip)
    {
      flights[i].skip = true;
      return flights[i].distance;
    }
  }

  return 0; // not found
}

// Given from, find any connection.
FlightInfo find(String from)
{
  for(int i=0; i < numFlights; i++) {
    if(flights[i].from.equals(from) &&
```

```
              !flights[i].skip)
      {
        FlightInfo f = new FlightInfo(flights[i].from,
                          flights[i].to,
                          flights[i].distance);
        flights[i].skip = true; // prevent reuse

        return f;
      }
    }
    return null;
}

// Determine if there is a route between from and to.
void isflight(String from, String to)
{
  int dist;
  FlightInfo f;

  // See if at destination.
  dist = match(from, to);
  if(dist != 0) {
    btStack.push(new FlightInfo(from, to, dist));
    return;
  }

  // Try another connection.
  f = find(from);
  if(f != null) {
    btStack.push(new FlightInfo(from, to, f.distance));
    isflight(f.to, to);
  }
  else if(btStack.size() > 0) {
    // Backtrack and try another connection.
    f = (FlightInfo) btStack.pop();
    isflight(f.from, f.to);
  }
}

// Reset all skip fields.
void resetAllSkip() {
  for(int i=0; i< numFlights; i++)
    flights[i].skip = false;
}
```

```
  // Remove a connection.
  void remove(FlightInfo f) {
    for(int i=0; i< numFlights; i++)
      if(flights[i].from.equals(f.from) &&
          flights[i].to.equals(f.to))
            flights[i].from = "";
  }
}
```

This program finds the following routes:

```
From? New York
To? Los Angeles
New York to Chicago to Denver to Los Angeles
Distance is 2900
New York to Chicago to Denver to Houston to Los Angeles
Distance is 4400
New York to Toronto to Los Angeles
Distance is 3000
```

In this case, the second solution is the worst possible route, but two fairly good solutions are also found. Notice that the set of solutions found by the node-removal method differs from that found by the path-removal approach. Different approaches to generating multiple solutions can often yield different results.

Finding the "Optimal" Solution

All of the previous search techniques were concerned, first and foremost, with finding a solution—any solution. As you saw with the heuristic searches, efforts can be made to improve the likelihood of finding a good solution; but no attempt was made to ensure that an optimal solution was found. However, at times you may want *only* the optimal solution. Keep in mind that "optimal," as it is used here, simply means the best route that can be found by using one of the multiple-solution generation techniques—it may not actually be the best solution. (Finding the best solution would, of course, require the prohibitively time-consuming exhaustive search.)

Before leaving the well-used flight scheduling example, consider a program that finds the optimal route given the constraint that distance is to be minimized. To do this, the program employs the path-removal method of generating multiple solutions and uses a least-cost search to minimize distance. The key to finding the shortest path is to keep a solution that is shorter than the previously generated solution. When there are no more solutions to generate, the optimal solution remains.

The entire "optimal solution" program is shown here. Notice that the program creates an additional stack, called **optimal**, which holds the optimal solution, and an instance variable, called **minDist**, which keeps track of the distance. There are also changes to **route( )** and some minor modifications to **main( )**.

```java
// Find "optimal" solution using least-cost.
import java.util.*;
import java.io.*;

// Flight information.
class FlightInfo {
  String from;
  String to;
  int distance;
  boolean skip; // used in backtracking

  FlightInfo(String f, String t, int d) {
    from = f;
    to = t;
    distance = d;
    skip = false;
  }
}

class Optimal {
  final int MAX = 100;

  // This array holds the flight information.
  FlightInfo flights[] = new FlightInfo[MAX];

  int numFlights = 0; // number of entries in flight array

  Stack btStack = new Stack(); // backtrack stack

  Stack optimal; // holds optimal solution

  int minDist = 10000;

  public static void main(String args[])
  {
    String to, from;
    Optimal ob = new Optimal();
    BufferedReader br = new
      BufferedReader(new InputStreamReader(System.in));
    boolean done = false;
    FlightInfo f;

    ob.setup();

    try {
```

```
        System.out.print("From? ");
        from = br.readLine();
        System.out.print("To? ");
        to = br.readLine();
        do {
          ob.isflight(from, to);

          if(ob.btStack.size() == 0) done = true;
          else {
            ob.route(to);
            ob.btStack = new Stack();
          }
        } while(!done);

        // Display optimal solution.
        if(ob.optimal != null) {
          System.out.println("Optimal solution is: ");

          int num = ob.optimal.size();
          for(int i=0; i < num; i++) {
            f = (FlightInfo) ob.optimal.pop();
            System.out.print(f.from + " to ");
          }

          System.out.println(to);
          System.out.println("Distance is " + ob.minDist);
        }
      } catch (IOException exc) {
        System.out.println("Error on input.");
      }
    }

    // Initialize the flight database.
    void setup()
    {
      addFlight("New York", "Chicago", 900);
      addFlight("Chicago", "Denver", 1000);
      addFlight("New York", "Toronto", 500);
      addFlight("New York", "Denver", 1800);
      addFlight("Toronto", "Calgary", 1700);
      addFlight("Toronto", "Los Angeles", 2500);
      addFlight("Toronto", "Chicago", 500);
      addFlight("Denver", "Urbana", 1000);
      addFlight("Denver", "Houston", 1000);
      addFlight("Houston", "Los Angeles", 1500);
```

```
    addFlight("Denver", "Los Angeles", 1000);
  }

  // Put flights into the database.
  void addFlight(String from, String to, int dist)
  {
    if(numFlights < MAX) {
      flights[numFlights] =
        new FlightInfo(from, to, dist);

      numFlights++;
    }
    else System.out.println("Flight database full.\n");
  }

  // Save shortest route.
  void route(String to)
  {
    int dist = 0;
    FlightInfo f;
    int num = btStack.size();
    Stack optTemp = new Stack();

    for(int i=0; i < num; i++) {
      f = (FlightInfo) btStack.pop();
      optTemp.push(f); // save route
      dist += f.distance;
    }

    // If shorter, keep this route
    if(minDist > dist) {
      optimal = optTemp;
      minDist = dist;
    }
  }

  /* If there is a flight between from and to,
     return the distance of flight;
     otherwise, return 0. */
  int match(String from, String to)
  {
    for(int i=numFlights-1; i > -1; i--) {
      if(flights[i].from.equals(from) &&
         flights[i].to.equals(to) &&
         !flights[i].skip)
```

```
      {
        flights[i].skip = true; // prevent reuse
        return flights[i].distance;
      }
    }
  }

  return 0; // not found
}

// Given from, find any connection using least-cost.
FlightInfo find(String from)
{
  int pos = -1;
  int dist = 10000; // longer than longest route

  for(int i=0; i < numFlights; i++) {
    if(flights[i].from.equals(from) &&
       !flights[i].skip)
    {
      // Use the shortest flight.
      if(flights[i].distance < dist) {
        pos = i;
        dist = flights[i].distance;
      }
    }
  }

  if(pos != -1) {
    flights[pos].skip = true; // prevent reuse
    FlightInfo f = new FlightInfo(flights[pos].from,
                        flights[pos].to,
                        flights[pos].distance);

    return f;
  }

  return null;
}

// Determine if there is a route between from and to.
void isflight(String from, String to)
{
  int dist;
  FlightInfo f;
```

```
      // See if at destination.
      dist = match(from, to);
      if(dist != 0) {
        btStack.push(new FlightInfo(from, to, dist));
        return;
      }

      // Try another connection.
      f = find(from);
      if(f != null) {
        btStack.push(new FlightInfo(from, to, f.distance));
        isflight(f.to, to);
      }
      else if(btStack.size() > 0) {
        // Backtrack and try another connection.
        f = (FlightInfo) btStack.pop();
        isflight(f.from, f.to);
      }
    }
  }
}
```

The output from the program is shown here:

```
From? New York
To? Los Angeles
Optimal solution is:
New York to Chicago to Denver to Los Angeles
Distance is 2900
```

In this case, the "optimal" solution is not quite the best one, but it is still a very good one. As explained, when using AI-based searches, the best solution to be found by one search technique will not always be the best solution that exists. You might want to try substituting another search technique in the preceding program, observing what type of "optimal" solution it finds.

The one inefficiency in the preceding method is that all paths are followed to their conclusion. An improved method would stop following a path as soon as the length equaled or exceeded the current minimum. You might want to modify this program to accommodate such an enhancement.

Back to the Lost Keys

To conclude this chapter on problem solving, it seems only fitting to provide a Java program that finds the lost car keys described in the first example. The accompanying code employs the same techniques used in the problem of finding a route between two cities, so the program is presented without further explanation.

```java
// Find the lost keys!
import java.util.*;
import java.io.*;

// Room information.
class RoomInfo {
  String from;
  String to;
  boolean skip;

  RoomInfo(String f, String t) {
    from = f;
    to = t;
    skip = false;
  }
}

class Keys {
  final int MAX = 100;

  // This array holds the room information.
  RoomInfo room[] = new RoomInfo[MAX];

  int numRooms = 0; // number of rooms

  Stack btStack = new Stack(); // backtrack stack

  public static void main(String args[])
  {
    String to, from;
    Keys ob = new Keys();

    ob.setup();

    from = "front_door";
    to = "keys";

    ob.iskeys(from, to);

    if(ob.btStack.size() != 0)
      ob.route(to);
  }
```

```java
// Initialize the room database.
void setup()
{
  addRoom("front_door", "lr");
  addRoom("lr", "bath");
  addRoom("lr", "hall");
  addRoom("hall", "bd1");
  addRoom("hall", "bd2");
  addRoom("hall", "mb");
  addRoom("lr", "kitchen");
  addRoom("kitchen", "keys");
}

// Put rooms into the database.
void addRoom(String from, String to)
{
  if(numRooms < MAX) {
    room[numRooms] = new RoomInfo(from, to);
    numRooms++;
  }
  else System.out.println("Room database full.\n");
}

// Show the route.
void route(String to)
{
  Stack rev = new Stack();
  RoomInfo r;
  int num = btStack.size();

  // Reverse the stack to display path.
  for(int i=0; i < num; i++)
    rev.push(btStack.pop());

  for(int i=0; i < num; i++) {
    r = (RoomInfo) rev.pop();
    System.out.print(r.from + " to ");
  }

  System.out.println(to);
}

/* If there is a path between from and to,
   return true, otherwise return false. */
```

```java
boolean match(String from, String to)
{
  for(int i=numRooms-1; i > -1; i--) {
    if(room[i].from.equals(from) &&
       room[i].to.equals(to) &&
       !room[i].skip)
    {
      room[i].skip = true; // prevent reuse
      return true;
    }
  }

  return false; // not found
}

// Given from, find any path.
RoomInfo find(String from)
{
  for(int i=0; i < numRooms; i++) {
    if(room[i].from.equals(from) &&
       !room[i].skip)
    {
      RoomInfo r = new RoomInfo(room[i].from,
                        room[i].to);
      room[i].skip = true; // prevent reuse

      return r;
    }
  }
  return null;
}

// Determine if there is a path between from and to.
void iskeys(String from, String to)
{
  int dist;
  RoomInfo r;

  // See if at destination.
  if(match(from, to)) {
    btStack.push(new RoomInfo(from, to));
    return;
  }
```

```
      // Try another connection.
      r = find(from);
      if(r != null) {
        btStack.push(new RoomInfo(from, to));
        iskeys(r.to, to);
      }
      else if(btStack.size() > 0) {
        // Backtrack and try another connection.
        r = (RoomInfo) btStack.pop();
        iskeys(r.from, r.to);
      }
    }
  }
```

Index

INTERNATIONAL CONTACT INFORMATION

AUSTRALIA
McGraw-Hill Book Company Australia Pty. Ltd.
TEL +61-2-9900-1800
FAX +61-2-9878-8881
http://www.mcgraw-hill.com.au
books-it_sydney@mcgraw-hill.com

CANADA
McGraw-Hill Ryerson Ltd.
TEL +905-430-5000
FAX +905-430-5020
http://www.mcgraw-hill.ca

GREECE, MIDDLE EAST, & AFRICA
(Excluding South Africa)
McGraw-Hill Hellas
TEL +30-210-6560-990
TEL +30-210-6560-993
TEL +30-210-6560-994
FAX +30-210-6545-525

MEXICO (Also serving Latin America)
McGraw-Hill Interamericana Editores S.A. de C.V.
TEL +525-117-1583
FAX +525-117-1589
http://www.mcgraw-hill.com.mx
fernando_castellanos@mcgraw-hill.com

SINGAPORE (Serving Asia)
McGraw-Hill Book Company
TEL +65-6863-1580
FAX +65-6862-3354
http://www.mcgraw-hill.com.sg
mghasia@mcgraw-hill.com

SOUTH AFRICA
McGraw-Hill South Africa
TEL +27-11-622-7512
FAX +27-11-622-9045
robyn_swanepoel@mcgraw-hill.com

SPAIN
McGraw-Hill/Interamericana de España, S.A.U.
TEL +34-91-180-3000
FAX +34-91-372-8513
http://www.mcgraw-hill.es
professional@mcgraw-hill.es

UNITED KINGDOM, NORTHERN, EASTERN, & CENTRAL EUROPE
McGraw-Hill Education Europe
TEL +44-1-628-502500
FAX +44-1-628-770224
http://www.mcgraw-hill.co.uk
computing_europe@mcgraw-hill.com

ALL OTHER INQUIRIES Contact:
McGraw-Hill/Osborne
TEL +1-510-420-7700
FAX +1-510-420-7703
http://www.osborne.com
omg_international@mcgraw-hill.com